• FOOD FACTS

• FOOD FACTS

CAROL ANN RINZLER

B L O O M S B U R Y

This book is for
My agents, Phyllis Westberg and Jacqueline Korn, who made it work;
My editors, Beverly Jane Loo, Kathy Rooney and Sian Facer, who made it real;
And my husband, Perry Luntz, who made it possible.

First published 1987

This paperback edition published 1988

Copyright © 1987 by Carol Ann Rinzler.
Additional material © 1987 Bloomsbury Publishing
Limited.

Bloomsbury Publishing Limited, 2 Soho Square,
London W1V 5DE

British Library Cataloguing in Publication Data

Rinzler, Carol Ann
  Food facts and what they mean.
  1. Food
  I. Title
  641.3   TX353

ISBN 0 7475 0283 8

Designed by Fielding Rowinski
Typeset by Sprint Productions Limited, London
Printed and bound in Great Britain by Richard Clay Ltd,
Bungay, Suffolk

• A note to the reader

The material in this book regarding the medical benefits or side effects of certain foods and possible interactions between food and drugs is drawn from sources current at the time the book was written. It is for your information only and should never be substituted for your own doctor's advice or used without his or her consent. Because your doctor is the person most familiar with your medical history and current health, he or she is always the person best qualified to advise you on medical matters, including the use or avoidance of specific foods. Please note also that the adverse effects attributed to some of the foods listed here may not happen to everyone who eats the food or every time the food is served, another reason why your own doctor is your best guide to your personal nutritional requirements.

• Contents

• Preface

Think of an orange.

Think of an aspirin.

Now think how similar they are.

Both affect your health. The aspirin by relieving your headache, the orange by contributing vitamin C to the diet. Both may have side effects. The aspirin may give you hives or make your stomach bleed; the orange may give you hives or trigger a flare-up of canker sores. Both interact with drugs or other chemicals in your body. The aspirin can make anti-coagulants stronger and anti-depressants weaker. The vitamin C in the orange may inactivate the active ingredient in a test for hidden blood in the stool which produces a false-negative result or it can assist the body in absorbing iron from food.

In short, they both influence health. But if you want to find out more about the aspirin's chemistry, benefits, side effects and interactions all you have to do is walk down to the library and check out the latest 'drug book.' Ask about an orange, and the librarian will direct you to the diet books or the cookbooks or the books on popular nutrition.

Which is strange when you consider that all foods, like all drugs, are mixtures of chemicals and that we have always used them as medicines. The Romans sterilized wounds with wine. The Egyptians poured in honey to help them heal. The Aztecs used chocolate as an aphrodisiac. Every Jewish grandmother cured a cold with chicken soup; every Italian mama heaped the plate with olive-oiled pasta to keep her brood in trim.

Today, we recognize the germ of science in everything they did. Wine 'sterilized' with alcohol. The hydrophilic ('water loving') honey soaked up liquids from a wound, killed bacteria and nourished new cell growth. Chocolate's methylxanthine stimulants (caffeine, theophylline, theobromine) elevated moods. The steam from chicken soup (not to mention its aroma) stimulated the flow of liquids that clear the nasal passages. Pasta was high-fibre food, and olive oil low in saturated fatty acids that damage the heart.

But it has taken a long time for science to move beyond the parlour game of validating folklore and begin to explore the serious medical and physical effects of the natural chemicals in food. Only recently have we identified the omega-3 fatty acids in fish that appear to ameliorate all kinds of inflammatory conditions from heart disease to psoriasis. Only now are we beginning to appreciate that the foods we eat may stimulate the production of mood altering chemicals in the brain. What was once folklore is now backed by science.

And that's why this book was written, to pull together in one place what science now shows about the medical effects of food.

• Acknowledgments

As a writer who deals with technical matters, I am always grateful to the experts and working scientists who are kind enough to read and comment upon my manuscript. Among them are the following people, whose patience and good humour were virtually boundless:

Harold R. Bolin of the US Department of Agriculture Western Regional Research Center; John L. Brady; Diane Goetz of the American Heart Association; Klaus Grohmann of Hunter College of the City University of New York; Joseph L. Jeraci of Cornell University; Manfred Kroger of the Pennsylvania State University; Judith Krzynowek of the National Marine Fisheries Service; Jan Lipman of the American Diabetes Association; Alfred C. Olson of the US Department of Agriculture Western Regional Research Center; Dennis O'Mara of the Centers for Disease Control; Joe M. Regenstein of Cornell University; Edward G. Remmers of the American Council on Science and Health; Dr Seymour Rosenblatt; J. Scott Smith of the Pennsylvania State University; Linda Troiano; Merle L. Weaver of the US Department of Agriculture Western Regional Research Center; and John H. Ziegler of the Pennsylvania State University.

I am also particularly grateful to Christopher Robbins who has adapted my book for the British market.

• How to use this book

The information in this book is organized into over a hundred entries, in alphabetical order. Most foods are described individually, but some are so similar in composition and effects that they are grouped together. For example, chives, leeks, shallots and spring onions are all covered under ONIONS and chicory and endive are listed under LETTUCE. The **Table of Contents** will show you where the food you are interested in is listed.

Each entry begins with a **Nutritional profile**, an easy-to-read chart that provides both the actual quantities and summarizes the relative proportions of some of the basic constituents in the food (energy, protein, fat, cholesterol, carbohydrates, fibre, sodium), as well as the food's most prominent vitamins and minerals.

The calculations for these **Nutritional profiles** are based on information from McCance and Widdowson's *The Composition of Foods*, Fourth Revised Edition, 1974, published by HMSO and from various reports of the *Household Food Consumption and Expenditure* survey, published annually by the Ministry of Agriculture, Fisheries and Food.

The nutrients for each food are described in terms of what you might expect to find in a 100g (approx 4 oz) portion of the food. Each nutrient is also graded as LOW, MEDIUM (MED) or HIGH. These values are based on a combination of the food table analyses and an understanding of the contribution each food makes to both the daily and the total diet, as shown in the *Household Food Consumption and Expenditure* survey and may include such factors as the availability of nutrients and the effects of cooking, processing and storage.

The table of **Recommended Daily Amounts of Nutrients** (RDA) on page xx shows the daily intake of each nutrient required for healthy living. The main vitamins and minerals needed for health, their function and the types of food in which they are found are listed in the chart on **Main vitamins and minerals** on page xviii.

The **Nutritional profile** is a general, overall description of the food. You will find more specific information in the text.

For example: is the food higher in starch or sugars? What kinds of fibre does it contain? Are its fats highly saturated or primarily unsaturated? Are its proteins 'complete' or 'incomplete'? You may not understand some of these terms. What is starch? What is the difference between saturated and unsaturated fats? These and other important terms are explained in the **Glossary of basic terms** (page xxv) and where you might like more information about them they appear in capital letters in the text.

Of course, you will want to know **The most nutritious way to serve this food**, since how you serve a food or what you serve it with may make it more nutritious. For example, the proteins in beans are deficient in the essential amino acids which are abundant in grains and vice versa. Serving

XVI · FOOD FACTS

beans and grains together 'completes' their proteins, a clear nutritional bonus.

If you have a medical problem or are on a special diet, you need to know about the **Diets that may restrict or exclude this food**. Sometimes, the problems are not as obvious as they should be. For example, if you are sensitive to milk, you may want to avoid sausages, some of which contain milk protein as a filler or binder. Remember that this list is only a guide; for more detailed personal advice, check with your doctor.

As a consumer, you should know how to choose the freshest, safest, most nutritious food. In short, what to look for when you are **Buying**. Even when you know the basics (avoid lettuce that has yellowed), you may be intrigued by the chemistry (as lettuce ages, its green chlorophyll fades, allowing its yellow carotenoid pigment to show through).

At home, your challenge is to protect the food from spoiling. Some foods, such as meat, must be refrigerated. Others, like pasta, can be stored in any cool, dry cupboard. Still others are more complicated. Tomatoes are a good example. Vine-ripened tomatoes have not turned completely red on picking will get juicier and tastier after a few days at room temperature, but artificially-ripened tomatoes (also known as 'hard ripe' tomatoes) will rot before they soften. That information you will find under the heading **Storing**.

Are you ready to eat? Then it's time to begin **Preparation**. Here's where you will learn how to handle food you are about to cook or serve. Of course, that includes an explanation of the chemical reactions involved. For example, we beat egg whites in a copper bowl whose ions will stabilize the egg white foam. We slice onions under running water to dilute the sulphur compounds that make our eyes water. And once we've done all that, we are ready to cook.

Now the most interesting development is the chemistry of **Cooking reactions**. When you heat food, its sugars and proteins caramelize to form a tasty crust. Aroma molecules begin to move more quickly, creating scents as subtle as a baking apple or as harsh as boiling cabbage. Pigments combine with oxygen or other chemicals in the food; meat turns brown and stringbeans, darker green. We have all seen this happen; this section will explain the 'how' and 'why.'

If you use frozen, canned or dried food, you should know about the **Effects of processing**. Often, processing changes taste and texture. Sometimes, it alters the nutritional balance one way or the other. Canned asparagus has less vitamin C than fresh asparagus, but dried apricots are much higher in iron than fresh ones. In a few rare cases, processing may create hazards that didn't exist before. For example, dried fruit treated with sulphur compounds to keep it from turning brown is potentially dangerous for people sensitive to sulphur.

Which leads us quite naturally to the **Medical uses and/or benefits** of food. The information under this heading is drawn from sources current as the book was written, but research in this area is so new and it is expanding so rapidly that it is almost always considered a 'work in progress' rather than a firm conclusion. It's possible that your morning newspaper has a story making something in this book obsolete even as you turn these pages. Think of what you read here as a guide, not a final answer.

The same thing goes for the **Adverse effects**. Allergies may be our most common side effect from foods. Some of us have a metabolic disorder that makes us unable to digest a component in food such as lactose (milk sugar) or gluten (a protein in wheat and other grains). People with thyroid problems may have to avoid the cruciferous vegetables (cabbage, Brussels sprouts, broccoli, radishes), all of which contain chemicals called goitrogens that can inhibit the production of thyroid hormones. More prosaically, if you eat an excessive amount of carrots and tomatoes over a long period of time, their pigments may turn your skin orange. These are some of the side effects you'll find listed here.

Finally, there is the question of **Food/drug interactions**, such as the ability of the calcium ions in dairy foods to bind tetracyclines into insoluble compounds your body cannot use. Like medical benefits and side effects, this is a category that is growing (and changing) every day.

Some medical benefits, adverse effects and food/drug interactions common to a number of foods are indicated by symbols under the relevant headings in the text. These are preceded by a ✓ where the food has a beneficial effect and a ✗ where the food has an adverse effect.

For example, under **Medical uses and/or benefits**

✓ DIABETES THERAPY
indicates that this food is particularly useful in the treatment of diabetes

and under **Adverse effects**

✗ HEART DISEASE
indicates that this food should be avoided by people at risk from heart disease. Where these symbols appear you should turn to the **Symbol key** on page xxi where you will find a more detailed explanation of each one.

For some foods you may find a dash appearing below a heading such as **Adverse effects**. This does not necessarily mean that there are no adverse effects associated with the food but that there are none of which we are aware.

When you are done, I hope that all this will give you a new way of looking at what you eat and the ability to see foods not merely as pleasant to eat but as important influences on both illness and good health.

If you are interested in learning more about the areas dealt with by this book you will find suggested **Further reading** on page 261 and a list of **Useful addresses** of organizations to contact on page 262.

• Main vitamins and minerals

The chart shows the main minerals and vitamins needed for health:

Mineral	Source	Function
Calcium	Skim part of milk, yoghurt, cheese, sardines, watercress, bread, hard tap water	Necessary for healthy bones and teeth; important in the blood and for healthy heart muscles and nerves
Iron	Meat, liver, eggs, white bread flour, figs, dried apricots, cocoa	Found in the red colour of blood and muscle protein
Magnesium	Almost all foods, especially all green vegetables, bread, milk, eggs, meat, peanuts	Important for good bones and enzymes
Phosphorus	Nearly all foods, vegetables, meat, milk, bread	Found in bone, all cells and necessary for many regular functions of the body
Potassium	Most foods but vegetables, fruit and meat are good sources	Found in all cells and has a role in the fluid balances
Sodium and Chloride	Small amounts in nearly all foods	Maintain the water and fluid balance of the body

Trace elements (needed in very small amounts)

Chromium	Cereals, fruits	Metabolism of fat and sugar
Cobalt	Vitamin B_{12} in meats and yeast extract	Necessary for Vitamin B_{12}
Copper	Most foods	Necessary for some enzymes to function
Fluorine	Water, tea, fish bones	For strong teeth and bones
Iodine	Fish, fruit and vegetables	Found in the hormone Thyroxine
Manganese	Cereals and nuts, tea	Necessary in enzymes

Trace element	Source	Function
Selenium	Most foods	Necessary for Vitamin E
Zinc	Most foods	Important for enzymes to function

Vitamin		
Vitamin A	Liver, cheese, eggs, green leafy vegetables, carrots, dried apricots, tomatoes	Seeing in dim light and healthy skin
Thiamin (B_1)	Skim of milk, pork, peas, cereals, potatoes	Metabolism of carbohydrate
Riboflavin (B_2)	Skim of milk, cheese, liver, meat, eggs	Utilization of energy from food
Nicotinic acid	Skim of milk, cheese, eggs, meat, peas, white flour	Utilization of energy from food
Vitamin B_6	Meat, eggs, fish, cereals, green vegetables	Metabolism of amino acids (in proteins)
Vitamin B_{12}	Liver, meat, eggs, yeast extract	Essential for cells to divide in growth and blood formation
Folic acid	Offal meats and green vegetables, peas and beans, bread, bananas	Works with B_{12} and other functions in healthy blood
Pantothenic acid	In most meats, cereals and vegetables	Release of energy from fat
Biotin	Offal, egg yolks	Metabolism of fat
Vitamin C	Green vegetables, potatoes, blackcurrants, citrus fruit, tomatoes	Essential for connective tissue
Vitamin D	Eggs, oily fish, margarine, Ovaltine	Important for movement and holding of calcium
Vegetable E	Vegetable oil, cereals, eggs	Not clear, but can get anaemia if deficient
Vitamin K	Most vegetables and cereals	Necessary for blood clotting

• Recommended Daily Amounts of

The table presents the RDAs which are published by the DHSS for use in the UK. They cover only the important nutrients. RDAs must be used with care. They are intended to indicate the 'safe' levels of intake which would maintain the adequate nutrition of nearly all healthy members of the population. They

Age ranges years		Energy		Protein	Calcium	Iron	Vitamin A (retinol equivalent)
		MJ^2	kcal	g	mg	mg	μg^3
Boys							
Under 1		3.25	780	19	600	6	450
1		5.0	1,200	30	600	7	300
2		5.75	1,400	35	600	7	300
3–4		6.5	1,560	39	600	8	300
5–6		7.25	1,740	43	600	10	300
7–8		8.25	1,980	49	600	10	400
9–11		9.5	2,280	56	700	12	575
12–14		11.0	2,640	66	700	12	725
15–17		12.0	2,880	72	600	12	750
Girls							
Under 1		3.0	720	18	600	6	450
1		4.5	1,100	27	600	7	300
2		5.5	1,300	32	600	7	300
3–4		6.25	1,500	37	600	8	300
5–6		7.0	1,680	42	600	10	300
7–8		8.0	1,900	48	600	10	400
9–11		8.5	2,050	51	700	12[4]	575
12–14		9.0	2,150	53	700	12[4]	725
15–17		9.0	2,150	53	600	12[4]	750
Men							
18–34	Sedentary	10.5	2,510	62	500	10	750
	Moderately active	12.0	2,900	72	500	10	750
	Very active	14.0	3,350	84	500	10	750
35–64	Sedentary	10.0	2,400	60	500	10	750
	Moderately active	11.5	2,750	69	500	10	750
	Very active	14.0	3,350	84	500	10	750
65–74		10.0	2,400	60	500	10	750
75 and over		9.0	2,150	54	500	10	750
Women							
18–54	Most occupations	9.0	2,150	54	500	12[4]	750
	Very active	10.5	2,500	62	500	12[4]	750
55–74		8.0	1,900	47	500	10	750
75 and over		7.0	1,680	42	500	10	750
Pregnant		10.0	2,400	60	1,200	13	750
Lactating		11.5	2,750	69	1,200	15	1,200

[1] Most people who go out in the sun need no dietary source of vitamin D, but children and adolescents in winter, and housebound adults, are recommended to take 10 μg vitamin D daily.
[2] Mega joules

Source: DHSS (1979) Recommended daily amounts of food, energy and nutrients for groups of

Nutrients (RDA)

allow for different needs but are intended to be applied only to groups of people. RDAs are, however, a useful guide for assessing the general nutritional value of different foods.

Thiamin	Riboflavin	Nicotinic acid equivalent	Vitamin C	Vitamin D[1]
mg	mg	mg	mg	μg^3
0.3	0.4	5	20	7.5
0.5	0.6	7	20	10
0.6	0.7	8	20	10
0.6	0.8	9	20	10
0.7	0.9	10	20	–
0.8	1.0	11	20	–
0.9	1.2	14	25	–
1.1	1.4	16	25	–
1.2	1.7	19	30	–
0.3	0.4	5	20	7.5
0.4	0.6	7	20	10
0.5	0.7	8	20	10
0.6	0.8	9	20	10
0.7	0.9	10	20	–
0.8	1.0	11	20	–
0.8	1.2	14	25	–
0.9	1.4	16	25	–
0.9	1.7	19	30	–
1.0	1.6	18	30	–
1.2	1.6	18	30	–
1.3	1.6	18	30	–
1.0	1.6	18	30	–
1.1	1.6	18	30	–
1.3	1.6	18	30	–
1.0	1.6	18	30	–
0.9	1.6	18	30	–
0.9	1.3	15	30	–
1.0	1.3	15	30	–
0.8	1.3	15	30	–
0.7	1.3	15	30	–
1.0	1.6	18	60	10
1.1	1.8	21	60	10

[3] Microgram
[4] These iron recommendations may not cover heavy menstrual losses.

people in the United Kingdom. Report on Health and Social Subjects, No 15. HMSO; London.

• Symbol key

✗ ANTICOAGULANTS

Plants such as asparagus, cruciferous greens (cabbage, Brussels sprouts, cauliflower), lettuce, spinach and even tea contain vitamin K, the blood-clotting vitamin produced naturally by bacteria in our intestines. Additional intake of vitamin K may reduce the effectiveness of anticoagulant drugs so that larger doses are required.

✓ DIABETES THERAPY

Foods such as beans, whole grain cereals, and even pasta, are digested very slowly, producing only a gradual rise in blood-sugar levels. As a result, the body needs less insulin to control blood sugar after eating beans than after eating some other high-carbohydrate foods such as bread or potatoes. A bean, whole-grain, vegetable, and fruit-rich diet, enables patients with Type I diabetes (who do not produce any insulin themselves) to cut their daily insulin intake. For patients with Type II diabetes (who can produce some insulin), the bean diet can reduce and sometimes stop the need for injected insulin. This diet is in line with the nutritional guidelines of the British Diabetic Association, but people with diabetes should alway consult their doctors and/ or dieticians before altering their diet.

There have been dramatic changes in diets recommended for diabetics and the British Diabetic Association will give guidance (see address list page 262).

✗ ENLARGED THYROID GLAND

Also known as goitre. Cruciferous vegetables, including broccoli, Brussels sprouts, cauliflower, kohlrabi, radishes and turnips contain goitrin, tyhiocynate and isothiocynate, chemical compounds that inhibit the formation of thyroid hormones and cause the thyroid to enlarge in an attempt to produce more. These chemicals, known collectively as goitrogens are not hazardous for healthy people who eat moderate amounts of cruciferous vegetables, but they may pose problems for people who have thyroid problems or are taking thyroid medication.

✘ FALSE RESULT IN TESTS FOR CANCER

1) Cancers of the endocrine or intestine secrete a chemical, serontin, which makes blood vessels expand and contract. Testing for serontin in the blood is used to show if one of these cancers is present. Foods such as walnuts, pineapples, plums, and tomatoes contain serontin and can give false positive results.

2) A tumour of the adrenal gland secretes vanillylmandelic acid (VMA) which used to be tested for in the blood to confirm the presence of this type of adrenal tumour. Foods such as cheese and chocolate which contain VMA would upset this test.

3) The occult blood tests for the presence of blood in faeces. The active ingredient in the test is alphaguaiaconic acid, a chemical that turns blue in the presence of blood. Some foods such as carrots, artichokes, broccoli, radishes and mushrooms contain peroxidase, a natural chemical that also turns alphaguaiaconic acid blue. Lamb and other meats which contain blood can leave sufficient traces of blood in the stool to turn the test chemical blue. Any of these foods may produce a positive test in people who do not actually have blood in the stool.

To reduce the chances of a false reading in any of these tests, none of these foods should be eaten in the 72 hours before taking the test.

✘ GOUT

Purines are the natural metabolic by-products of protein metabolism in the body. They eventually break down into uric acid, which can form sharp crystals that may cause gout if they collect in your joints or kidney stones if they collect in urine. Dried beans (including split peas, lentils, haricots, and soya beans) as well as meats (including sausages, offal and shellfish) are sources of purines; eating them raises the concentration of purines in your body. Although controlling the amount of purine-producing foods in the diet may not significantly affect the course of gout (which is treated with medication such as allo-purinol, which inhibits the formation of uric acid), limiting these foods is still part of many gout regimens.

✘ HEART DISEASE

Fats in the diet, especially saturated fats, increase the chances of a heart attack. Saturated fat leads to an increase in the cholesterol in the blood which encourages the 'furring' of the arteries and is seen as one of the main causes of heart attacks. Cholesterol in food may also lead to a raised level of blood cholesterol but it is believed this effect is weaker than that of the saturated fats. Both the NACNE (National Advisory Committee on Nutrition Education) and the Government's COMA (Committee on Medical Aspects of Food Policy) have recommended that the whole population should aim to eat less of saturated fats and less of all fats to reduce heart disease deaths. People at high risk would be advised to cut out all dietary cholesterol as well. However most of us should aim to reduce the amount of high cholesterol foods (offal meats, egg yolks, shellfish) as part of healthy eating. Saturated fats are found in all meat and dairy fats, as well as in palm or coconut oils used in manufactured foods. The hydrogenation process used to make margarines from vegetable oils tends to increase the amount of saturated fat in the product.

✓ HEART DISEASE

Polyunsaturated fatty acids (in fish oils, and oils like soya, maize, sunflower) may help reduce the risk of heart disease. Monounsaturated fatty acids are found in all fats and oils to some degree but have no known harmful or beneficial effects in heart disease and are called 'neutral'. Olive oil is low in both saturated and polyunsaturated fatty acids, but is high in the neutral mono-type which may be why Italians and Greeks can eat so much olive oil and have so little heart disease.

There is some evidence that foods rich in gums and pectins (pulses and beans), foods rich in bran (whole cereals), natural yoghurt and even garlic and onions tend to lower raised blood cholesterol which reduces the risk of heart disease. Apart from its role in helping make people overweight (which is a risk factor in heart disease), it is no longer believed that sugar can be a direct cause of heart disease.

✗ MONOAMINE OXIDASE (MAO) INHIBITORS

Monoamine oxidase (MAO) inhibitors are drugs used as antidepressants or antihypertensives. They inhibit the action of natural enzymes that break down tyramine so that that it can be eliminated from the body. Tyramine is a pressor amine, a chemical that constricts blood vessels and raises blood pressure. Tyramine, a natural by-product of protein metabolism, occurs naturally in many foods, particularly fermented or aged foods. If you eat a food rich in tyramine while you are taking a MAO inhibitor, the pressor amines cannot be efficiently eliminated from your body and the result may be a hypertensive crisis (sustained elevated blood pressure). Food containing large amounts of tyramine include cheese, chocolate, Marmite, Bovril, game. But foods such as avocado, aubergine, banana, sauerkraut (pickled cabbage), soya beans and spinach have also interfered with MAO inhibitor drugs.

✗ NITRATE/NITRITE POISONING

Beetroot, aubergine, lettuce, radish, spinach, collard and turnip greens and celery contain nitrates that convert naturally into nitrites in your stomach and then react with the amino acids in proteins to form nitrosamines. Although some nitrosamines are known or suspected carcinogens, this natural chemical conversion presents no known problems for a healthy adult. However, when these nitrate-rich vegetables are cooked and left to stand at room temperature, bacterial enzyme action (and perhaps some enzymes in the plants) convert the nitrates to nitrites at a much faster rate than normal. These higher-nitrite foods may be hazardous for infants; several cases of 'spinach poisoning' been reported among children who ate cooked spinach that had been left standing at room temperature. Nitrates and nitrites are also added to foods, especially meat products as curing or preserving agents. They will be listed on food labels as potassium nitrate (E249) or nitrite (saltpetre) (E252), sodium nitrate (E251), or its nitrite form (E250).

✓ POTASSIUM REPLACEMENT
Patients on diuretics may be advised to increase their consumption of potassium to replace that lost in urine. There is also some good evidence that eating more potassium in relation to the amount of sodium in foods may help control or even avoid raised blood pressure. Fresh fruit especially apricots, bananas, grapefruit, guava, pears, peaches, oranges and tangerines and dried fruits like figs and prunes are high in potassium. Fresh vegetables are also good sources of potassium.

✓ PROTECTION AGAINST CANCER
Epidemiological research has shown that people whose diets are relatively abundant in foods rich in vitamin A and C tend to have fewer cancers of the respiratory and gastro-intestinal tracts. Although no explanation for this has been found, doctors in both the USA and the UK recommend eating plenty of the fresh vegetables and fruits rich in these vitamins: carrots, pumpkin, sweet potato, all green leaves, papaya, mango, persimmons and dried apricots and prunes.

✘ SULPHITE SENSITIVITY
Many foods, especially dried fruits, fruit juices, pre-peeled potatoes and crisps and even sausage meat can contain one or more sulphur oxides to preserve food, mainly as an anti-oxidant, or to help retain vitamin C. People who are sensitive to sulphites can suffer a range of reactions from skin rashes to fatal anaphylactic shock. Sulphur oxides will be listed on packets as sulphur dioxide (E220), sulphite (E221), sodium bisulphite (E222), or sodium metabisulphite (E223).

• Glossary of basic terms

BROWNING REACTIONS are of two types.

1) This is called enzymatic browning and occurs when some plant tissues are injured by cutting or bruising. An enzyme called polyphenoloxidase reacts with phenols in the injured cells to produce a brown coloured compound. This browning can occur within minutes in bananas, avocados and potatoes. It is not harmful but the discolouring is not appreciated. Extensive browning can produce slight flavour changes in some foods. Once begun, the reaction cannot be stopped but it can be slowed significantly by refrigeration or by coating the cut surfaces with a mild acid solution of lemon juice or vinegar.

2) This is produced by the heat of cooking and is called the *Maillard reaction* after the Frenchman who discovered it. Heat produces an irreversible reaction between amino acids in food and sugars, producing a brown colour. The browning of toast is an example. New compounds are formed in the reaction and the flavour of food, as well as the colour, is changed.

CARBOHYDRATES include simple sugars such as sucrose, plus starch, cellulose and the materials which make up plant cell walls. They are important in the diet as a source of energy (calories) and dietary fibre which is a mixture of compounds which are not digested in our stomachs. When healthy eating advice says 'eat more carbohydrate foods' it always means starchy carbohydrate foods like cereals and root vegetables, and not sugars. Starchy carbohydrate contributes to dietary fibre as well as giving a source of energy. Sugars give only calories.

CHOLESTEROL is a substance related to fats and is an important part of all living cells in the body. It is essential for the proper functioning of cell membranes, the production of hormones and the bile acids so necessary for the digestion of fats. The body makes all the cholesterol it needs and none is necessary in the diet. Cholesterol becomes a problem if the body makes too much, or if the added amount from animal fats in the diet overloads the body's disposal system so that an excess accumulates in the blood. Cholesterol is insoluble in water and so any excess tends to be deposited in the walls of the blood vessels through which it is transported around the body. These deposits can help cause heart attacks by blocking the arteries. Eating too much saturated fat, from animal or plant sources, can increase the production of surplus cholesterol in the body.

ESSENTIAL FATTY ACIDS. Although fats are used as a source of energy in our diet, it is not thought fats are an essential part of our nutrition except to supply two fatty acids which our bodies cannot synthesize; linolenic and linoleic acids. These are called essential fatty acids and since both are polyunsaturated, it follows that there is no nutritional need to eat any saturated fats.

FATS are important for the normal functioning of our bodies. Fats are widespread in animal and plant tissues. The difference between fats and oils is that fats are solid at room temperature while oils are liquid. Most culinary fats and oils are triglycerides, made of a molecule of glycerol combined with three different fatty acids. Fatty acids are based on chains of carbon atoms ranging between 4 and 22 carbons in length. The three fatty acids are different and are drawn from over 20 possible forms. The mix of fatty acids in each fat determines their physical and chemical properties. Fats which have a majority of saturated fatty acids in their composition are called *saturated fats* (eg dairy fat and coconut oil), those with mostly monounsaturated fatty acids are *monounsaturated fats* (eg olive oil), while those made up largely of polyunsaturated types are called *polyunsaturated fats* (eg soya and sunflower oils). All fats contain some of each type of fatty acid. Butter has 63% saturated fatty acids and only 3% polyunsaturated types.

PROTEIN is made of combinations of *amino acids*, the combinations of which determine the physical and chemical properties of the protein in a similar way to the fatty acids in fats (see FATS). 20 different amino acids are found in proteins and, like fatty acids, only some are essential to our diet. They are made of carbon, hydrogen, and oxygen atoms but also have nitrogen, phosphorus and sulphur atoms in their molecules. The body can make most of the amino acids it needs from a surplus of other amino acids in food. However there are 9 which must be eaten as they cannot be made in the body. These 9 are known as 'essential amino acids'. Proteins are graded according to the proportion of these 'essential amino acids' in their formulae. Proteins that contain sufficient amounts of all the essential amino acids are called 'complete' or 'high quality' proteins. Proteins that are deficient in one or more of the essential amino acids are called 'incomplete' or 'limited' proteins. Complete proteins are found in foods of animal origin such as meat, milk and eggs. Incomplete proteins are found in plant foods. Egg white protein is closest to the proportion needed for our nutrition. Cereal proteins tend to be low in the amino acids lysine and tryptophan, legumes are low in methionine. This is why dietitians often talk about mixing cereals or legumes with animal protein to 'complement' their individual amino acid mixes. However, this is not necessary whenever we eat protein because in the UK we eat 2-3 times the minimum safe level for protein and tend to eat a mix of protein sources, which means we are not likely to run short of any one essential amino acid. Only when protein intakes are close to the minimum requirement does the quality of that protein become important.

Excess protein in the diet cannot be stored as protein; it is converted into glucose in the liver or even can be used as energy in the same way as starch and sugar in the diet.

RECOMMENDED DAILY AMOUNTS (RDAs) of nutrients are published by the Department of Health and Social Security in the UK. The RDAs (see the table, on page xx) give suggested amounts of most, but not all, nutrients which are necessary for health, growth, physical activity, and successful reproduction. They are given for both sexes, and for different ages, activity levels and for pregnancy. The amounts are the estimates of safe, *minimum* levels to be eaten, on average, in the daily diet of healthy people. The levels are set to cover the needs of over 95% of the population to allow for the fact that some people may need more or less of particular nutrients to be healthy. They are set for the greatest need which ensures that everyone will have enough while some will have a small, but safe, surplus. The RDAs for some nutrients, such as vitamin C, which can't be stored in the body need to be eaten daily. Others such as vitamin A, which can be stored in the liver, are not necessary every day so long as the total amount eaten over time matches, or exceeds, the RDA. The RDAs do not give the levels of consumption at which harmful effects occur. Nor do they give advice on important non-nutrients like dietary fibre, sugar or alcohol intake. These recommendations are found in Dietary Guidelines like the NACNE report.

It is important to realise that the RDAs are not intended to be applied to individual diets. Exact requirements vary from person to person. They are based on the needs of groups of people and are designed for use in assessing the adequacy of a group's diet and for planning the meals in hospitals, schools etc. They can be used, however, as a guide to a healthy diet for individuals.

SATURATED FATTY ACIDS have only single chemical bonds (or linkages) between the carbon atoms making up their chain structure. Without any double bonds, these fatty acids are less able to react with hydrogen atoms.

STARCH can be of different types in different plants, but all are long chains (which can be straight or branching) of glucose molecules. Starch is insoluble in water and is used as a storage of energy in plants. We have enzymes which break the long chains into single glucose molecules so they can be taken into our blood to supply cells.

SUGARS are made up of carbon, hydrogen and oxygen atoms. Sucrose, or table sugar, is made of two joined, or bonded, molecules of the simple sugars, fructose and glucose. Sucrose is found in most plants and is the product of plant photosynthesis which traps the energy of light in a chemical form which plants, and ourselves, can release and use. Glucose is also found in plants, especially in fruits along with other sugars, and also in our blood where it is a form of travelling energy for cells to use, produced when we digest foods. Fructose is also found in fruits and especially in honey. Sucrose, glucose and fructose are very soluble and are easily digested sources of dietary energy.

Lactose is the sugar found in milk. It is formed from a molecule of glucose and one of galactose, another sugar.

UNSATURATED FATTY ACIDS have one or more double bonds between adjacent carbon atoms in their chain. They can be monounsaturated, with only one double bond in the entire chain, or can have two or more double bonds when they are called polyunsaturated fatty acids. The more double bonds the more chemically reactive the fatty acids, which also means they can react easily with hydrogen which makes them more saturated.

• Apples

Nutritional profile per 100g food (raw)		
Energy value:	Low	35 Kcal
Protein:	Low	0.2 g
Fat:	Low	Trace
Cholesterol:	None	None
Carbohydrates:	Med	9.2 g
Fibre:	Low	2.0 g
Sodium:	Low	2 mg
Major vitamin contribution:	Vitamin C	Low
Major mineral contribution:	Potassium	Med

Apples are rich in SUGARS (glucose, fructose and sucrose) but have only a trace of STARCH. They provide all the CARBOHYDRATE food fibres, cellulose, hemi-cellulose, pectins (which comprise 70 percent of total fibre in an apple's flesh), plus the noncarbohydrate food fibre lignin, in the peel. Apples have a little PROTEIN, very little FAT, and no CHOLESTEROL.

Apples have small amounts of vitamin A and the B vitamins, plus vitamin C. A medium apple supplies 6 mg vitamin C, 20 percent of the RDA for a healthy adult. Ounce for ounce, apples have about a quarter the potassium of fresh oranges.

The most nutritious way to serve this food
Fresh and unpeeled, to take advantage of the fibre in the peel and preserve the vitamin C, which is destroyed by the heat of cooking.

Diets that may restrict or exclude this food
Antiflatulence diet (raw apples)
Low-fibre diet
Sucrose-restricted diet

Buying
Choose: Apples that are firm and brightly coloured: shiny Starkings and Red Delicious; clear-green Granny Smith; Golden Delicious.
The sour taste of an immature apples (and some varieties, even when ripe) comes from malic acid. As an apple ripens, the amount of malic acid declines and the apple becomes sweeter.
Avoid: Bruised apples. When an apple is damaged it develops soft brown

bruises under the skin. It's easy to check loose apples; if you buy them packed in a plastic bag, turn the bag around.

Storing

Store apples in the refrigerator. Cool storage keeps them from losing the natural moisture that makes them crisp. It also keeps them from turning brown inside, near the core, a phenomenon that occurs when apples are stored at warm temperatures. Apples can be stored in a cool, dark cabinet with plenty of circulating air.

Check the apples from time to time. They store well, but the longer the storage, the greater the natural loss of moisture and the more likely chance that even the crispest apple will begin to taste mealy.

Preparation

Don't peel or slice an apple until you are ready to use it. When you cut the apple you trigger the BROWNING REACTION. Acid slows the browning reaction (but will not stop it completely). Dip raw sliced and or peeled apples into a solution of lemon juice and water, or vinegar and water, or mix them with citrus fruits in a fruit salad.

Cooking reactions

When you cook an unpeeled apple, insoluble cellulose and lignin will hold the peel intact through all normal cooking. The flesh of the apple, though, will fall apart as the pectin in its cell walls dissolves and the water inside its cells swells, rupturing the cell walls and turning the apples into apple sauce. Commercial bakers keep the apples in their apple pies firm by treating them with calcium; home bakers have to rely on careful timing. To prevent baked apples from melting into mush, core the apple and fill the centre with sugar or raisins to absorb the moisture released as the apple cooks. Cutting away a circle of peel away at the top will allow the fruit to swell without splitting the skin.

Red apple skins are coloured with red anthocyanin pigments. When an apple is cooked with sugar, the anthocyanins and the sugars combine to form irreversible brownish compounds.

Effects of processing

Juice. Clear apple juice has been filtered to remove the pulp; the pulp is left in 'natural' apple juice. Most commercial apple juice is pasteurized, then packed in vacuum-sealed packets to stop all natural enzyme action. Without pasteurization, the enzymes in the juice begin to turn sugars into alcohols, eventually producing a mildly alcoholic beverage know as hard cider. (Pasteurization also protects apple juice from the moulds that produce the neurotoxin patulin.)

Medical uses and/or benefits
As an antidiarrhoeal. The pectin in apple is a natural antidiarrhoeal that helps solidify stool. Grated raw apple is sometimes used as a folk remedy for diarrhoea, and purified pectin is an ingredient in many over-the-counter antidiarrhoeals such as kaolin.
Lower absorption of dietary fats. Apples are rich in pectin, which appears to interfere with the body's absorption of dietary fats. The exact mechanism by which this occurs is still unknown, but one theory is that the pectins in the apple form a gel in your stomach that soaks up fats and keeps them from being absorbed by your body.

Adverse effects associated with this food
Poisoning. Apple seeds contain amygdalin, a naturally occurring cyanide sugar compound that degrades into hydrogen cyanide. While accidentally swallowing an apple seed once in a while is not a serious hazard, cases of human poisoning after eating apple seeds have been reported, and swallowing only a few seeds may be lethal for a child.

Food/drug interactions
—

• Apricots

Nutritional profile per 100g food				
	Fresh		*Dried*	
Energy value:	Low	28 Kcal	Med	182 Kcal
Protein:	Low	0.6 g	Low	4.8 g
Fat:	Low	Trace	Low	Trace
Cholesterol:	None	None	None	None
Carbohydrates:	Low	6.7 g	(not available)	
Fibre:	Low	2.1 g	High	28 g
Sodium:	Low	Trace	Low	56 mg
Major vitamin contribution:	Vitamin A, Vitamin K	Med Low		High Med
Major mineral contribution:	Iron	Low		Med

About the nutrients in this food

Apricots are a rich source of carotenes, the natural yellow pigments the body uses to make vitamin A. 100g of fresh apricots provide about 250 micro g of vitamin A which is equivalent to about one third the daily requirement for an adult. Fresh apricots also provide vitamin C and potassium. Dried apricots contain four fifths the daily requirement of these nutrients. Dried apricots are rich in iron; 100g provides nearly one-third the daily requirement of iron for an adult woman (about half the daily requirement for an adult man).

The most nutritious way to serve this food

Ounce for ounce, dried apricots are richer in nutrients and fibre than fresh ones. Fresh is best, especially if you are worried about calories. Neither drying nor cooking cause any significant loss of useful nutrients.

Diets that may restrict or exclude this food

Low-fibre diet
Low-potassium diet
Low-sodium diet (dried apricots containing sodium sulphide)
Sucrose-restricted diet

Buying

Choose: Firm, plump orange fruit that gives slightly when you press with your thumb. The brighter the colour, the stronger the flavour.

Avoid: Bruised apricots. When apricots are bruised, cells are broken, releasing an enzyme that forms brown spots under the bruise.

Avoid apricots that are hard or mushy or withered; all are less tasty than ripe, firm apricots, and the withered ones will decay quickly.

Use greenish apricots only for cooking: they are low in carotenes and will never ripen satisfactorily at home.

Storing
Store ripe apricots in the refrigerator and use them within a few days. Apricots do not lose their vitamin A in storage, but they are very perishable and rot fairly quickly.

Preparation
To peel apricots easily, drop them into boiling water for a minute or two, then lift them out with a slotted spoon and plunge them into cold water. As with tomatoes, this works because the change in temperature damages a layer of cells under the skin so the skin slips off easily.

Dried apricots should be soaked in water for 12-24 hours to soften them before cooking.

Cooking reactions
Cooking dissolves pectin, the primary fibre in apricots, and softens the fruit. But it does not change the colour or lower the vitamin A content because carotenes are impervious to the heat of normal cooking.

Effects of processing
Drying. Five pounds of fresh apricots produce only a pound of dried ones. Drying removes water, not nutrients; ounce for ounce, dried apricots have ten time the iron, ten times the fibre, and twice the vitamin A of the fresh fruit.

To keep them from turning brown as they dry, apricots may be treated with sulphur dioxide. This chemical may cause serious allergic reactions, including anaphylactic shock, in people who are sensitive to sulphites.

Medical uses and/or benefits
✓ POTASSIUM REPLACEMENT

✓ PROTECTION AGAINST CANCER

Alternative cancer treatment. Extract of apricot pits, known medically as Laetrile, is used by some alternative practitioners to treat cancers. The theory behind this treatment is that the cyanide in amygdalin is released only when it comes in contact with beta-glucuronidase, an enzyme common in tumour cells, and that it does not affect healthy cells. No controlled test has proved this thesis.

Adverse effects
✗ SULPHITE SENSITIVITY

Poisoning. The bark, leaves, and inner stony pit of the apricot all contain amygdalin, a natural chemical that can break down into several components, including hydrogen cyanide (Prussic acid) in your stomach. Apricot oil, which is specially treated during processing to remove the cyanide, can be marked *FFPA* to show that it is 'free from Prussic acid.' Cases of fatal poisoning from apricot pits have been reported, including one in a three-year-old girl who ate fifteen apricot kernels.

Food/drug interactions
—

• Artichokes (Globe artichoke; Jerusalem artichoke)

Nutritional profile per 100g of food boiled				
	Globe artichoke		*Jerusalem artichoke*	
Energy value:	Low	7 Kcal	Low	18 Kcal
Protein:	Low	0.5 g	Low	1.6 g
Fat:	Low	Trace	Low	Trace
Cholesterol:	Low	None	Low	None
Carbohydrates:	Low	1.2 g	Low	3.2 g
Fibre:	Low	(not available)	Low	(not available)
Sodium:	Low	6 mg	Low	3 mg
Major vitamin contribution:	Vitamin C	Low		Low
Major mineral contribution:	Potassium, calcium	Low Low		Med —

Globe artichokes: Globe and Jerusalem artichokes are related only by their similar taste. Globe artichokes are members of the thistle family of plants, whereas Jersusalem artichokes are related to sunflower plants.

The thistly plants, from which we get artichoke hearts, are a moderate source of calcium, and potassium. A 100 g serving of cooked globe artichoke provides 19 mg calcium, about a sixth of the calcium you would get from the same size serving of whole milk plus 10 percent of the daily requirement for vitamin C.

Globe artichokes also contain cynarin, a sweet-tasting chemical that is soluble in water (including the saliva in your mouth) and can sweeten the taste of anything you eat after you eat the artichoke.

Jerusalem artichokes: Not true artichokes, these are the edible tubers of the American sunflower. Jerusalem artichokes are high in STARCH and indigestible CARBOHYDRATES, particularly the complex sugar known as inulin, which is made up of units of fructose. As the artichoke matures, its starches turn to SUGAR, making the vegetable sweeter and raising its calorie count after it is dug. A small Jerusalem artichoke tastes bland and starchy and provides about 7 calories; after it has been stored for a while, it tastes sweet and delivers up to 75 calories.

The most nutritious way to serve this food

Jerusalem artichokes can be sliced and eaten raw, but globe artichokes should always be cooked. Raw globe artichokes contain a natural chemical that makes it hard for our bodies to digest protein; the chemical is inactivated by cooking.

Diets that may restrict or exclude this food
Controlled-potassium diet
Low-sodium diet

Buying
Choose: Compact globe artichokes that feel heavy for their size. The leaves should be tighly closed. Globe artichokes are available all year, and the colour of their leaves may vary with the season — bright green in the spring and olive green or bronze in the winter, if they have been exposed to frost. All artichokes with greenish leaves taste equally good but yellow leaves mean that an artichoke is aging.
Choose: Firm, clean Jerusalem artichoke tubers with no soft or bruised spots. Jersualem artichokes are in season from December to March.

Storing
Refrigerate both globe artichokes and Jerusalem artichokes. Store them in plastic bags to retain their moisture.

Cook globe artichokes and refrigerate them in a covered container if you plan to hold them longer than a day or two.

Preparation
To clean a globe artichoke, fill a large bowl or pot with cold water and plunge the artichoke into it to rinse sand off the leaves. To core a globe artichoke, turn it upside down on a cutting board and remove the core with a grapefruit knife. To prepare a Jerusalem artichoke, scrub the root with a vegetable brush, then peel and slice.

When you slice into the base of a globe artichoke or peel and slice a Jerusalem artichoke, you trigger the BROWNING REACTION which discolours the fruit. Dip cut vegetables in water containing lemon juice or a little vinegar to slow the reaction.

Cooking reactions
When you heat a globe artichoke, the chlorophyll in its green leaves will react chemically with acids in the artichoke or in the cooking water to turn the leaves bronze.

When you cook a Jerusalem artichoke, the most obvious changes are in texture. In moist heat, the starch granules in the Jerusalem artichoke absorb water. Eventually the swollen granules will rupture cells and the starch and nutrients inside will be much more accessible and easier to digest.

Effects of processing
Canning. Globe artichoke hearts packed in brine are higher in sodium than

fresh artichokes. If they are marinated in olive oil, they are much higher in fat.

Freezing. Frozen artichoke hearts are comparable in nutritional value to fresh ones.

Medical uses and/or benefits
—

Adverse effects
Contact dermatitis. Globe artichokes contain essential oils that may cause contact dermatitis in sensitive people.

Food/drug interactions
✖ FALSE RESULT IN TESTS FOR CANCER

• Asparagus

Nutritional profile per 100g food (boiled)		
Energy value:	Low	9 Kcal
Protein:	Low	1.7 g
Fat:	Low	Trace
Cholesterol:	None	None
Carbohydrates:	Low	0.6 g
Fibre:	Low	0.8 g
Sodium:	Low	1 mg
Major vitamin contribution:	Vitamins, A, B, C	Med, Low, Med
Major mineral contribution:	Potassium	Low

Asparagus is a source of vitamin A, vitamin C, and the B vitamins, including folic acid. 100 g of fresh boiled asparagus provides 30 percent of the vitamin C, 20 percent of the vitamin A requirement of an adult.

The most nutritious way to serve this food
Fresh, boiled and drained. Canned asparagus may have less than half the nutrients found in freshly cooked spears and is high in sodium.

Diets that may restrict or exclude this food
Low-sodium diet (canned asparagus)

Buying
Choose: Bright green stalks. The tips should be purplish and tightly closed; the stalks should be firm. Asparagus is in season from May to June.
Avoid: Wilted stalks and asparagus whose buds have opened.

Storing
Store fresh asparagus in the refrigerator. To keep it as crisp as possible, wrap it in a damp paper towel and then put the whole package into a plastic bag.

Preparation
The white part of the fresh green-asparagus stalk is woody and tasteless, so snap the stalks where the green begins to turn white. If the skin is very thick, peel it, but save the parings for soup stock.

Cooking reactions
Chlorophyll, the pigment that makes green vegetables green, is sensitive to acid. When you heat asparagus, its cholorphyll will react chemically with acids in the asparagus or in the cooking water to form pheophytin, which is brown . As a result, cooked asparagus is brownish in colour. To avoid this effect cook asparagus quickly to retain its colour. Stand in a covered steamer or pan only until the base of the stems are easily pierced with a knife point — 10-15 minutes.

Effects of processing
Canning: The intense heat of canning makes asparagus soft, robs it of its bright green colour, and reduces the vitamin B and C content. (White asparagus, which is grown without light to stop it turning green, contains about 5 percent of the vitamin A of fresh asparagus.) With its liquid canned asparagus, green or white, contains about 90 times the sodium in fresh asparagus (348 mg in 100 g of canned against 4 mg in 100 g of fresh boiled asparagus).

Medical uses and/or benefits
—

Adverse effects
Odourous urine. After eating asparagus, we all excrete a smelly waste product, the sulphur compound methyl mercaptan, in our urine.

Food/drug interactions
✘ ANTICOAGULANTS

• Aubergines

Nutritional profile per 100 g food (raw)		
Energy value:	Low	14 Kcal
Protein:	Low	0.7 g
Fat:	Low	Trace
Cholesterol:	None	None
Carbohydrates:	Low	3.1 g
Fibre:	Low	2.5 g
Sodium:	Low	3 mg
Major vitamin contribution:	Vitamin B$_1$ and B$_2$	Med, Low
Major mineral contribution:	Potassium	Med

Aubergines have a little bit of everything — but not very much of any particular nutrient. They are low in calories and sodium, have very little fat and no CHOLESTEROL at all. Their primary virtue is their culinary adaptability. Aubergines can be sliced and used in place of veal for a vegetarian *parmigiana* dish, ground and added to spaghetti sauce, or minced with olive oil and seasonings to serve as a 'poor man's caviar.'

The most nutritious way to serve this food
Freshly cooked (but see *Adverse effects*, below).

Diets that may restrict or exclude this food
—

Buying
Choose: Firm, purple to purple-black or unblemished white aubergines that are heavy for their size.
Avoid: Withered, soft, bruised, or damaged aubergines. Withered aubergines will be bitter; damaged ones with be dark inside.

Storing
Handle aubergines carefully. If you bruise an aubergine, its damaged cells will release polyphenoloxidase, an enzyme that hastens the oxidation of phenols in the aubergine's flesh, producing brown compounds that darken the vegetable.
Refrigerate fresh aubergine to keep it from losing moisture and wilting.

Preparation

Do not slice or peel an aubergine until you are ready to use it since it will turn brown. You can slow this chemical reaction (but not stop it completely) by soaking sliced aubergine in iced water — which will reduce the aubergine's already slim supply of water-soluble vitamin C and B vitamins — or by painting the slices with a solution of lemon juice or vinegar.

To remove the liquid that can make a cooked aubergine taste bitter, slice the aubergine, salt the slices, pile them on a plate, and put a second plate on top to weight the slices down. Discard the liquid that results.

Cooking reactions

A fresh aubergine's cells are full of air that escapes when you heat the vegetable. If you cook an aubergine with oil, the empty cell will soak it up. Eventually, however, the aubergine's cell walls will collapse and the oil will leak out, which is why aubergine *parmigiana* often seems to be served in a pool of olive oil.

Aubergine should never be cooked in an aluminium pot, which will discolour the aubergine. If you cook the aubergine in its skin, adding lemon juice or vinegar to the dish will turn the skin, which is coloured with red anthocyanin pigments, a deeper red-purple.

Cooking reduces the aubergine's supply of water-soluble vitamins, but you can save the Bs if you serve the aubergine with its juices.

Effects of processing
—

Medical uses and/or benefits
—

Adverse effects
✖ NITRATE/NITRITE POISONING

Food/drug interactions
✖ MAO INHIBITORS

✖ FALSE RESULT IN TESTS FOR CANCER

• Avocados

Nutritional profile per 100 g food (raw)		
Energy value:	High	223 Kcal
Protein:	Low	4.2 g
Fat:	High	22.2 g
Cholesterol:	None	None
Carbohydrates:	Low	1.8 g
Fibre:	Low	2.0 g
Sodium:	Low	2 mg
Major vitamin contribution:	Vitamins A, B and C	Med, High, Med
Major mineral contribution:	Potassium	Med

The calories in avocados are supplied mostly by FAT, which accounts for about 23 percent of the weight of the fruit and is 79 percent monounsaturated and 9 percent polyunsaturated fatty acids. Avocados are a good source of vitamin C; a 100 g portion can provide all of the daily requirement of 30 mg for a healthy adult.

Diets that may restrict or exclude this food
Controlled-potassium diet
Low-fat diet

Buying
Choose: Fruit that feels heavy for its size. The Hass, which comes mainly from California or Israel is pear-shaped, with a thick bumpy skin that ranges in colour from dark green to purple black. Its flesh is oily and buttery in taste. The Fuerte or Nabal avocado, mainly from Florida or Israel, has smooth bright green skin. Its flesh is 'sweeter' and more watery than the Hass. Both are ripe if the fruit feels soft when pressed with the thumb. To test with minimum damage to the fruit, press at the stem end, not in the middle.
Avoid: Avocados with soft dark spots on the skin that indicate damage underneath.

Storing
Store hard, unripened avocados in a warm place; a bowl on top of the refrigerator will do. Avocados are shipped before they ripen, when the flesh is hard enough to resist bruising in transit, but they ripen off the tree and will soften nicely at home.

Store soft, ripe avocados in the refrigerator to slow the natural enzyme action that turns their flesh brown as they mature even when the fruit has not been cut.

Preparation
Cut avocado will brown (see BROWNING REACTIONS) if left exposed to air. Brush with lemon juice to slow the reaction. To store a cut avocado, brush it with lemon juice or vinegar, wrap it tightly in plastic, and keep it in the refrigerator — where it will eventually turn brown. Or you can store the avocado as guacamole; mixing it with lemon juice, tomatoes, onions, and mayonnaise (all of which are acid) is an efficient way to protect the colour of the fruit.

Cooking reactions
—

Effects of processing
—

Medical uses and/or benefits
—

Adverse effects
—

Food/drug interactions
✘ MAO INHIBITORS

✘ FALSE RESULT IN TESTS FOR CANCER

• Bananas (Plantains)

Nutritional profile per 100 g food		
Energy value:	Med	79 Kcal
Protein:	Low	1.1 g
Fat:	Low	0.3 g
Cholesterol:	None	None
Carbohydrates:	High	19.2 g
Fibre:	Med	3.4 g
Sodium:	Low	1 mg
Major vitamin contribution:	B vitamins and vitamin C	Med, Med
Major mineral contribution:	Potassium, magnesium	High, Med

A banana begins life with more STARCH than SUGAR, but as the fruit ripens its starches turn to sugar. The colour of a banana's skin is a fair guide to its starch/sugar ratio. When the skin is yellow-green, 40 percent of its CARBOHYDRATES are starch; when the skin is fully yellow and the banana is ripe, only 8 percent of the carbohydrates are still starch. The rest (91 percent) have broken down into sugars — glucose, fructose, and sucrose which is the most plentiful sugar in the fruit.

Bananas are a source of riboflavin and the B vitamins, a moderate source of vitamin C, and a good source of nicotinic acid, potassium, and magnesium. They are low in sodium. They also contain small quantities of the indigestible food fibres cellulose, hemicellulose, and lignin and moderate amounts of pectin, the food fibre that may prevent the absorption of fats and help lower blood levels of cholesterol.

Plantains are a variety of banana. Unlike 'eating' bananas, their starches do not turn to sugar as they mature. They remain a starchy food that must be cooked before being eaten. Plantains can be a good source of vitamin A: the amount of vitamin depends on the colour of the fruit — the yellower the plantain, the more vitamin A it contains.

The most nutritious way to serve this food

Fresh and ripe. Green bananas contain proteins that inhibit the actions of amylase, an enzyme that makes it possible for us to digest starch and other complex carbohydrates.

Plantains must be cooked before eating.

Diets that may restrict or exclude this food

Controlled-potassium diet

Sucrose-restricted diet

Buying

Choose: Bananas that will be good when you plan to eat them. Bananas with brown specks on the skin are ripe enough to eat immediately. Bananas with creamy yellow skin will be ready in a day or two. Bananas with mostly yellow skin and a touch of green at either end can be ripened at home and used in two or three days.

Choose: Plantains that are large and firm, with green peel that may be flecked with some brown spots. As the plantain ripens, its skin turns black, but black plantains are still good unless soft.

Avoid: Overripe bananas whose skin has turned brown or split open. A greyish-yellow skin means that the fruit has been damaged by cold storage. Plantains and bananas with soft spots under the skin may be rotten.

Storing

Store bananas that aren't fully ripe at room temperature for a day or two. Bananas are picked green, shipped hard to protect them from damage en route and then sprayed with ethylene gas to ripen them quickly. Untreated bananas release ethylene naturally to ripen the fruit and turn its starches to sugar, but natural ripening takes time.

Store ripe bananas in the refrigerator. The cold air will slow (but not stop) the natural enzyme action that ripens and eventually rots the fruit if you leave it at room temperature. Cold storage will darken the banana's skin but the fruit inside will remain pale and tasty for several days.

Preparation

Do not slice or peel bananas or plantains until you are ready to use them as they will discolour (see BROWNING REACTIONS). You can slow the browning (but not stop it completely) by dipping raw sliced or peeled bananas into a solution of lemon juice and water or by mixing the slices with citrus fruits in a fruit salad. Overripe, discoloured bananas can be used in baking, where the colour doesn't matter and their intense sweetness is an asset.

When you are ready to cook a plantain, cut off the ends, then slice down through the peel and remove the peel in strips. Do this under running water to keep the plantain from staining your hands.

Cooking reactions

When bananas are boiled or fried, they are cooked so quickly that there is very little change in colour or texture. Even so, they will probably taste sweeter and have a more intense aroma then uncooked bananas.

When you cook a plantain, which is very high in starch, the fruit softens and its nutrients become more available.

Effects of processing

Drying. Drying removes water and concentrates the nutrients and calories in bananas. Bananas may be treated with compounds such as sulphur dioxide to keep them from browning as they dry. People who are sensitive to sulphites may suffer severe allergic reactions, including anaphylactic shock, if they eat dried bananas treated with sulphur dioxide.

Freezing. Fresh bananas freeze well but will brown if you try to thaw them at room temperature. To protect the creamy colour, thaw frozen bananas in the refrigerator and use as quickly as possible.

Medical uses and/or benefits
✓ POTASSIUM REPLACEMENT

Healing gastric ulcers. In 1984, British researchers announced that research with laboratory rats suggested that eating powdered, dried plantains helped to prevent the formation of aspirin-induced gastric ulcers and to heal existing ulcers. The healing power of the plantain powder appeared to be due to its growth stimulation of the mucous membrane lining of the stomach.

Adverse effects
✗ SULPHITE SENSITIVITY

Food/drug interactions
✗ MAO INHIBITORS

✗ FALSE RESULT IN TESTS FOR CANCER

• Barley

Nutritional profile per 100 g food (boiled)		
Energy value:	Med	120 Kcal
Protein:	Low	2.7 g
Fat:	Low	0.6 g
Cholesterol:	None	None
Carbohydrates:	High	27.6 g
Fibre:	Med	2.2 g
Sodium:	Low	1 mg
Major vitamin contribution:	B vitamins	Med
Major mineral contribution:	Potassium	Low

Barley contains some PROTEINS, a little FAT, and a lot of complex CARBO-HYDRATES (starch and fibres). Its proteins are considered 'incomplete' because they are deficient in the amino acid, lysine, and two of its important nutrients, iron and calcium, are largely unavailable because barley, like other grains, contains phytic acid — which binds the minerals into insoluble, indigestible compounds. This presents no problem as long as your diet includes sufficient amounts of calcium and iron from other foods.

Barley is a good source of B vitamins, potassium, phosphorus, and magnesium.

The most nutritious way to serve this food
Cereals are good sources of carbohydrates but are best served with legume or meat protein foods to complement the cereal protein which is relatively low in some amino acids like lysine.

Diets that may restrict or exclude this food
Gluten-free diet

Buying
Choose: Barley in plastic or cellophane packs so you can see it is clean, free from stones and other rubbish and not mouldy.

Storing
Store barley in air- and moistureproof containers in a cool, dark, dry cabinet. Well-protected, it will keep for several months with no loss of nutrients.

Preparation
Pick over the barley and discard any damaged or darkened grains.

Cooking reactions
When you cook barley in water, its STARCH granules absorb water molecules, swell, and soften. If you continue to cook the barley, the starch granules will rupture, releasing molecules of starch which will absorb some of the water molecules in the liquid. This is why a little barley added to a soup or stew will make the soup or stew thicker.

The B vitamins in barley are water-soluble. You can save them by serving the barley with the liquid in which it was cooked.

Effects of processing
Pearling. Barley from which the outer layer has been removed is called pearled barley. Milling, the process by which the barley is turned into flour, also removes the outer coating (bran) of the grain. Since most of the B vitamins and fibre are concentrated in the bran, both pearled and milled barley are lower in nutrients and fibre than whole barley.

Malting. After barley is harvested, the grain may be left to germinate, during which complex carbohydrates in the grain change into the sugar mattose. The grain, now called malted barley, is used as the base for several fermented and distilled alcoholic beverages, including beer and whisky.

Medical uses and/or benefits
✓ HEART DISEASE

Adverse effects
—

Food/drug interactions
—

• Bean curd (Tofu)

See also SOYA BEANS

Nutritional profile per 100 g food (fresh)		
Energy value:	Med	70 Kcal
Protein:	Med	7.4 g
Fat:	Low	4.2 g
Cholesterol:	None	None
Carbohydrates:	Low	0.6 g
Fibre:	Low	0.3 g
Sodium:	Low	5 mg
Major vitamin contribution:	B vitamins	Med
Major mineral contribution:	Calcium, iron	High, Med

Bean curd is made by boiling soya beans with water, grinding the beans into a paste, and adding calcium sulphate that coagulates the curd and makes the bean curd a richer source of calcium than plain soya beans. (Japanese and Chinese bean curd is coagulated with an acid — lemon juice or vinegar.)

Bean curd supplies complete PROTEINS which are 90 percent digestible, a figure approaching that of milk. The iron in bean curd is three times more available than the iron in whole soya beans, which are high in iron but whose iron is in a form not easily assimilated by our bodies (see SOYA BEANS).

The most nutritious way to serve this food
Cooked. Uncooked soya bean curd may harbour bacteria than can cause food poisoning.

Diets that may restrict or exclude this food
Controlled-protein diet (for patients with kidney disease)

Buying
Choose: Clean blocks of fresh bean curd, submerged in clean water and stored in a refrigerated dairy case. Soya bean curd is a perishable, moist, protein-rich food that provides a perfect medium for bacterial growth. Check the sell by date on packets of prepacked curd. Dried curd can now be bought and is a good alternative to the fresh curd.
Avoid: Unrefrigerated fresh curd; bean curd with a rind (which only develops when the curd is left uncovered) or bean curd whose surface is not pure, creamy white (any bright orange, yellow, blue, or green spots are almost certainly mould).

Storing
Cover fresh bean curd with clean water and store it in the refrigerator. Change the water daily, using two clean spoons rather than your hands to lift the curd. Discard any mouldy curd immediately (throw out the whole block, not just the mouldy spot). Use fresh curd within a few days; prepacked curd should be used as indicated by the date on the bag.

Preparation
Rinse the curd and slice or cut into cubes.

Cooking reactions
Frying the soya bean curd evaporates its moisture and coagulates its proteins, making the curd more dense and chewy. It also makes the bean curd safer to eat because cooking kills microorganisms on the curd.

Effects of processing
Freezing. Bean curd-based frozen desserts may have as much fat and calories as ice creams or frozen yoghurt, but, unless other fats are added, their FATS are primarily unsaturated and there is no CHOLESTEROL in bean curd. And, because there is no lactose in bean curd, these desserts are used as an ice cream substitute for people who cannot digest the sugar in milk.

Medical uses and/or benefits
—

Adverse effects
—

Food/drug interactions
✖ MAO INHIBITORS

• Bean sprouts
See also BEANS

Nutritional profile per 100 g food		
Energy value:	Low	35 Kcal
Protein:	Low	3.8 g
Fat:	Low	0.2 g
Cholesterol:	None	None
Carbohydrates:	Low	5.9 g
Fibre:	Low	1.8 g
Sodium:	Low	5 mg
Major vitamin contribution:	B vitamins, vitamin C	Med, Med
Major mineral contribution:	Iron, potassium	Low, Med

As beans sprout they convert stored STARCHES and SUGARS into energy needed to grow. As a result, sprouts have less CARBOHYDRATE than beans do. They have three to five times more vitamin C than the beans from which they grew but less PROTEIN, less iron, less vitamin A and less B vitamins, and 8 times as much water which dilutes the nutrients.

The most nutritious way to serve this food
Fresh raw or steamed.

Diets that may restrict or exclude this food
Low-fibre, low-residue diet

Buying
Choose: Fresh, crisp sprouts. The tips should be moist, crisp and white. (The shorter the sprout, the more tender it will be.) It is sometimes difficult to judge bean sprouts packed in plastic bags, but you can see through to tell if the tip of the sprout looks fresh. Sprouts sold from water-filled bowls should be refrigerated, protected from dirt and debris, and served with a spoon or tongs, *not scooped up by hand*.
Avoid: Mushy sprouts (they may be decayed) and soft ones (they have lost moisture and vitamin C).

Storing
Refrigerate sprouts in a plastic bag to keep them moist and crisp. To get the most vitamin C, use the sprouts within a few days.

Preparation
Rinse the sprouts thoroughly under cold running water to get rid of dirt and sand. Discard any soft or browned sprouts. Use the sprouts whole.

Cooking reactions
Cooking destroys some of the heat-sensitive vitamin C in sprouts. To save it, steam the sprouts quickly, stir-fry them, or add them uncooked just before you serve the dish.

Effects of processing
Canning. Vitamin C is heat-sensitive, and heating the sprouts during the canning process reduces their vitamin C content.

Medical uses and/or benefits
—

Adverse effects
—

Food/drug interactions
—

Beans (Black beans, canellini beans, chickpeas, haricot beans, kidney beans)

See also BEAN CURD, BEAN SPROUTS, SOYA BEANS

Nutritional profile per 100 g food (raw)		
	Haricot beans	
Energy value:	Med	93 Kcal
Protein:	High	6.6 g
Fat:	Low	0.5 g
Cholesterol:	None	None
Carbohydrates:	High	16.6 g
Fibre:	High	7.4 g
Sodium:	Med	15 mg
Major vitamin contribution:	B vitamin, folic acid	Med, Med
Major mineral contribution:	Calcium, iron, potassium, magnesium, zinc	All medium

Beans are rich in CARBOHYDRATES: pectins, gums, STARCH, and SUGARS (including the indigestible complex sugars raffinose and stachyose, which make beans 'gassy' when they are fermented by bacteria in the human gut). Beans have no CHOLESTEROL and most types very little FAT. Up to 25 percent of the calories in beans come from their proteins, which are considered 'incomplete' because they are low in the essential amino acids methionine and cystine. Soya beans are the only beans that contain proteins considered 'complete' because they contain balanced amounts of all the essential amino acids.

All beans are a good source of B vitamins, particularly vitamin B_6. Dried beans are also a good source of folic acid.

Beans contain non-heme iron, the inorganic iron found in plant foods. You can improve the availability of the iron in beans by eating them with meat or with a food rich in vitamin C.

Raw beans also contain antinutrient chemicals that inhibit those enzymes that make it possible for your body to digest PROTEINS and STARCHES, factors that inactivate vitamin A and hemagglutinins, chemicals that make red blood cells clump together. These antinutrients are often inactivated by cooking the beans.

The most nutritious way to serve this food

With grains. The PROTEINS in grains are low in the essential amino acids lysine and isoleucine but contain sufficient tryptophan, methionine, and cystine; the proteins in beans are the opposite. When eaten in mixtures, these foods provide 'complete' proteins.

With a vitamin C-rich food (tomatoes) which enhances your body's ability to use the iron in the beans. The vitamin C may convert the ferric iron in beans into ferrous iron, which is more easily absorbed by the body.

Diets that may restrict or exclude this food
Low-calcium diet
Low-fibre diet
Low-purine (antigout) diet

Buying
Choose: Smooth-skinned, uniformly sized, evenly coloured beans that are free of stones and debris. Check the date on the packet. Beans older than one year become tough and lose their flavour.
Avoid: Beans sold in bulk. The open bins expose the beans to air and light and may allow insect contamination (tiny holes in the beans indicate than an insect has burrowed into or through the bean).

Storing
Store beans in air- and moistureproof containers in a cool, dark cabinet where they are protected from heat, light, and insects.

Preparation
Wash dried beans and pick them over carefully, discarding damaged or withered beans and any that float. (Only withered beans are light enough to float in water.)

Cover the beans with water, bring them to the boil, and then set them aside to soak. When you are ready to use the beans, discard the water in which beans have been soaked. Some of the indigestible sugars in the beans that cause intestinal gas when you eat the beans will leach out into the water, making the beans less 'gassy.'

Cooking reactions
When beans are cooked in liquid, their cells absorb water, swell, and eventually rupture, releasing the pectins and gums and nutrients inside. In addition, cooking destroys antinutrients in beans, making them more nutritious and safe to eat.

Effects of processing
Canning. The heat of canning destroys some of the B vitamins in the beans. You can recover the lost B vitamins simply by using the liquid in the can, but the liquid also contains the indigestible sugars that cause intestinal gas when you eat beans.

Preprocessing. Preprocessed dried beans have already been soaked. They take less time to cook but are lower in B vitamins.

Medical uses and/or benefits
✓ HEART DISEASE

✓ DIABETES THERAPY

As a slimming aid. Although beans are medium in calories, they are also high in bulk and fibre, and even a small serving can make you feel full. Because they are insulin-sparing, they delay the rise in insulin levels that makes us feel hungry again soon after eating. Research at the University of Toronto suggests the insulin-sparing effect may last for several hours after you eat the beans, perhaps until after the next meal.

Adverse effects
✗ GOUT

Intestinal gas
All legumes (beans and peas) contain raffinose and stachyose, complex SUGARS that human beings cannot digest. The sugars are fermented in the gut by intestinal bacteria which produce gas that distends the intestines and makes us uncomfortable. You can lessen this effect by covering the beans with water, bringing them to a boil for three to five minutes, and then setting them aside to soak for four to six hours so that the indigestible sugars leach out in the soaking water, which can be discarded. Then add new water and cook the beans as your recipe directs; drain them before serving.

Food/drug interactions
—

• Beef
See also SAUSAGES

Nutritional profile per 100 g food (raw)		
	Rump Steak	
Energy value:	Med	197 Kcal
Protein:	High	18.9 g
Fat:	Med to high	13.5 g
Cholesterol:	Med	65 mg
Carbohydrates:	None	None
Fibre:	None	None
Sodium:	Med	51 mg
Major vitamin contribution:	Vitamins B_1, B_2, nicotinic acid, vitamins B_6, B_{12}	All high
Major mineral contribution:	Iron, potassium, phosphorus, zinc	All high

Like other animal foods, beef provides high quality PROTEINS. Beef and pork fat contain more SATURATED FATTY ACIDS than lamb fat and slightly less CHOLESTEROL than an equal amount of chicken fat. There is no fibre in beef and no CARBOHYDRATES other than the small amounts of glycogen (sugar) stored in the animal's muscles and liver.

Beef is an excellent source of B vitamins, including nicotinic acid, vitamin B_6, and vitamin B_{12}, which is found only in animal foods. Lean beef provides heme iron, the organic iron that is about five times more useful to the body than the inorganic form of iron found in plant foods. Beef is also an excellent source of zinc.

The most nutritious way to serve this food
With a food rich in vitamin C. Ascorbic acid increases the absorption of iron from meat. Eat the lean with as little fat as possible.

Diets that may restrict or exclude this food
Controlled-fat, low-cholesterol diet
Low-protein diet

Buying
Choose: Choose lean cuts of beef with as little internal marbling (streaks of

fat) as possible. The leanest cuts are rump and fillet steak; brisket, and chuck have the most fat.

Choose the cut of meat that is right for your recipe. Generally, the cuts from the centre of the animal's back — the rib, the T-bone, the porterhouse steaks — are the most tender. They can be cooked by dry heat — grilling, roasting, pan frying. Cuts from around the legs, the underbelly, and the neck — the shank, the brisket, the round — contain muscles used for movement. They must be tenderized by stewing or boiling.

Storing
Refrigerate raw beef immediately, carefully wrapped to prevent its drippings from contaminating other foods. Refrigeration slows the natural multiplication of bacteria on the meat surface. Unchecked, these bacteria will cause the meat to spoil.

Minced beef, with many surfaces where bacteria can live should be used within 24 to 48 hours. Other cuts of beef will stay fresh in the refrigerator for 3-5 days.

Beef can be frozen raw or after cooking.

Preparation
Trim the beef carefully. By judiciously cutting away all visible fat you can significantly reduce the amount of fat and cholesterol in each serving.

Cooking reactions
Cooking changes the appearance and flavour of beef, alters its nutritional value, makes it safer, and extends its storage life.

Browning meat before you cook it does not 'seal in the juices,' but it does change the flavour by caramelizing proteins and sugars on the surface (see BROWNING REACTIONS). Because beef's only sugars are the small amounts of glycogen in the muscles, we add sugars in marinades or basting liquids that may also contain acids (vinegar, lemon juice, wine) to break down muscle fibres and tenderize the meat.

An obvious nutritional benefit of cooking is the fact that heat lowers the fat content of beef by liquifying the fat so it can run off the meat.

Finally, cooking makes beef safer by killing Salmonella and other organisms in the meat. As a result, cooking also serves as a short-term natural preservative. Fresh beef can be refrigerated for two or three days, then cooked and held safely for another day or two because the heat of cooking destroys bacteria on the surface of the meat and temporarily interrupts the natural process of deterioration.

Effects of processing
Aging. Hanging fresh meat exposed to the air in a refrigerated room reduces

the moisture content and shrinks the meat slightly. As the meat ages, enzymes break down muscle proteins 'tenderizing' the beef.

Canning. The high temperatures used in canning food and the long cooking process alter proteins in the meat so that they act as antioxidants. Once the can is open, however, the meat should be protected from oxygen that will change the flavour of the beef.

Curing. Salt-curing preserves meat by surrounding the meat cells and bacteria with a concentrated salt solution which draws moisture from the bacterial cells and kills them. Salt-cured meat is much higher in sodium than fresh meat.

Freezing. Home-frozen beef is sometimes dryer when thawed than fresh beef is. It may also be lower in B vitamins. When you freeze beef, the water inside its cells freezes into sharp ice crystals that can puncture cell membranes. When the beef thaws, moisture (and some of the B vitamins) will leak out through these torn cell walls. The loss of moisture is irreversible, but some of the vitamins can be saved by using the drippings when the meat is cooked. Freezing may also cause freezer burn — dry spots left when moisture evaporates from the surface of the meat.

Smoking. Hanging cured or salted meat over an open fire slowly dries the meat, kills microorganisms on its surface, and gives the meat a rich, 'smoky' flavour that varies with the wood used in the fire. Meats smoked over an open fire are exposed to carcinogenic chemicals in the smoke, including a-benzopyrene. Meats treated with 'artifical smoke flavouring' are not, since the flavouring is commercially treated to remove tar and a-benzopyrene.

Medical uses and/or benefits

Meat is one of the best sources of iron, especially from liver which is the richest food source. Iron is more efficiently absorbed from beef than from foods like flour, dried apricots and chocolate. Meat provides a quarter of the iron in the average British diet.

Adverse effects

✖ HEART DISEASE

Antibiotic sensitivity. Cattle are given antibiotics to protect them from infection. The antibiotic treatment must stop several days before the animal is slaughtered. Theoretically, the beef should then be free of antibiotic residues, but some people who are sensitive to penicillin or tetracycline may have an allergic reaction to the meat, although this is rare.

Antibiotic-resistant Salmonella and toxoplasmosis. Cattle treated with antibiotics may produce meat contaminated with antibiotic-resistant strains of *Salmonella*, and all raw beef may harbour ordinary *Salmonella* as well as *T. gondii*, the parasite that causes toxoplasmosis. *Toxoplasmosis* is particularly hazardous for pregnant women. It can be passed on to the foetus and may trigger a series of birth defects including blindness and mental retardation.

Both *Salmonella* and the *T. gondii* can be eliminated by cooking meat thoroughly and washing all utensils, cutting boards, and work surfaces as well as your hands with hot soapy water before touching any other food.

Food/drug interactions
✖ MAO INHIBITORS

Papain (see PAPAYA). Papain meat tenderizers work by enzymatic action, which breaks down the proteins in beef and may produce vasoactive amines similar to tyramine (see MAO INHIBITORS).

• Beetroot

Nutritional profile per 100 g food (raw)		
Energy value:	Low	28 Kcal
Protein:	Low	1.3 g
Fat:	Low	Trace
Cholesterol:	None	None
Carbohydrates:	Low	6.0 g
Fibre:	Low	3.1 g
Sodium:	Med	84 mg
Major vitamin contribution:	Vitamin C	Low
Major mineral contribution:	Potassium	Med

Beetroot are storage roots rich in complex CARBOHYDRATES — STARCH, SUGARS, and the indigestible fibres cellulose and hemicellulose. They have some vitamin C and some B vitamins, but because their red colour comes from anthocyanin pigments, not carotene, they have negligible amounts of vitamin A.

The most nutritious way to serve this food
Cooked, to dissolve the stiff cell walls and make the nutrients inside available.

Diets that may restrict or exclude this food
Low-sodium diet

Buying
Choose: Smooth, firm globes.
Avoid: Beetroot with soft spots or blemishes that suggest decay underneath.

Storing
Protect the nutrients in beetroot by storing the vegetables in a cool place, such as the vegetable crisper in your refrigerator. When stored, the beetroot converts its starch into sugars; the longer it is stored, the sweeter it becomes.

Remove any leaves from beetroot before storing and store the leaves like other leafy vegetables, in plastic bags in the refrigerator to keep them from drying out and losing vitamins.

Use both beetroot and the leaves within a week.

Preparation
Scrub the globes with a vegetable brush under cold running water. They are

best boiled whole to preserve both colour and vitamins. When cooked and cooled, the skin can be rubbed off easily.

Cooking reactions
Betacyanin and betaxanthin, the red betalain pigments in beetroot, are water-soluble. (That's why borscht is a scarlet soup.) They turn more intensely red when you add acids; think of scarlet sweet-and-sour beetroot in lemon juice or vinegar with sugar. They turn slightly blue in a basic (alkaline) solution such as baking soda and water.

Like carrots, beetroot have such stiff cell walls that it is hard for the human digestive tract to extract the nutrients inside. Cooking will not soften the cellulose in the root cell walls, but it will dissolve enough hemicellulose so that digestive juices are able to penetrate.

Effects of processing
Canning. Beetroot lose neither their colour nor their texture in canning.

Medical uses and/or benefits
—

Adverse effects
✘ NITRATE/NITRITE POISONING

Pigmented urine and faeces. The ability to metabolize betacyanins and betaxanthins is a genetic trait. People with two recessive genes for this trait cannot break down these red pigments, which will be excreted, bright red, in urine. Eating beetroots can also turn faeces red, but it will not cause a false-positive result in a test for occult blood in the stool. Neither coloured urine nor faeces are harmful.

Food/drug interactions
—

• Blackberries

Nutritional profile per 100 g food (raw)		
Energy value:	Low	29 Kcal
Protein:	Low	1.3 g
Fat:	Low	Trace
Cholesterol:	None	None
Carbohydrates:	Low	6.4 g
Fibre:	Low	7.3 g
Sodium:	Low	4 g
Major vitamin contribution:	Vitamins C, E	High, Med
Major mineral contribution:	Calcium, potassium	Med, Med

Blackberries have no STARCH but do contain SUGARS and dietary fibre —
including primarily pectin, which dissolves as the fruit matures, and
vitamin C.

The most nutritious way to serve this food
Fresh

Diets that may exclude or restrict this food
—

Buying
Choose: Plump, firm dark berries with no hulls.
Avoid: Baskets of berries with juice stains or liquid leaking out of the berries.
The stains and leaks are signs that there are crushed — and possibly
mouldy — berries inside.

Storing
Cover berries and refrigerate them. Then use them in a day or two.
  Do not wash berries before storing. The moisture collects in spaces on the
surface of the berries which may mould in the refrigerator. Also, handling
the berries may damage their cells, releasing enzymes that can destroy
vitamins.

Preparation
Rinse the berries under cool running water, then drain them and pick them
over carefully to remove all stems and leaves.

Cooking reactions

Cooking destroys some of the vitamin C in fresh blackberries and lets water-soluble B vitamins leak out. Cooked berries are likely to be mushy because the heat and water dissolve their pectin and the skin of the berry collapses. Cooking may also change the colour of blackberries, which contain soluble red anthocyanin pigments that stain cooking water and turn blue in basic (alkaline) solutions. Adding lemon juice to a blueberry pie stablises these pigments; it is a practical way to keep the berries a deep, dark reddish-blue.

Effects of processing

Canning. The intense heat used in canning reduces the vitamin C content of blackberries. Berries packed in juice have more nutrients, ounce for ounce than berries packed in either water or syrup.

Medical uses and/or benefits

—

Adverse effects

Hives and angioedema (swelling of the face, lips, and eyes). These are common allergic responses to berries, virtually all of which have been known to trigger allergic reactions in susceptible people.

Food/drug interactions

—

• Blackcurrants (Gooseberries)

Nutritional profile per 100 g food (raw)				
	Blackcurrants		*Gooseberries*	
Energy value:	Low	28 Kcal	Low	17 Kcal
Protein:	Low	0.9 g	Low	1.1 g
Fat:	Trace	Trace	Trace	Trace
Cholesterol:	None	None	None	None
Carbohydrates:	Low	6.6 g	Low	3.4 g
Fibre:	High	8.7 g	Low	3.2 g
Sodium:	Low	3 mg	Low	2 mg
Major vitamin contribution:	Vitamin C	High		High
Major mineral contribution:	Potassium	High		High

Nutritionally, fresh blackcurrants, the berries used to make crème de cassis, are more valuable than fresh red currants, white currants and gooseberries. They have nearly twice as much vitamin A; one and a half times the potassium, calcium, and phosphorus; and nearly 5 times as much vitamin C — 200 mg/ 100 grams versus 41 mg/100 grams. (All currants and gooseberries are rich in vitamin C, which is lost when the berries are cooked to make jams and jellies.)

The most nutritious way to serve this food
Fresh

Diets that may restrict or exclude this food
Sucrose-restricted diet
Low-fibre diet

Buying
Choose: Plump, firm, well-coloured currants. Gooseberries, which are members of the same family as currants, should have a slight golden blush.
Avoid: Sticky packets of currants or berries and mouldy fruit.

Storing
Refrigerate ripe currants or gooseberries and use them within a day or so.

Preparation
Wash fresh currants or gooseberries under cold running water, pull off stems and leaves, and drain the berries.

Cooking reactions
When fresh currants and gooseberries are heated, the water under the skin expands; if you cook them long enough, the berries will eventually burst.

Effects of processing
Canning. The heat of canning destroys vitamin C; canned gooseberries have only about one-third the vitamin C of fresh gooseberries.

Medical uses and/or benefits
—

Adverse effects
Allergic reactions. Virtually all berries have been implicated as the cause of classic allergic symptoms — hives, angioedema (swelling of the lips and eyes), and upset stomach — in sensitive individuals.

Food/drug interactions
—

• Blueberries

Nutritional profile per 100 g food (raw)		
Energy value:	Low	56 Kcal
Protein:	Low	0.6 g
Fat:	Low	Trace
Cholesterol:	None	None
Carbohydrates:	Med	14.3 g
Fibre:	Med	4.3 g
Sodium:	Low	1 mg
Major vitamin contribution:	Vitamin C	Med
Major mineral contribution:	Calcium	Low

Blueberries have no STARCH but do contain SUGARS and dietary fibre — primarily pectin, which dissolves as the fruit matures and vitamin C.

The most nutritious way to serve this food
Fresh

Diets that may exclude or restrict this food
—

Buying
Choose: Plump, firm dark blue berries. The whitish shine on the berries is a natural protective coating. Fresh berries are now available but frozen packs are more common.
Avoid: Baskets of berries with juice stains or liquid leaking out of the berries. The stains and leaks are signs that there are crushed (and possibly mouldy) berries inside.

Storing
Cover berries and refrigerate them. Then use them in a day or two.
   Do not wash berries before storing. The moisture increases the chance that they will mould in the refrigerator.
   Do not store blueberries in metal containers. The anthocyanin pigments in the berries can combine with metal ions to form dark, unattractive pigment/metal compounds that stain the containers and the berries.

Preparation
Rinse the berries under cool running water, then drain them and pick them

over carefully to remove all stems, leaves, and hard (immature) or soft (overripe) berries.

Cooking reactions

Cooking destroys some of the vitamin C in fresh blueberries. Cooked berries are likely to be mushy because the berries' skin collapses when heat dissolves the pectin inside.

Blueberries may also change colour when cooked. The berries are coloured with blue anthocyanin pigments. Ordinarily, anthocyanin-pigmented fruits and vegetables turn reddish in acids (lemon juice, vinegar) and deeper blue in bases (baking soda).

Effects of processing

Canning and freezing. The intense heat used in canning the fruit or in blanching it before freezing reduces the vitamin C content of blueberries by half.

Medical uses and/or benefits

—

Adverse effects

Hives and angioedema (swelling of the face, lips, and eyes). These are common allergic responses to berries, virtually all of which have been reported to trigger these reactions.

Food/drug interactions

—

• Bread

Nutritional profile per 100 g food						
	White sliced		Wholemeal		Chapatis	
Energy value:	Med	Kcal 233	Med	Kcal 216	High	Kcal 336
Protein:	Med	7.8 g	Med	8.8 g	Med	8.1 g
Fat:	Low	1.7 g	Low	2.7 g	Med	12.8 g
Cholesterol:	None*		None*		None*	
Carbohydrates:	High	49.7 g	High	41.8 g	High	50.2 g
Fibre:	Low	2.7 g	Med	8.5 g	Med	3.7 g
Sodium:	High	540 g	High	540 g	High	130 mg
Major vitamin contribution: B vitamins	Med		Med		Med	
Major mineral contribution: Calcium,	Med		Med		Med	
Iron	High		High		High	
Potassium	Med		Med		Med	

* Depends on composition of added fat.

Nutritional content depends on the type of flour used and the other ingredients. All white flours have less B vitamins and fibre than wholemeal, bran enriched or granary flour. All white bread in Britain is enriched with iron, calcium and B vitamins. Speciality breads like Vienna loaves and rich buns contain milk or eggs which add extra PROTEIN and calcium. Most bought bread is high in sodium.

Breads generally are a good source of starchy CARBOHYDRATE, B vitamins, protein and dietary fibre.

Homemade breads share the basic nutritional characteristics of commercially made breads, but you can vary the recipe to suit your own taste, lowering the salt, sugar, or fat and raising the fibre content, as you prefer.

The most nutritious way to serve this food
Fresh with little butter and margarine, and with low sugar spreads. Sandwiches with meat, eggs, sardines, cheese or salads make well balanced meals. These foods supply the essential amino acid lysine to 'complete' the proteins in grains.

Diets that may restrict or exclude this food
Gluten-free diet (excludes breads made with wheat, oats, rye, buck-wheat and barley flour)
Lactose-free diet (for milk enriched breads)
Low-fibre diet (excludes coarse whole-grain breads)
Low-sodium diet

Buying
Choose: Fresh bread. Bread from a small baker which will be fresher than white sliced or other packet breads in supermarkets and corner shops.

Storing
Store bread at room temperature, in a tightly closed plastic bag (the best protection) or in a breadbin. How long bread stays fresh depends to a great extent on how much fat it contains. Bread made with some butter or other fat will keep for about three days at room temperature. Bread made without fat (most Italian bread, French bread) will dry out in just a few hours; for longer storage, wrap it in foil, put it inside a plastic bag, and freeze it. When you are ready to serve the French or Italian bread, you can remove it from the plastic bag and put the foil-wrapped loaf directly into the oven.

Throw away mouldy bread. The moulds that grow on bread may produce the same carcinogenic toxins (aflatoxins) as those made by moulds on peanuts, milk, or rice.

Do not store fresh bread in the refrigerator; bread stales most quickly at temperatures just above freezing. The one exception: in warm, humid weather, refrigerating bread slows the growth of moulds.

Serving
The fresher the bread the more tasty. Slightly stale bread can be refreshed by placing in a warm oven for ten minutes.

Cooking reactions
Toasting is a chemical process that caramelizes sugars and amino acids (proteins) on the surface of the bread, turning the bread a golden brown (see BROWNING REACTIONS). Some of the sugars become indigestible food fibre and some of the amino acids break into smaller fragments that are no longer nutritionally useful. Thus toast has more fibre and less protein than plain bread. However, the role of heat-generated fibres in the human diet is poorly understood. Toasting has no significant effect on the nutritional value.

Effects of processing
Freezing. Frozen bread releases moisture that collects inside the paper, foil,

or plastic bag in which it is wrapped. If you unwrap the bread before defrosting it, the moisture will be lost and the bread will be dry. Always defrost bread in its wrappings.

Drying. Since moulds require moisture, the less moisture a food contains, the less likely it is to support mould growth. That is why breadcrumbs and crispbreads, which are relatively moisture-free, keep better than fresh bread. Both can be ground fine and used as a toasty-flavoured thickener in place of flour or cornflour.

Medical uses and/or benefits
—

Adverse effects
Allergic reactions and/or gastric distress. Bread contains several ingredients that may trigger allergic reactions, aggravate digestive problems, or upset a specific diet among them gluten (prohibited on gluten-free diets); milk (prohibited on a lactose- and galactose-free diet or for people who are sensitive to milk proteins); sugar (prohibited on a sucrose-free diet); salt (controlled on a sodium-restricted diet); and fats (restricted or prohibited on a controlled-fat, low-cholesterol diet).

Food/drug interactions
—

Broccoli
See also CABBAGE, GREENS

Nutritional profile per 100 g food (raw)		
Energy value:	Low	23 Kcal
Protein:	Low	3.3 g
Fat:	Low	Trace
Cholesterol:	None	None
Carbohydrates:	Low	2.5 g
Fibre:	Med	3.6 g
Sodium:	Low	12 mg
Major vitamin contribution:	Vitamins C and A	High, High
Major mineral contribution:	Calcium, potassium	Med, High

Broccoli has negligible amounts of PROTEINS, virtually no FAT, and a small amount of dietary fibre (cellulose and hemicellulose) and CARBOHYDRATES, primarily sugar with a trace of STARCH.

It is a good source of vitamin A drawn from yellow caretenoids hidden under the chlorophyll that makes its stalks and florets green and a good source of vitamin C. 100 g raw broccoli provides about 100 mg vitamin C, three times the RDA for a healthy adult and twice as much as you get from an equal amount of orange juice. Broccoli also contains vitamin E and vitamin K, the blood-clotting vitamin manufactured by bacteria that live in our intestines.

Broccoli contains a little iron, and it is a good source of calcium. Ounce for ounce, it has approximately as much calcium as milk, and the calcium in broccoli is almost as easily assimilated by the body.

The most nutritious way to serve this food
Fresh, lightly steamed, to protect its vitamin C.

Diets that may restrict or exclude this food
Anti-flatulence diet
Low fibre diet

Buying
Choose: Broccoli with tightly closed buds. The stalk, leaves, and florets should be fresh, firm, and deeply coloured. Broccoli is usually green; some varieties are tinged with purple.
Avoid: Broccoli with woody stalk or florets that are open or turning yellow.

When the green chlorophyll pigments fade enough to let the yellow cartenoids underneath show through, the buds are about to bloom and the broccoli is past its prime.

Storing
Pack broccoli in a plastic bag and store it in the refrigerator or in the vegetable crisper to protect its vitamin C. At 32°F (0°C), fresh broccoli can hold onto most of its vitamin C for as long as two weeks.

Preparation
First, rinse the broccoli under cool running water to wash off any dirt and debris clinging to the florets. Then put the broccoli, florets down, into a pan of salt water (1 tsp. salt to 2 pints water) and soak for 15 to 30 minutes to drive out insects hiding in the florets. Then cut off the leaves and trim away woody section of stalks.

Cooking reactions
The broccoli stem contains a lot of cellulose and will stay firm for a long time even through the most vigorous cooking, but the cell walls of the florets are not so strongly fortified and will soften, eventually turning to mush if you cook the broccoli too long.

Like all cruciferous vegetables, broccoli contains mustard oils, natural chemicals that break down into a variety of smelly sulphur compounds (including hydrogen sulphide and ammonia) when the broccoli is heated. The reaction is more intense in aluminium pots. The longer you cook broccoli, the more smelly compounds there will be, although broccoli will never be as odorous as cabbage or cauliflower.

Effects of processing
Freezing. Frozen broccoli usually contains less vitamin C than fresh broccoli. The vitamin is lost when the broccoli is blanched to inactivate enzymes that would otherwise continue to ripen the broccoli in the freezer. On the other hand, according to researchers at Cornell University, broccoli blanched in a microwave oven kept 90 percent of its vitamin C, compared to 56 percent for broccoli blanched in a pot of boiling water on top of a stove.

Medical uses and/or benefits
✓ PROTECTION AGAINST CANCER

Adverse effects
✗ ENLARGED THYROID GLAND

Food/drug interactions
✗ FALSE RESULT IN TESTS FOR CANCER

• Brussels sprouts

See also CABBAGE

Nutritional profile per 100 g food (raw)		
Energy value:	Low	26 Kcal
Protein:	Low	4.0 g
Fat:	Low	Trace
Cholesterol:	None	None
Carbohydrates	Low	2.7 g
Fibre:	Med	4.2 g
Sodium:	Low	4 mg
Major vitamin contribution:	Vitamins A and C	Med, High
Major mineral contribution:	Potassium	Med

Brussels sprouts are an excellent source of vitamins C and A. 100 g of boiled drained Brussels sprouts provide 40 mg vitamin C (over 100 percent of the RDA). The vitamin A comes from carotenes, whose yellow colour is masked by the chlorophyll that makes the leaves green. The darkest leaves have the most vitamins.

Brussels sprouts also contain an antinutrient, a natural chemical that splits the thiamin (vitamin B_1) molecule so that it is no longer nutritionally useful. This thiamin inhibitor is inactivated by cooking.

The most nutritious way to serve this food
Fresh, lightly steamed to preserve the vitamin C and inactivate the antinutrient.

Diets that may restrict or exclude this food
Antiflatulence diet
Low-fibre diet

Buying
Choose: Firm, compact heads with bright, dark-green leaves.
Avoid: Puffy, soft sprouts with yellow or wilted leaves. The yellow carotenes in the leaves show through only when the leaves age and their green chlorophyll pigments fade. Wilting leaves and puffy, soft heads are also signs of aging.

Storing
Store the Brussels sprouts in the refrigerator. While they are most nutritious

if used soon after harvesting, sprouts will keep their vitamins (including their heat-sensitive vitamin C) for several weeks in the refrigerator.

Store the sprouts in a plastic bag to protect them from moisture loss.

Preparation

First, drop the sprouts into salted iced water to flush out any small insects hiding inside. Next, trim them. Remove yellow leaves and leaves with dark spots or tiny holes, but keep as many of the darker, vitamin A-rich outer leaves as possible.

Cooking reactions

Brussels sprouts contain mustard oils, natural chemicals that break down into a variety of smelly sulphur compounds when the sprouts are heated, a reaction that is intensified in aluminium pots. The longer you cook the sprouts, the more smelly compounds there will be.

To keep cooked Brussels sprouts green, and retain the most vitamin C steam the sprouts quickly in very little water.

Effects of processing

Freezing. Frozen Brussels sprouts contain the same amounts of vitamins as fresh boiled sprouts.

Medical uses and/or benefits

✓ PROTECTION AGAINST CANCER

Adverse effects

✗ ENLARGED THYROID GLAND

Intestinal gas. Bacteria that live naturally in the gut degrade the indigestible carbohydrates (food fibre) in Brussels sprouts and produce gas that some people find distressing.

Food/drug interactions

✗ ANTICOAGULANTS

• Butter

Nutritional profile per 100 g food		
Energy value:	High	740 Kcal
Protein:	Low	0.4 g
Fat:	High	82 g
Cholesterol:	High	230 mg
Carbohydrates:	None	None
Fibre:	None	None
Sodium:	High	850 mg
Major vitamin contribution:	Vitamins A and D	High, Med
Major mineral contribution:	None	

FATS are concentrated sources of energy. Ounce for ounce, they contain nearly twice as many calories as PROTEINS and CARBOHYDRATES. They are digested more slowly than proteins and carbohydrates and keep us feeling full longer.

Except for fats from marine animals, animal fats (butter, lard) contain more SATURATED than UNSATURATED FATTY ACIDS and are high in CHOLESTEROL compared with most vegetable oils. Two-thirds (by weight) of the fatty acids in butter are saturated, one-third are monounsaturated, and there is a trace of polyunsaturated fatty acids. By comparison, 60 percent of the fatty acids in corn oil are polyunsaturated, 24 percent are monounsaturated, and 13 percent are saturated. One tablespoon of butter has 31 mg cholesterol; there is no cholesterol in vegetable oil.

Butter has a trace of protein and no fibre at all. It provides vitamin A and vitamin D. The amounts of vitamins A and D vary with the season and the animals' feed.

The most nutritious way to serve this food
—

Diets that may restrict or exclude this food
Low-cholesterol, controlled-fat diet
Sodium-restricted diet (salted butter)

Buying
Choose: Fresh butter. Check the sell by date on the pack.

Storing
Store butter in the refrigerator, tightly wrapped to protect it from air and

prevent it from picking up the odours of other foods. Even refrigerated butter will eventually turn rancid but this reaction is slowed by cold. Salted butter stays fresh longer than plain butter.

Preparation
—

Cooking reactions
Fats are very useful in cooking. They keep foods from sticking to the pot or pan; add flavour and, as they warm, transfer heat from the pan to the food. In doughs and batters, fats separate the flour's starch granules from each other. The more closely the fat mixes with the starch, the smoother the bread or cake will be.

Heat speeds the oxidation and decomposition of fats. When fats are heated, they can catch fire spontaneously without boiling first at what is called the smoke point. Butter will burn at 250°F (121°C).

Effects of processing
Freezing. Freezing slows the oxidation of fats more effectively than plain refrigeration; frozen butter keeps for up to nine months.

Medical uses and/or benefits
—

Adverse effects
✖ HEART DISEASE

Increased risk of hypertension and some forms of cancer. There is a statistical but as yet unexplained correlation between consumption of fat and the risk of colon and breast cancer. The current search for a link between fat and cancer centres on an examination of the ways in which fat metabolism affects the human body chemistry, including cholesterol metabolism and hormone cycles. As for hypertension, some controlled studies have shown that reducing fat consumption may lower blood pressure.

Food/drug interactions
—

• Cabbage (Chinese leaf, green cabbage, red cabbage, Savoy cabbage)

See also BROCCOLI, BRUSSELS SPROUTS, CAULIFLOWER, GREENS, RADISHES, TURNIPS

Nutritional profile per 100 g food (raw)		
Energy value:	Low	26 Kcal
Protein:	Low	3.3 g
Fat:	Low	Trace
Cholesterol:	None	None
Carbohydrates	Low	3.3 g
Fibre:	Med	3.1 g
Sodium:	Low	23 mg
Major vitamin contribution:	Vitamin A and C	Low, High
Major mineral contribution:	Calcium	Low

Cabbage supplies moderate amounts of vitamin A from the carotenoids hidden under the green chlorophyll pigments in Savoy and green cabbage and the red anthocyanin pigments in red cabbage. Vitamin A is most abundant in the deep green outer leaves; Savoy cabbage has more vitamin A than other green cabbage, which has more than red cabbage. Raw cabbage is a good source of vitamin C.

Raw red cabbage contains an antinutrient enzyme that splits the thiamin molecule so that the vitamin is no longer nutritionally useful. This thiamin inhibitor is inactivated by cooking.

The most nutritious way to serve this food
Fresh, lightly steamed

Diets that may restrict or exclude this food
Antiflatulence diet
Low-fibre diet

Buying
Choose: Cabbages that feel heavy for their size. The leaves should be tightly closed. The outer leaves on a Savoy cabbage may curl back from the head, but the centre leaves should still be relatively tightly closed.

Also look for green cabbages that still have their dark-green vitamin-rich outer leaves.

Avoid: Green and Savoy cabbage with yellow or wilted leaves. Wilted leaves mean a loss of moisture and vitamins.

Storing

Store cabbage in a cool, dark place, preferably a refrigerator. In cold storage, cabbage can retain as much as 75 percent of its vitamin C for as long as six months. Cover the cabbage to keep it from drying out and losing vitamin A.

Preparation

Do not slice the cabbage until you are ready to use it; slicing tears cabbage cells and released the enzyme that hastens the oxidation and destruction of vitamin C.

To separate the leaves for stuffing, immerse the entire head in boiling water for a few minutes, then lift it out and let it drain until it is cool enough to handle comfortably. The leaves should pull away easily. If not, put the cabbage back into the hot water for a few minutes.

Cooking reactions

Cabbage contains mustard oils that break down into a variety of smelly sulphur compounds when the cabbage is heated. The longer you cook the cabbage the more smelly the compounds will be.

Keeping red cabbage red is another problem. This cabbage is coloured with red anthocyanins pigments that turn redder in acids (lemon juice, vinegar) and blue-purple in bases (such alkaline chemicals as baking soda). Here the solution is simple: Make sweet-and-sour cabbage. But be careful not to make it in an iron or aluminium pot, since vinegar (which contains tannins) will react with these metals to discolour the pot and the vegetable. Glass, stainless-steel, or enamelled pots do not produce this reaction.

Effects of processing

Pickling: Sauerkraut is a fermented and pickled product, made by immersing the cabbage in a salt solution strong enough to kill off harmful bacteria but allow beneficial ones to survive, breaking down proteins in the cabbage and producing the lactic acid that gives sauerkraut its distinctive flavour. Sauerkraut contains more than thirty-five times as much sodium as fresh cabbage (661 mg sodium/100 grams sauerkraut) but only half the vitamin C and one-third the vitamin A.

Medical uses and/or benefits
✓ PROTECTION AGAINST CANCER

Adverse effects
✗ ENLARGED THYROID GLAND

Intestinal gas. Bacteria that live naturally in the gut degrade the indigestible carbohydrates (food fibre) in cabbage, producing gas that some people find distressing.

Food/drug interactions

✘ ANTICOAGULANTS

✘ MAO INHIBITORS

• Carob

Nutritional profile per 100 g food (powder)		
Energy value:	High	177 Kcal
Protein:	Low	4.5 g
Fat:	Low	0.7 g
Cholesterol:	None	None
Carbohydrates:	High	81 g
Fibre:	Med	7 g
Sodium:	Med	100 mg
Major vitamin contribution:	B vitamins	Med
Major mineral contribution:	Calcium, iron, potassium	High, High, High

Carob flour which is milled from the dried pod of a Mediterranean evergreen tree, *Ceratonia siliqua* looks like cocoa but has a starchy, beanlike flavour. It can be mixed with sweeteners to make a cocoalike powder or combined with fats and sweeteners to produce a sweet that looks like and has the same rich mouthfeel as milk chocolate but tastes more like honey.

Carob, which is also known as locust bean gum, has less PROTEIN, carbohydrtates, fibre, and calcium and fewer calories than cocoa. Its CARBOHYDRATES include the sugars sucrose, D-mannose, and D-galactose. (D-galactose is a simple sugar that links up with other sugars to form the complex indigestible sugars raffinose and stachyose.) Carob also contains gums and pectins, the indigestible food fibres commonly found in seeds.

The most nutritious way to serve this food
In milk as a cocoa substitute.

Diets that may restrict or exclude this food
Low-carbohydrate diet
Sucrose-restricted diet

Buying
Choose: Tightly sealed containers that will protect the flour from moisture and insects.

Storing
Store carob flour in a cool, dark place in a container that protects it from air, moisture, and insects.

Keep carob 'chocolate' cool and dry.

Preparation
Measure out carob flour by filling a cup or tablespoon and levelling it off with a knife. To substitute carob for plain flour, use one part carob flour to three parts plain flour. To substitute for chocolate, use 3 tablespoons of carob flour plus 2 tablespoons of water for each ounce of plain chocolate.

Cooking reactions
Unlike cocoa powder, carob flour contains virtually no fat. It will burn, not melt, if you heat it in a saucepan. When the flour is heated with water, its starch granules soften and form a mixture which can be used as a stabilizer, thickener, or binder in processed foods and cosmetics. In cake batters, it performs just like other flours (see FLOUR).

Effects of processing
—

Medical uses and/or benefits
Absorbent and demulcent. Medically, carob flour has been used as a soothing skin powder.
As a chocolate substitute. People who are sensitive to chocolate can usually use carob instead. Like cocoa beans, carob is free of CHOLESTEROL. Unlike cocoa, which contains the central-nervous-system stimulant caffeine and the muscle stimulant theobromine, carob does not contain any stimulating methylxanthines.

Adverse effects
—

Food/drug interactions
—

• Carrots

Nutritional profile per 100 g food (raw)		
Energy value:	Low	23 Kcal
Protein:	Low	0.7 g
Fat:	None	Trace
Cholesterol:	None	None
Carbohydrates:	Low	5.4 g
Fibre:	Med	2.9 g
Sodium:	Med	95 mg
Major vitamin contribution:	Vitamin A	High
Major mineral contribution:	Potassium	Med

Carrots are roots. Their crisp texture comes from water pressure on the cell walls stiffened with the indigestible food fibres cellulose, hemicellulose, and lignin. Carrots also provide pectin, and they contain small amounts of sugar (primarily sucrose), very little STARCH and PROTEIN, a trace of FAT, and no CHOLESTEROL.

They are an excellent source of the deep yellow carotenoids from which we produce vitamin A. 100 g of boiled, drained carrots supplies 25,000 times the RDA for a healthy adult. Carrots also have small amounts of vitamin C, the B vitamins, a form of calcium easily absorbed by the body and potassium.

The most nutritious way to serve this food
Raw or cooked. Cooking does not destroy vitamin A.

Diets that may restrict or exclude this food
Low-fibre diet
Low-sodium diet (fresh and canned carrots)

Buying
Choose: Firm, bright orange-yellow carrots.
Avoid: Wilted or shrivelled carrots, pale carrots, or carrots with brown spots on the skin.

Storing
Trim off any leaves before you store carrots. The leafy tops will wilt and rot long before the sturdy root.

Keep carrots cool. They will actually gain vitamin A during their first five months in storage. Protected from heat and light, they can hold their vitamins at least another two and a half months.

Store carrots in perforated plastic bags or containers. Circulating air prevents the natural formation of the terpenoids that make the carrots taste bitter. Storing carrots near apples also encourages the development of terpenoids.

Store peeled carrots in iced water in the refrigerator to keep them crisp for as long as 48 hours.

Preparation

Scrape the carrots. Very young, tender carrots can be cleaned by scrubbing with a vegetable brush.

Soak carrots that are slightly limp in iced water to firm them up. Don't discard slightly wilted intact carrots; use them in soups or stews where texture doesn't matter.

Cooking reactions

Since carotenes do not dissolve in water and are not affected by the normal heat of cooking, carrots stay yellow and retain their vitamin A when you heat them. But cooking will dissolve some of the hemicellulose in the carrot's stiff cell walls, changing the vegetable's texture and making it easier to reach and absorb the nutrients inside.

Effects of processing

Freezing. The characteristic crunchy texture of fresh carrots depends on the integrity of its cellulose- and hemicellulose-stiffened cell walls. Freezing cooked carrots creates ice crystals that rupture these membranes so that the carrots usually seem soft when defrosted. If possible, remove the carrots before freezing a soup or stew and add fresh or canned carrots when you defrost the dish.

Medical uses and/or benefits

✓ PROTECTION AGAINST CANCER

Protection against vitamin A-deficiency blindness. In the body, the vitamin A from carrots aids a protein found in the rods (the cells inside your eyes that let you see in dim light) that makes vision possible. One raw carrot a day provides more than enough vitamin A to maintain vision in a normal healthy adult. Vitamin A deficiency is very rare in the UK.

Adverse effects

Oddly pigmented skin. The carotenoids in carrots are fat-soluble. If you eat large amounts of carrots day after day, these carotenoids will be stored in your fatty tissues, including the fat just under your skin, and eventually your skin will look yellow. If you eat large amounts of carrots *and* large amounts of tomatoes (which contain the red pigment lycopene), your skin may be tinted orange. This effect has been seen in people who ate very large amounts of carrots and tomatoes a day for several months; when the excessive amounts of these vegetables were eliminated from the diet, skin colour returned to normal. Large amounts of concentrated carrot juice over long periods can cause vitamin A poisoning.

Food/drug interactions

✘ FALSE RESULT IN TESTS FOR CANCER

• Cauliflower

See also CABBAGE

Nutritional profile per 100 g food (raw)		
Energy value:	Low	13 Kcal
Protein:	Low	1.9 g
Fat:	Low	Trace
Cholesterol:	None	None
Carbohydrates:	Low	1.5 g
Fibre:	Med	2.1 g
Sodium:	Low	8 mg
Major vitamin contribution:	B vitamins, vitamin C	Med, Low
Major mineral contribution:	Potassium	High

Cauliflower contains indigestible food fibres cellulose, hemicellulose, and pectin; a little PROTEIN and FAT: some SUGAR and a trace of STARCH. It is a low source of vitamin C and a source of B vitamins and potassium.

The most nutritious way to serve this food
Raw or boiled

Diets that may restrict or exclude this food
Antiflatulence diet
Low-fibre diet

Buying
Choose: Creamy white heads with tight, compact florets and fresh green leaves. The size of the cauliflower has no bearing on its nutritional value or its taste.
Avoid: Cauliflower with brown spots or patches.

Storing
Keep cauliflower in a cool, humid place to safeguard its vitamin C content and texture.

Preparation
Pull off and discard any green leaves still attached to the cauliflower and slice off the woody stem and core. Then plunge the cauliflower, head down, into a bowl of salted iced water to flush out any insects hiding in the head. To keep the cauliflower crisp when cooked, add a teaspoon of vinegar to the water.

You can steam or bake the cauliflower head whole or break it up into florets for faster cooking.

Cooking reactions

Cauliflower contains mustard oils, natural chemicals that give the vegetable its taste but break down into a variety of smelly sulphur compounds (including hydrogen sulphide and ammonia) when the cauliflower is heated. The longer you cook the cauliflower, the better it will taste but the worse it will smell. Adding a slice of bread to the cooking water may lessen the odour.

To keep cauliflower white, add a tablespoon of lemon juice, vinegar, or milk to the cooking water.

Steaming or stir-frying cauliflower preserves the vitamin C that would be lost if the vegetable were cooked for a long time or in a lot of water.

Effect of processing

Freezing. Before it is frozen, cauliflower must be blanched to inactivate catalase and peroxidase, enzymes that would otherwise continue to ripen and eventually deteriorate the vegetable.

Medical uses and/or benefits
—

Adverse effects
✖ ENLARGED THYROID GLAND

Intestinal gas. Bacteria that live naturally in the gut degrade the indigestible carbohydrates (food fibre) in cauliflower, producing intestinal gas that some people find distressing.

Food/drug interactions
✖ ANTICOAGULANTS

✖ FALSE RESULT IN TESTS FOR CANCER

• Caviar

Nutritional profile per 100 g food		
Energy value:	High	262 Kcal
Protein:	High	26.9 g
Fat:	Low	15.0 g
Cholesterol:	High	(not available)
Carbohydrates:	Low	3.3 g
Fibre:	None	None
Sodium:	High	2,200 mg
Major vitamin contribution:	B vitamins	High
Major mineral contribution:	Calcium, iron, phosphorus	(not available)

Caviar is a low fat, high-CHOLESTEROL, high-PROTEIN, low-CARBOHYDRATE
FOOD. It is extremely high in sodium and, ounce for ounce, contains twice as
much calcium as milk.

The most nutritious way to serve this food
—

Diets that may restrict or exclude this food
Low-cholesterol, controlled-fat diet
Low-salt/low-sodium diet

Buying
Choose: Shiny, transclucent, large-grained grey fresh caviar (sturgeon roe)
with a clean aroma and tightly sealed tins and jars of less expensive roe.
Lumpfish roe is small-grained and usually black. Cod, salmon, carp, pike, and
tuna roe are large-grained and orangey red or pinkish.

Storing
Store fresh caviar in the coldest part of the refrigerator; it will spoil within
hours at temperatures above 39°F (4°C).
   Store jars of caviar in a cool, dark place.

Preparation
Always serve caviar in a dish (or jar) nestled in ice to keep it safe at room
temperature. The roe contains so much salt that it will not freeze.

When making canapés, add the caviar last so that the oil does not spread and discolour the other ingredients.

Cooking reactions
—

Effects of processing
Pressing. Pressed caviar is caviar with 10 percent of its moisture removed. As a result it contains more nutrients per ounce than regular caviar and is even higher in sodium.

Medical uses and/or benefits
Omega-3 fish oils. Caviar contains the same protective oils found in other fish (see FISH).

Adverse effects
—

Food/drug interactions
✘ MAO INHIBITORS

• Celery (Celeriac)

Nutritional profile per 100g food				
	Celery (raw)		Celeriac (boiled)	
Energy value:	Low	8 Kcal	Low	14 Kcal
Protein:	Low	Trace	Low	1.9g
Fat:	Low	Trace	Low	Trace
Cholesterol:	None	None	None	None
Carbohydrates:	Low	1.3g	Low	2.0g
Fibre:	Low	1.8g	Med	4.9g
Sodium:	High	140mg	Low	28mg
Major vitamin contribution:	Vitamins B and C	Low, Med	Low, Low	
Major mineral contribution:	Potassium, phosphorus	Med, Low	High, Med	

Celery stalks get their crispness from the water pressure in their strong cells. Celery has some SUGAR but almost no STARCH. It is a source of vitamins B and C and some folic acid.

Celeriac, a swollen root of a plant similar to celery, has more starch, fibre, and about the same amount of vitamin C but less sodium and more potassium.

The most nutritious way to serve this food
Fresh

Diets that may restrict or exclude this food
Low-fibre diet
Low-sodium diet

Buying
Choose: Crisp, medium-size pale green celery with fresh leaves. Darker stalks have more vitamin A but are likely to be more stringy.
Choose: Celeriac roots that are firm and small, with no sprouts on top. The larger roots contain more cellulose and lignin, which makes them woody.
Avoid: Wilted or yellowed stalks. Wilted stalks have lost moisture and are low in vitamin C. Yellowed stalks are no longer fresh; their chlorophyll pigments have faded enough to let the yellow carotenes show through.
Avoid: Bruised or rotten celery. Celery cells contain natural chemicals that can become mutagenic or carcinogenic when the cell membranes are damaged.

Bruised or rotting celery may contain up to a hundred times the chemicals in fresh celery.

Storing
Handle celery carefully to avoid damaging the stalks and releasing mutagenic or irritating chemicals.

Remove green tops from celeriac before storing the root.

Refrigerate celery and celeriac in plastic bags or in the vegetable drawer to keep them moist and crisp. They will stay fresh for about a week.

Preparation
Rinse celery under cold running water to remove all sand and dirt. Cut off the leaves, blanch them, dry them thoroughly, and rub them through a sieve or food mill. The dry powder can be used to season salt or frozen for later use in soups or stews.

Scrub celeriac under cold running water. Cut off leaves, small roots, and root buds. Peel and slice the celeriac and use it raw in salads or boil it. When you cut celeriac it will brown. Dip raw sliced and/or peeled celeriac into lemon juice or vinegar and water to slow the BROWNING REACTION. Refrigeration also slows the enzyme action, but not as effectively as an acid bath.

Cooking reactions
When you cook celery the green flesh will soften as the pectin inside its cells dissolves in water, but the virtually indestructible cellulose and lignin 'strings' on the ribs will stay intact. If you don't like the strings, pull them off before you cook the celery.

Cooking also changes the colour of celery. Chlorophyll, the pigment that makes green vegetables green, is very sensitive to acids. When you heat celery, the chlorophyll in its stalks reacts chemically with acids in the celery or in the cooking water to form pheophytin, which is brown.

You can keep the celery green by cooking it quickly or by cooking it in lots of water.

Like other roots, celeriac softens when cooked as the hemicellulose in its cell walls dissolves and the pectin inside leaks out.

Effects of processing
—

Medical uses and/or benefits
✓ PROTECTION AGAINST CANCER

Adverse effects
✗ NITRATE/NITRITE POISONING

Contact dermatitis. Celery contains limonene, an essential oil known to cause contact dermatitis in sensitive individuals. (Limonene is also found in dill, caraway seeds, and the peel of lemon and limes.)

Photosensitivity. The chemicals released by damaged or mouldy celery are photosensitizers as well as potential mutagens and carcinogens. Constant contact with these chemicals can make skin very sensitive to light, a problem most common among food workers who handle large amounts of celery without wearing gloves.

Food/drug interactions
—

• Cheese

Nutritional profile per 100g food				
		Typical Cheeses		
		Cottage		*Cheddar*
Energy value:	Low	Kcal 96	High	Kcal 406
Protein:	High	13.6g	High	26.0g
Fat:	Low	4.0g	High	33.5g
Cholesterol:	Med	13 mg	High	70mg
Carbohydrates:	Low	Trace	Low	Trace
Fibre:	None	None	None	None
Sodium:	High	450mg	High	610mg
Major vitamin contribution:	Vitamin A, D, B vitamins	Low, Low, Low,		High, Med Low,
Major mineral contribution:	Calcium, phosphorous	Low, Med,		High, Med

Cheese is an excellent source of high-quality, complete PROTEINS. Most cheese is high in CHOLESTEROL and FATS, although the fat content of individual cheeses varies widely.

All cheeses supply vitamin A. Orange and yellow cheeses are coloured with carotenoid pigments, including bixin (the carotenoid pigment in annatto) and synthetic beta-carotene.

Hard cheeses are an excellent source of calcium; softer cheeses are a good source: cream cheese and cottage cheese are poor sources. A 100g portion of cheddar cheese, or 1 kg of cottage cheese each contain about as much calcium as one pint of milk. But, ounce for ounce, cheese has much less thiamin (vitamin B_1), riboflavin (vitamin B_2), nicotinic acid, magnesium, and potassium than milk because these water-soluble nutrients are lost when the whey is discarded during cheese making.

All cheese (unless otherwise labeled) is high in sodium.

The most nutritious way to serve this food
Eat it as it comes, in salads, on sandwiches. There are no significant losses in nutrients if it is toasted or browned.

Fat content of common cheeses

Low Fat up to 15% by weight	%	Med Fat 15–25% by weight	%	High Fat over 25% by weight	%
Bon blanc	0	Bon Bel	20	Cambozola	42
Cottage	4–7	Brie	23	Cheddar type	35
Petit Suisse	11	Camembert	23	Cream cheese	47
		Chèvre	23	Danish Blue	29
		Edam	22	Dolcelatte	28
		Gorgonzola	25	Lymeswold	40
		Gouda	22	Port Salut	26
		Gruyère	24	Roquefort	32
		Leiden	22	St André	40
		Mozzarella	24	Stilton	46
		Processed types	25		

Source: Robbins, C.J. *Eating for Health* Granada, London, 1985.

Cholesterol content of cheeses

mg per 100g

Camembert	72mg
Cheddar	70mg
Danish Blue	88mg
Edam	72mg
Stilton	120mg
Cottage cheese	13mg ·
Cream cheese	94mg
Processed cheese	88mg

Source: McCance and Widdowson's *The Composition of Foods,* HMSO, London 1978.

Diets that may restrict or exclude this food
Antiflatulence diet
Controlled-fat, low-cholesterol diet

Lactose and galactose-free diet (lactose, a disaccharide [double sugar] is composed of one unit of galactose and one unit of glucose)
Low-calcium diet (for patients with kidney disease)

Buying

Choose: White rind on brie type cheeses and avoid 'chalky' textured brie which may not ripen if it has been refrigerated or stored for long before you buy it. Check the sell by date on packaged cheese.

Avoid: Any cheese with mould that is not, as with blue cheese, an integral part of the cheese itself. Watch for strong smelling soft cheeses which are over-ripe.

Storing

All cheese should be kept in a cool place or referigerator except grated cheeses treated with preservatives and labelled to show that they can be kept outside the refrigerator. Some sealed packets of processed cheeses can be stored at room temperature but must be refrigerated once the packet is opened.

Wrap cheeses tightly to protect them from contamination by microorganisms in the air and to keep them from drying out. Well-wrapped, refrigerated hard cheeses that have not been cut or sliced will keep for up to six months; sliced hard cheeses will keep for about two weeks. Soft cheeses (cottage cheese, ricotta, cream cheese, and Neufchâtel) should be used within five to seven days. Use all packaged or processed cheeses by the date stamped on the packet.

Throw out mouldy cheese (unless the mould is an integral part of the cheese, as with blue cheese or Stilton).

Preparation

For easily grated cheese, chill the cheese first so it won't stick to the grater.

When serving cheese with fruit or crackers, bring it to room temperature to activate the taste and aroma.

Cooking reactions

Heat changes the structure of proteins and may force moisture out of the protein tissue, which is why overcooked cheese is often stringy. Whey proteins, contain the sulphur atoms that give hot or burned cheese an unpleasant 'cooked' odour. To avoid both strings and an unpleasant odour, add cheese to sauces at the last minute and cook just long enough to melt the cheese.

Effects of processing

Freezing. All cheese loses moisture when frozen; semisoft cheeses will freeze and thaw better than hard cheeses, which may be crumbly when defrosted.

Drying. The more moisture cheese contains, the more able it is to support the growth of organisms like mould. So, dried cheeses will keep significantly longer than ordinary cheeses.

Medical uses and/or benefits
Protection against tooth decay. Cheddar cheese appears to have an inhibiting effect on the bacteria that cause tooth decay. The mechanism is still unclear.

Adverse effects
✖ HEART DISEASE

Allergy to milk proteins. Milk is one of the foods most frequently implicated as a cause of allergic reactions, particularly upset stomach. However, in many cases the reaction is not a true allergy but the result of lactose intolerance (see below).

Lactose intolerance. Lactose intolerance — the inability to digest the sugar in milk — is an inherited metabolic deficiency that affects two thirds of all adults, including 90 to 95 per cent of all Orientals, 70 to 75 percent of all blacks, and 6 to 8 percent of Caucasians. These people do not have sufficient amounts of lactase, the enzyme that breaks the disaccharide lactose into its easily digested components, galactose and glucose. When they drink milk, the undigested sugar is fermented by bacteria in the gut, causing bloating, diarrhoea, flatulence, and intestinal discomfort. Some milk is now sold with added lactase to digest the lactose and make the milk usable for lactase-deficient people. In making cheese, most of the lactose in milk is broken down into glucose and galactose. There is very little lactose in cheeses other than the fresh ones—cottage cheese, cream cheese, and curd cheese.

Galactosemia. Galactosemia is an inherited metabolic disorder in which the body lacks the enzymes needed to metabolize galactose, a component of lactose. Galactosemia is a recessive trait; you must receive the gene from both parents to develop the condition. Babies born with galactosemia will fail to thrive and may develop brain damage or cataracts if they are given milk. To prevent this, children with galactosemia are usually kept on a protective milk-free diet for several years, until their bodies have developed alternative pathways by which to metabolize galactose. Pregnant women who are known carriers of galactosemia may be advised to give up milk and milk products while pregnant lest the unmetabolized galactose in their bodies cause brain damage to the foetus (damage not detectible by amniocentesis). Genetic counselling is available to identify galactosemia carriers and assess their chances of producing a baby with the disorder.

Food poisoning. Raw (unpasteurized) milk and cheeses made from raw milk may contain various microorganisms, including *Salmonella* and *Listeria*, that are destroyed by pasteurization. *Salmonella* poisoning produces gastrointestinal symptoms that, in the very young, the elderly, and the debilitated, may be life-threatening. *Listeria* poisoning is a flulike infection that may be especially hazardous to infants, for those who are already ill, and for pregnant women, all of whom face the risk of encephalitis or blood infections if exposed to the *Listeria* bacteria.

Pencillin sensitivity. People who experience a sensitivity reaction the first time they take penicillin may have been sensitised by exposure to the *Pencillium* moulds in the environment, including the *Pencillium* moulds used to make Brie, Camembert, Roquefort, Stilton, and other 'blue' cheeses.

Food/drug interactions

✘ MAO INHIBITORS

✘ FALSE RESULT IN TESTS FOR CANCER

Tetracyclines. The calcium ions in milk products, including cheese, bind tetracyclines into insoluble compounds. If you take tetracyclines with cheese, your body may not be able to absorb and use the drug efficiently.

Tyramine. Many cheeses contain tyramine, formed when bacteria digest the proteins in milk to make the cheese. As a general rule, there is more tyramine nearer the rind than in the interior of the cheese. Tyramine disposal from the body is interfered with by MAO inhibitors (see above), antidepressants and antihypertensive drugs.

Tyramine content of cheeses

High
Camembert, Cheddar, Emmenthal, Stilton

Medium to high
Brie, Gruyère, Mozzarella, Parmesan, Romano, Roquefort

Low
Processed cheese

Very little or none
Cottage and cream cheese

Sources: *The Medical Letter Handbook of Adverse Drug Interactions* (1985); *Handbook of Clinical Dietetics* (The American Dietetic Association, 1981).

• Cherries

Nutritional profile per 100g fruit		
Energy value:	Low	47 Kcal
Protein:	Low	0.6g
Fat:	Low	Trace
Cholesterol:	None	None
Carbohydrates:	Med	11.9g
Fibre;	Low	1.7g
Sodium:	Low	3mg
Major vitamin contribution:	Vitamin C, Vitamin A	Low, Low
Major mineral contribution:	Potassium	Med

Cherries contain no STARCH: all their CARBOHYDRATES are SUGARS. Fresh cherries contain vitamin A and are a source of vitamin C. A 100g serving of uncooked cherries provides about 5 mg vitamin C, 15% of the adult daily requirement.

The most nutritious way to serve this food
Eaten raw to protect their vitamin C.

Diets that may restrict or exclude this food
Low-sodium diet (maraschino cherries)
Sucrose-restricted diet

Buying
Choose: Plump, firm, brightly coloured cherries with glossy skin whose colour may range from pale golden yellow to deep red to almost black, depending on the variety. The stems should be green and fresh, bending easily and snapping back when released.
Avoid: Sticky cherries (they've been damaged and are leaking), red cherries with very pale skin (they're not fully ripe), and bruised cherries whose flesh will be discoloured under the bruise.

Storing
Store cherries in the refrigerator to conserve their nutrients and flavour. Cherries are highly perishable; use them as quickly as possible.

Preparation
—

Cooking reactions

Depending on the variety, cherries get their colour from either red anthocyanin pigments or yellow-to-orange-to-red carotenoids. The anthocyanins dissolve in water, turn redder in acids and bluish in bases (alkalis). The carotenoids are not affected by heat and do not dissolve in water, which is why cherries do not lose vitamin A when you cook them. Vitamin C, however, is vulnerable to heat.

Effects of processing

Canning and freezing. Canned and frozen cherries contain less vitamin C and vitamin A than fresh cherries. Sweetened canned or frozen cherries contain more sugar than fresh cherries.

Glacé cherries. Crystalized cherries are much higher in calories and sugar than fresh cherries. Maraschino cherries contain about twice as many calories per serving as fresh cherries and are high in sodium.

Medical uses and/or benefits
—

Adverse effects

Poisoning. Like apple seeds and apricot, peach, or plum stones, cherry stones contain amygdalin, a naturally occurring cyanide/sugar compound that breaks down into hydrogen cyanide in the stomach. While accidentally swallowing a cherry stone once in a while is not a serious hazard, cases of human poisoning after eating apple seeds have been reported (see APPLES). *Note*: Some wild cherries are poisonous.

Food/drug interactions
—

• Chocolate (Cocoa, milk chocolate, sweet chocolate)

Nutritional profile per 100g food				
	Milk Chocolate		*Cocoa Powder*	
Energy value:	High	529 Kcal	High	312 Kcal
Protein:	Med	8.4g	High	18.5g
Fat:	High	30.3g	High	21.7g
Cholesterol:	Low	(not available)	None	None
Carbohydrates:	High	59.4g	Med	11.5g
Fibre:	Low	None	Low	4.3g
Sodium:	Med	120mg	High	950mg
Major vitamin contribution:	B vitamins	Low		Med
Major mineral contribution:	Calcium, potassium, iron, copper	Med, Med, Med, Med		Low, High, High, High

Like other seeds, cocoa beans are a good source of PROTEINS, CARBOHYDRATES (starch), fibre (cellulose, pectins, gums, and the noncarbohydrate fibre lignin). B vitamins, and minerals. Cocoa is usually eaten mixed with fats and sugars in confectionery and drinks which make significant changes to its nutritional value in food.

The proteins in cocoa beans, cocoa, and plain chocolate are considered 'incomplete' because they are deficient in the essential amino acids lysine and isoleucine (which are supplied by the milk in milk chocolate). Cocoa butter, the fat in cocoa beans, has no CHOLESTEROL but it is the third most highly saturated vegetable fat, coconut and palm kernel oils. As a food, cocoa butter had two attractive special properties: it rarely becomes rancid and it melts at 92–95°F (33–35°C), the temperature of the human tongue.

Cocoa and chocolate are a good source of thiamin (Vitamin B_1), riboflavin (Vitamin B_2) and nicotinic acid plus phosphorus, iron, potassium, and copper. Cocoa and chocolate also contain oxalic acid, which binds with calcium to form calcium oxalate, an insoluble salt. That is the basis for the old wives' tale that chocolate milk is not nutritious. The fact, though, is that there is more calcium in the milk than can bind with the cocoa or chocolate syrup you add to it; chocolate-flavoured milk is still a good source of calcium.

The most nutritious way to serve this food

With milk. The proteins in milk, which contain adequate amounts of all the essential amino acids, including lysine and isoleucine, complement the proteins in cocoa.

Diets that may restrict or exclude this food

Antiflatulence diet
Low-calcium and low-oxalate diet (to prevent the formation of calcium oxalate kidney stones)
Low-calorie diet
Low-carbohydrate diet
Low-fat diet
Low-fat, controlled cholesterol diet (milk chocolates)
Low-fibre diet
Potassium-regulated (low potassium) diet
Low-sodium diet

Buying

Choose: Tightly sealed boxes or bars. When you open a box of chocolates or unwrap a chocolate bar, the chocolate should be glossy and shiny. Chocolate that looks dull may be stale, or it may be inexpensively made without enough cocoa butter to make it gleam and give it the rich creamy mouthfeel we associate with the best chocolate. (Fine chocolate melts evenly on the tongue.) Chocolate should also smell fresh, not dry and powdery, and when you break a bar or piece of chocolate it should break cleanly, not crumble. One exception: if you have stored a bar of chocolate in the refrigerator, it may splinter if you break it without bringing it to room temperature first.

Storing

Store chocolate at a constant temperature, preferably below 78°F (25°C). At higher temperatures, the fat in the chocolate will rise to the surface and, when the chocolate is cooled, the fat will solidify into a whitish powdery *bloom*. Bloom is unsightly but doesn't change the chocolate's taste or nutritional value. To get rid of bloom, melt the chocolate. The chocolate will turn dark, rich brown again when its fat recombines with the other ingredients. Chocolate with bloom makes a perfectly satisfactory chocolate sauce.

Dark chocolate (plain chocolate, semisweet chocolate) ages for at least six months after it is made, and its flavour becomes deeper and more intense. Wrapped tightly and stored in a cool, dry cupboard, it can stay fresh for a year or more. Milk chocolate ages only for about a month after it is made and holds its peak flavour for about three to six months, depending on how carefully it is stored. Plain cocoa, with no added milk-powder or sugar, will stay fresh for up to a year if you keep it tightly sealed and cool.

Preparation
—

Cooking reactions
Chocolate is high in STARCH; it burns easily. To melt chocolate without mishap, put it in a bowl over a pot or bowl full of very hot water and stir gently.

Effects of processing
Freezing. Chocolate freezes and thaws well. Pack it in a moistureproof container and defrost it in the same package to let it reabsorb moisture it gave off while frozen.

Medical uses and/or benefits
—

Adverse effects
Allergic reactions. Chocolate is often implicated as a cause of the classic allergy symptoms hives, angioedema (swelling of the face, lips, eyes), and upset stomach, plus headaches.
Apthous ulcers. Eating chocolate sometimes triggers a flare-up of apthous ulcers (canker sores) in sensitive people, but eliminating chocolate from the diet will not prevent or cure the canker sores.
Gastric upset. In people prone to heartburn, the caffeine and fat in chocolate may provoke secretion of gastric acid creating the uncomfortable sensation we call heartburn.
Stimulants. Cocoa and chocolate contain the methylxanthine central nervous system stimulants caffeine; theophylline, and theobromine. Theobromine, the weakest CNS stimulant of the three, is also a muscle stimulant. A cup of filter coffee has 110 to 150 mg caffeine; a cup of cocoa made with a tablespoon of plain cocoa powder has about 18 mg caffeine.

Food/drug interactions
✘ MAO INHIBITORS

✘ FALSE RESULT IN TESTS FOR CANCER

• Coconuts

See also NUTS

Nutritional profile per 100g food		
	Dessicated Coconut	
Energy value:	High	604 Kcal
Protein:	Med	5.6g
Fat:	High	62g
Cholesterol:	None	
Carbohydrates:	Med	6.4g
Fibre:	High	23.5g
Sodium:	Low	28mg
Major vitamin contribution:	B vitamins	Med
Major mineral contribution:	Iron, potassium phosphorus, magnesium	Low, High Med, Med

The coconut, which has SUGARS but no STARCH, is a good source of dietary fibre. Like other nuts, its PROTEINS are 'incomplete' because they are deficient in the essential amino acid lysine and isoleucine. The coconut's most plentiful nutrient is FAT. Coconut meat is one-third fat. Unlike other vegetable fats, coconut oil has very little vitamin E and almost no polyunsaturated fatty acids but a higher concentration of SATURATED FATTY ACIDS than any other food. It has no CHOLESTEROL.

The most nutritious way to serve this food
Fresh from the nut.

Diets that may restrict or exclude this food
Low-fat diet
Low-fibre, low-residue diet
Sucrose restricted diet

Buying
Choose: Coconuts that are heavy for their size. You should be able to hear the liquid sloshing around inside when you shake a coconut; if you don't, the coconut has dried out. Avoid nuts with a wet 'eye' (the three sunken spots at the top of the nut) or with mould anywhere on the shell.

Storing

Store whole fresh coconuts in a cool place.

Keep dessicated or shredded coconut in an air- and moistureproof container once you have opened the can or bag.

Preparation

Puncture one of the 'eyes' of the coconut with a sharp, pointed tool. Pour out the liquid. Then crack the coconut by hitting it with a hammer in the middle, where the shell is widest. Continue around the nut until you have cracked the shell in a circle around the middle and can separate the two halves. Pry the meat out of the shell.

To shred coconut meat, break the shell into small pieces, peel off the hard shell and the brown papery inner covering, then rub the meat against a food grater.

Cooking reactions

Toasting caramelizes sugars on the surface of the coconut meat and turns it golden. Toasting also reduces the moisture content of the coconut meat, concentrating the nutrients.

Effects of processing

Drying. Drying concentrates all the nutrients in coconut. *Unsweetened* dessicated or shredded coconut has about twice as much protein, fat, carbohydrate, iron, and potassium as an equal amount of fresh coconut. *Sweetened* desicated or shredded coconut has six times as much sugar.

Coconut milk and cream. Coconut cream is the liquid wrung out of fresh coconut meat; coconut milk is the liquid wrung from fresh coconut meat that has been soaked in water; coconut water is the liquid in the centre of the whole coconut. Coconut milk and cream are high in fat, coconut water is not. All coconut liquids should be refrigerated if not used immediately.

Medical uses and/or benefits

—

Adverse effects

Hives and angioedema (swelling of the eyes and lips). All nuts, including coconuts, are common allergens.

Apthous ulcers. All nuts, including coconuts, may trigger a flare-up of apthous ulcers (canker sores) in sensitive people, but eliminating nuts from the diet won't cure or prevent the canker sores.

Food/drug interactions

—

• Coffee

Nutritional profile per 100g food				
	Ground Roasted Beans		*Infusion*	
Energy value:	High	287 Kcal	Low	2 Kcal
Protein:	High	10.4g	Low	0.2g
Fat:	Med	15.4g	Trace	Trace
Cholesterol:	None	None	None	None
Carbohydrates:	Med	28.5g	Trace	Trace
Fibre:	Trace	Trace	None	None
Sodium:	Low	74mg	Trace	Trace
Major vitamin contribution:	Vitamin B₂, Nicotinic acid	Low, Low		Low, Low,
Major mineral contribution:	Potassium, calcium, magnesium, phosphorus, iron	High, Med, High, Med, Med		Low, Trace, Trace, Trace, Trace

Coffee beans (the roasted seeds from the fruit of the evergreen *Coffea* trees) are about 11 percent PROTEIN, 8 percent sucrose and other SUGARS, 10–15 percent oils, 6 percent assorted acids, and 1–2 percent caffeine. Coffee beans contain the B vitamins riboflavin and nicotinic acid, iron, potassium, and sodium, but brewed coffee has only negligible amounts of nicotinic acid, potassium, sodium, and iron.

Like spinach, rhubarb, and tea, coffee contains oxalic acid (which binds calcium ions into insoluble compounds your body cannot absorb), but this is of no nutritional consequence so long as your diet contains adequate amounts of calcium-rich foods.

The most nutritious way to serve this food
Decaffeinated.

Diets that may restrict or exclude this food
Bland diet
Gout diet
Ulcer diet

Caffeine content (cup of coffee)	
Filter coffee	110-150mg
Percolated coffee	64-124mg
'Instant' coffee	40-108mg
Decaffeinated coffee	2-5mg

Source: Briggs, George M. and Calloway, Doris Howes, *Nutrition and Physical Fitness*, 11th ed. (New York: Holt, Rinehart and Winston, 1984).

Buying
Choose: Freshly ground coffee and coffee beans in tightly sealed, air- and moisture-proof containers.
Avoid: Bulk coffees or coffee beans stored in open bins over a period of time. When coffee is exposed to air, the volatile molecules that give it its distinctive flavour and richness escape, leaving the coffee flavourless and/or bitter.

Storing
Store unopened vacuum-packed cans of ground coffee or coffee beans in a cool place where they will stay fresh for six months to a year. They will lose some flavour in storage, though, because it is impossible to can coffee without trapping some flavour-destroying air inside the can.

Once the can or paper bag has been opened, the coffee or beans should be sealed as tight as possible and stored in the regrigerator. Tightly wrapped, regrigerated ground coffee will hold its freshness and flavour for about a week, whole beans for about three weeks. For longer storage, freeze the coffee or beans in an air- and moistureproof container. (You can brew coffee directly from frozen ground coffee and you can grind frozen beans without thawing them.)

Preparation
If you make your coffee with tap water, let the water run for a while to add oxygen. Soft water makes 'cleaner'-tasting coffee than mineral-rich hard water. Coffee made with chlorinated water will taste better if you refrigerate the water overnight in a glass (not plastic) bottle so that the chlorine evaporates.

Never make coffee with hot tap water or water that has been boiled. Both lack oxygen, which means that your coffee will taste flat.

Always brew coffee in a scrupulously clean pot. Each time you make coffee, oils are left on the inside of the pot. If you don't scrub them off, they will turn rancid and the next pot of coffee you brew will taste bitter. To clean a coffee pot, wash it with detergent, rinse it with water in which you have dissolved a few teaspoons of baking soda, then rinse one more time with boiling water.

Cooking reactions

In making coffee, your aim is to extract flavourful solids (including coffee oils and sucrose and other sugars) from the ground beans without pulling bitter, astringent tannins along with them. How long you brew the coffee determines how much solid material you extract and how the coffee tastes. The longer the brewing time, the greater the amount of solids extracted. If you brew the coffee long enough to extract more than 30 percent of its solids, you will get bitter compounds along with the flavourful ones. (These will also develop by letting coffee sit for a long time after brewing it.)

Ordinarily, filter coffee tastes less bitter than percolator coffee because the water in a filter coffeemaker goes through the coffee only once, while the water in the percolator pot is circulated through the coffee several times. To make strong but not bitter coffee, increase the amount of coffee — not the brewing time.

Effects of processing

Drying. Instant coffees are made by dehydrating concentrated brewed coffee. These coffees are often lower in caffeine than ground coffees because some caffeine, which dissolves in water, is lost when the coffee is dehydrated.

Decaffeinating. Decaffeinated coffee is made with beans from which the caffeine has been extracted, either with an organic solvent (methylene chloride) or with water. How the coffee is decaffeinated has no effect on its taste, but many people prefer water-processed decaffeinated coffee because it is not a chemically treated food. (Methylene chloride is an animal carcinogen, but the amounts that remain in methylene-chloride decaffeinated coffees are small and are considered harmless by health authorities. The carcinogenic organic solvent trichloroethylene [TCE], a chemical that causes liver cancer in laboratory animals, is no longer used to decaffeinate coffee.)

Medical uses and/or benefits

As a stimulant. Caffeine is a stimulant that may increase alertness and concentration, intensify muscle responses, speed up the heartbeat, and elevate mood (which is why it is often combined with analgesics in over-the-counter painkillers). Its effects vary widely from person to person and if you drink coffee every day its effects may be less than if you only drink it once in a while. Some people even find coffee relaxing.

Changes in blood vessels. Caffeine dilates systemic blood vessels and constricts cerebral blood vessels, which is one possible explanation of coffee's ability to relieve headaches caused by engorged blood vessels. Conversely, it may also be why one study at the Long Beach Veterans Hospital in California showed that ordinary (but not decaffeinated) coffee appeared to increase pain-free exercise time in patients with angina. (Caffeine dilates the coronary arteries and increases the coronary blood flow but also increases heartbeat; medical opinion is divided as to whether or not heart patients should be allowed coffee.)

As a diuretic. Caffeine is a mild diuretic sometimes included in over-the-counter remedies for premenstrual tension or menstrual discomfort.

Adverse effects

Stimulation of acid secretion in the stomach. Both ordinary and decaffeinated coffees increase the secretion of stomach acid, which suggests that the culprit is the oil in coffee, not its caffeine.

Elevated levels of serum cholesterol. In several studies, people who drink coffee appear to have higher levels of serum cholesterol than people who do not drink coffee. Some research suggests that the problem may occur in men who drink two or more cups of coffee a day and women who drink four or more cups a day.

Caffeine. Coffee's best known constituent is the methylxanthine central nervous system stimulant caffeine. How much caffeine you get in a cup of coffee depends on how the coffee was processed and brewed. Caffeine is water-soluble. *Instant, freeze-dried,* and *decaffeinated* coffees all have less caffeine than ground roasted coffee.

Withdrawal symptoms. Caffeine is a drug for which you develop a toler-ance; the more often you use it, the more likely you are to require a larger dose to produce the same effects and the more likely you are to experience withdrawal symptoms (headache, irritation) if you stop using it. The symptoms of coffee-withdrawal can be relieved immediately by drinking a cup of coffee.

Unproved/disproved allegations

Birth defects. There is no proved link between coffee consumption by a pregnant woman and birth defects in the child she is carrying.

Nursing infants. Only 0.6–1.5 percent of the caffeine a nursing mother drinks show up in her breast milk; this amount is not considered harmful to the nursing infant.

Fibrocystic breast disease. Although giving up coffee and other caffei-nated beverages reduces symptoms in some women with fibrocystic breast disease, there is no proved causal link between caffeine and fibrocystic breast disease.

Hypertension. Although coffee seems to raise blood pressure slightly in some people, it has not yet been shown to have any special effect on people with hypertension.

Food/drug interactions

◄ FALSE RESULT IN TESTS FOR CANCER

Allopurinol. Coffee and other beverages containing methylxanthine stimulants (caffeine, theophylline, and theobromine) reduce the effectiveness of the antigout drug allopurinol, which is designed to inhibit xanthines.

Antibiotics. Coffee increases stomach acidity, which reduces the rate at which ampicillin, erythromycin, penicillin, and tetracyclines are absorbed when they are taken by mouth. (There is no effect when the drugs are administered by injection.)

Antiulcer medication. Coffee increases stomach acidity and reduces the effectiveness of normal doses of cimetidine and other antiulcer medications.

Iron supplements. Caffeine binds with iron to form insoluble compounds your body cannot absorb. Ideally, iron supplements and coffee should be taken at least two hours apart.

Nonprescription drugs containing caffeine. The caffeine in coffee may add to the stimulant effects of the caffeine in over-the-counter cold remedies, diuretics, pain relievers, stimulants, and weight-control products containing caffeine. Some cold tablets contain 30 mg caffeine, some pain relievers 130, and some weight-control products as much as 280 mg caffeine. There are 110—150 mg caffeine in a cup of filter coffee.

Sedatives. The caffeine in coffee may counteract the drowsiness caused by sedative drugs; this may be a boon to people who get sleepy when they take antihistamines. Coffee will not, however, 'sober up' people who are experiencing the inebriating effects of alcohol beverages.

Theophylline. Caffeine relaxes the smooth muscle of the bronchi and may intensify the effects (and/or increase the risk of side effects) of this antiasthmatic drug.

• Courgettes (Marrow, yellow squash)

Nutritional profile per 100g food (raw)		
Energy value:	Low	16 Kcal
Protein:	Low	0.6g
Fat:	Low	Trace
Cholesterol:	None	None
Carbohydrates:	Low	3.7g
Fibre:	Low	1.8g
Sodium:	Low	1mg
Major vitamin contribution:	Vitamin C	Low
Major mineral contribution:	Potassium	High

Courgettes and the yellow summer squash have moderate amounts of SUGAR, as well as the CARBOHYDRATE food fibres cellulose and hemicellulose, pectins, and gums. The seeds and peel are a source of the noncarbohydrate food fibre lignin, which is found in stems, leaves, and seed coverings. Courgettes have a little PROTEIN and FAT. Like other vegetables, they have no CHOLESTEROL. Yellow summer squash is a moderately good source of carotene, the yellow pigment that your body can convert to vitamin A.

100g of raw courgettes has about 5 mg vitamin C, 15 percent of the RDA for a healthy adult.

The most nutritious way to serve this food
Steamed quickly in very little water, to preserve the vitamin C.

Diets that may restrict or exclude this food
Low-fibre diet
Sucrose-restricted diet

Buying
Choose: Dark green, slender courgettes. Yellow squash should be brightly coloured with lightly pebbled skin.

Choose smaller (and therefore more tender) squash. The best courgettes are 4 to 9 inches long.

Avoid: Limp courgettes. They have lost moisture and vitamins. Avoid squash and marrows whose skin is bruised or cut; handle gently to avoid bruising them yourself. Bruising tears cells, activating ascorbic acid oxidase, an enzyme that destroys vitamin C. Avoid squash with a hard rind; the harder the rind, the older the squash and the larger and harder the seeds inside.

Storing
Refrigerate courgettes, which are perishable and should be used within a few days.

Preparation
Cut off each round end. Peel older, larger squash or marrows, then slice them in half and remove the hard seeds. Younger, more tender courgettes can be cooked with the peel and seeds.

Cooking reactions
As marrow and squash cooks, cells absorb water, the pectins in their cell walls dissolve, and the vegetable gets softer. The seeds, stiffened with insoluble cellulose and lignin, will remain firm.

Yellow squash stays bright-yellow no matter how long you cook it; its carotene pigments are impervious to the normal heat of cooking.

Effects of processing
—

Medical uses and/or benefits
—

Adverse effects
—

Food/drug interactions
—

• Cranberries

Nutritional profile per 100g food (raw)		
Energy value:	Low	15 Kcal
Protein:	Low	0.4g
Fat:	Trace	Trace
Cholesterol:	None	None
Carbohydrates:	Low	3.5g
Fibre:	Med	4.2g
Sodium:	Low	2mg
Major vitamin contribution:	Vitamin C	Low
Major mineral contribution:	Iron, potassium	Low, Med

Cranberries are nearly 90 percent water. The rest is CARBOHYDRATES (SUGARS and indigestible gums, pectins, and cellulose, but no STARCH), plus a little protein and a trace of FAT. Since pectin dissolves as the fruit ripens, the older and riper the berries, the less pectin they contain. The only important vitamin in cranberries is vitamin C.

The most nutritious way to serve this food
Fresh or raw frozen berries.

Diets that may restrict or exclude this food
Low-fibre diet

Buying
Choose: Firm, round, plump, bright red berries that feel dry to the touch.
Avoid: Shrivelled, damp, or mouldy cranberries.

Storing
Store cranberries in the refrigerator. Fresh cranberries will turn brownish if stored at high temperatures, when oxygen and the vitamin C in the berries combine to destroy the anthocyanin pigments that make cranberries red.

Preparation
Wash the berries under running water, drain them, and pick them over carefully to remove shrivelled, damaged, or mouldy berries.

Cooking reactions
First, the heat will make the water inside the cranberry swell, so that if you

cook it long enough the berry will burst. Next, the anthocyanin pigments that make cranberries red will dissolve and make the cooking water red. Cooking cranberries in lemon juice and sugar preserves the colour as well as brightens the taste. Finally, the heat of cooking will destroy the vitamin C in cranberries. Cranberry sauce has about one-third the vitamin C of an equal amount of fresh cranberries.

Effects of processing
—

Medical uses and/or benefits
Urinary antiseptic. In 1985, researchers at Youngstown State University in Ohio found a special factor in cranberries that seems to interfere with the ability of pathogenic bacteria to cling to the surface of cells in the bladder and urinary tract. The factor has shown up in the urine of both animal and human subjects within one to three hours after drinking cranberry juice and may stay potent for as long as twelve to fifteen hours. If the Youngstown research proves out, it may well provide a scientific explanation for the longstanding use of cranberry juice as a folk remedy for urinary infections.

Adverse effects
—

Food/drug interactions
Methenamine. Foods that acidify urine appear to make this urinary antiseptic more effective. Cranberry juice produces hippuric acid which makes urine more acid.

• Cucumbers (Gherkins)

Nutritional profile per 100g food (raw)		
Energy value:	Low	10 Kcal
Protein:	Low	0.6g
Fat:	Low	0.1g
Cholesterol:	None	None
Carbohydrates:	Low	1.8g
Fibre:	Low	0.4g
Sodium:	Low	13mg
Major vitamin contribution:	Vitamin C	Med
Major mineral contribution:	Iron, potassium	Low, Low

Fresh cucumbers are a source of vitamin C, and provide some potassium but provide no other useful nutrients.

The most nutritious way to serve this food
Raw, fresh-sliced.

Diets that may restrict or exclude this food
Antiflatulence diet
Low-fibre diet

Buying this food
Choose: Firm cucumbers with a green skin. Fresh cucumbers will still have a withered yellow flower attached to the non-stalk end.

Choose cucumbers with a clean break at the stem end; a torn, uneven stem end means that the cucumber was pulled off the vine before it was ready. Technically, all the cucumbers we buy are immature; truly ripe cucumbers have very large, hard seeds that make the vegetable unpalatable.

Avoid: Cucumbers with yellowing skin; the vegetable is so old that its chlorophyll pigments have faded and the carotenes underneath are showing through. Puffy, soft cucumbers are also past their prime.

Storing
Store cucumbers in the refrigerator and use them as soon as possible.

Preparation
Rinse the cucumber under cold, running water. You can peel the cucumber —

but not until you are ready to use it, since slicing the cucumber tears its cell walls, releasing an enzyme that oxidizes and destroys vitamin C.

Cooking reactions
—

Effects of processing
Pickling. Cucumbers are not a good source of iron, but pickled cucumbers and gherkins may be. If processed in iron vats, the pickled cucumbers have picked up iron and will give you about 1 mg per pickle. Pickled cucumbers made in stainless steel vats have no iron, nor do pickles made at home in glass or earthenware.

Medical uses and/or benefits
—

Adverse effects
Intestinal gas. Some sensitive people find cucumbers 'gassy.' Pickling, marinating, and heating, which inactivate enzymes in the cucumber, may reduce this gasiness for certain people — although others find pickles even more upsetting than fresh cucumbers.

Food/drug interactions
✗ FALSE RESULT IN TESTS FOR CANCER

• Dates

Nutritional profile per 100g food (dried)		
Energy value:	High	248 Kcal
Protein:	Low	2.0g
Fat:	Low	Trace
Cholesterol:	None	None
Carbohydrates:	High	63.9g
Fibre:	High	8.7g
Sodium:	Low	5mg
Major vitamin contribution:	Vitamin B$_1$ nicotinic acid	Low, Med,
Major mineral contribution:	Iron, potassium	Low, High

Dates are a high-CARBOHYDRATE food, rich in fibre and packed with SUGAR (as much as 70 percent of the total weight of the fruit). Dates are also a source of non-heme iron, the inorganic iron found in plant foods, plus potassium, nicotinic acid, thiamin, and riboflavin, but they are an unusual fruit because they have no vitamin C at all.

The most nutritious way to serve this food
With meat or with a vitamin C-rich food. Both enhance your body's ability to use the non-heme iron in plants (which is ordinarily much less useful than heme iron, the organic iron in foods of animal origin).

Diets that may restrict or exclude this food
Disaccharide-intolerance (sucrase- or invertase-deficiency) diet
Low-carbohydrate diet
Low-fibre/low-residue diet
Low-potassium diet
Low-sodium diet (dried dates, if treated with sodium sulphite)
Sucrose-restricted diet

Buying
Choose: Soft, shiny brown or golden brown whole dates in tightly sealed, airtight packages, or packets of compressed dried dates.

Storing
Store opened packets of dates in a cool place. Properly stored dates will stay fresh for weeks.

Preparation

To slice dates neatly, chill them in the refrigerator or freezer for an hour first. The colder they are, the easier it will be to slice them.

If you're adding dates to a cake or bread dough, coat them first with flour to keep them from dropping through the dough and clustering at the bottom of the pan.

Cooking reactions

The dates will absorb moisture from a cake or bread dough and soften.

Effects of processing

—

Medical uses and/or benefits

✓ POTASSIUM REPLACEMENT

Adverse effects

✗ SULPHITE SENSITIVITY

Food/drug interactions

—

• Eggs

Nutritional profile per 100g (whole, raw)		
Energy value:	Med	147 Kcal
Protein:	High	12.3g
Fat:	Med	10.9g
Cholesterol:	None (white), High (yolk)	1260mg
Carbohydrates:	None	None
Fibre:	None	None
Sodium:	Med	140g
Major vitamin contribution:	Vitamin A, riboflavin, vitamin D	Med, Med, Med
Major mineral contribution:	Iron, calcium, potassium, phosphorus	Med, Low, Med, High

Egg white is a high-protein, low-fat food with virtually no cholesterol and only about 13 percent of the calories in an equal weight of egg yolk. The only important vitamin in egg white is riboflavin (vitamin B_2), a 'visible vitamin' that gives egg white its slightly greenish tint.

Egg yolks are a good source of PROTEIN, but they are high in FAT and CHOLESTEROL. 30 percent of the fatty acids in the yolk are saturated (see SATURATED FATTY ACIDS), and one large egg yolk has 1260 mg cholesterol. The yolk is a good source of calcium, phosphorus, and heme iron, the organic form of iron found in foods of animal origin. Its retinol makes it a good source of vitamin A but, since the yolk also contains xanthophylls (carotenoid pigments with little vitamin A activity), you can't judge the vitamin content by the colour. Egg yolks also supply vitamin D, thiamin (vitamin B_1), riboflavin (vitamin B_2), and nicotinic acid. Both egg whites and egg yolks are moderately high in sodium.

Together, the yolk and white make a high-protein, relatively low-calorie food, with a calcium-rich shell that can be ground and added to cooked eggs as a calcium supplement. The proteins in eggs are considered 'complete,' with a rating of 100 on an arbitrary scale established by the Food and Agriculture Organization of the World Health Organization to measure the relative quality of food proteins. Like the proteins in milk, they are 99 percent digestible, the most useful single proteins available for human beings. Eggs have no sugar and no fibre.

The most nutritious way to serve this food
Boiled, poached or in omelettes with extra whites and fewer yolks (for example, two whites and one yolk) to reduce the fat and cholesterol content.

Diets that may restrict or exclude this food
Controlled-fat, low-cholesterol diet
Low-protein diet

Buying
Choose: Eggs that fit your needs. Eggs are graded by weight from size 1 (large) to size 7 (small). The colour of the egg's shell depends on the breed of the hen that laid the egg and has nothing to do with the egg's food value.

Storing
Store fresh eggs in the refrigerator in an egg-keeper section or keep them in the original carton, which is designed to keep them from breaking or absorbing strong odours through their shells. *Never* wash eggs before storing them: the water will make the egg shell more porous, allowing harmful microorganisms to enter.

Store separated leftover yolks and whites in small, tightly covered containers in the refrigerator, where they may stay fresh for up to a week. Raw eggs are very susceptible to *Salmonella* and other bacterial contamination: discard *any* egg that looks or smells the least bit unusual.

Refrigerate hard boiled eggs, including decorated Easter eggs. They, too, are susceptible to *Salmonella* contamination and should *never* be left at room temperature.

Preparation
First, find out how fresh the eggs really are. The freshest one are the eggs that sink and lie flat on their sides when submerged in cool water. These eggs can be used for any dish. By the time the egg is a week old, the air pocket inside, near the broad end, has expanded so that the broad end tilts up as the egg is submerged in cool water. The yolk and the white inside have begun to separate; these eggs are easier to peel when hard boiled. A week or two later, the egg's air pocket has expanded enough to cause the broad end of the egg to point straight up when you put the egg in water. By now the egg is runny and should be used in sauces where it doesn't matter if it isn't picture-perfect. If the egg floats, throw it away.

When you whip an egg white, you change the structure of its protein molecules which unfold, breaking bonds between atoms on the same molecule and forming new bonds to atoms on adjacent molecules. The result is a network of protein molecules that hardens around air trapped in bubbles in the net. If you beat the whites long enough, the foam will turn stiff enough to hold its shape even if you don't cook it, but it will be too stiff to expand naturally if you heat it, as in a soufflé. When you do cook properly whipped egg white foam, the hot air inside the bubbles will expand. Ovalbumin, an elastic protein in the white, allows the bubble walls to bulge outward until they are cooked firm and the network is stabilized as a puffy soufflé.

The bowl in which you whip the whites should be absolutely free of fat or grease, since the fat molecules will surround the protein molecules in the egg white and keep them from linking up together to form a puffy white foam. Egg whites will react with metal ions from the surface of an aluminium bowl to form dark particles that discolour the egg-white foam. You can whip eggs successfully in an enamel or glass bowl, but they will do best in a copper bowl because copper ions from its surface bind to the egg and stabilize the foam.

Cooking reactions

When you heat a whole egg, its protein molecules behave exactly as they do when you whip an egg white. They unfold, form new bonds, and create a protein network, this time with molecules of water caught in the net. As the egg cooks, the protein network tightens, squeezing out moisture, and the egg becomes opaque. The longer you cook the egg, the tighter the network will be. If you cook the egg too long, the protein network will contract strongly enough to force out all the moisture. That is why overcooked egg custards run and why overcooked eggs are rubbery.

If you mix eggs with milk or water before you cook them, the molecules of liquid will surround and separate the egg's protein molecules so that it takes more energy (higher heat) to make the protein molecules coagulate. Scrambled eggs made with milk are softer than plain scrambled eggs cooked at the same temperature.

When you boil an egg in its shell, the air inside expands and begins to escape through the shell as tiny bubbles. Sometimes, however, the force of the air is enough to crack the shell. Since there's no way for you to tell in advance whether any particular egg is strong enough to resist the pressure of the bubbling air, the best solution is to create a safety vent by sticking a pin through the broad end of the egg before you start to boil it. Or you can slow the rate at which the air inside the shell expands by starting the egg in cold water and letting it warm up naturally as the water warms rather than plunging it cold into boiling water — which makes the air expand so quickly that the shell is virtually certain to crack.

As the egg heats, a little bit of the protein in its white will decompose, releasing sulphur that links up with hydrogen in the egg, forming hydrogen sulphide, the gas that gives rotten eggs their distinctive smell. The hydrogen sulphide collects near the coolest part of the egg — the yolk. The yolk contains iron, which now displaces the hydrogen in the hydrogen sulphide to form a green iron-sulphide ring around the hard-cooked yolk.

Effects of processing

Drying. Dried eggs, when reconstituted, have virtually the same nutritive value as fresh eggs. Always refrigerate dried eggs in an air- and moistureproof container. At room temperature, they will lose about a third of their vitamin A in six months.

Medical uses and/or benefits
—

Adverse effects
✘ HEART DISEASE

Allergy. Eggs are among the foods most often linked to the classic symptoms of true food allergy: abdominal pain, nausea or vomiting, cramps, dizziness, hives, angioedema (swollen lips and eyes), hay-feverlike reactions, and eczema.
Antinutrients. Egg white contains the antinutrient avidin. The avidin in raw egg whites binds biotin into an insoluble compound your body cannot absorb, and people who eat large amounts of raw egg whites might end up with a biotin deficiency. However, since avidin is inactivated simply by cooking the egg, this is very rare.
Cholesterol. People at high risk of heart disease especially with raised blood CHOLESTEROL levels are advised to restrict their consumption of egg *yolks* to a maximum of 3—5 per week. Because the yolks are one of the most concentrated sources of dietary cholesterol the less eaten the better for high risk people. Egg whites are free from cholesterol.

Food/drug interactions
Sensitivity to vaccines. Live-virus measles vaccine, live-virus mumps vaccine, and the vaccines for influenza are grown in either chick embryo or egg culture. They may all contain minute residual amounts of egg proteins that may provoke a hypersensitivity reaction in people with a history of anaphylactic reactions to eggs (hives, swelling of the mouth and throat, difficulty breathing, a drop in blood pressure, or shock).

• Figs

Nutritional profile per 100g food (dried)		
Energy value:	High	213 Kcal
Protein:	Low	3.6g
Fat:	Trace	Trace
Cholesterol:	None	None
Carbohydrates:	High	52.9g
Fibre:	High	18.5g
Sodium:	High	87mg
Major vitamin contribution:	B vitamins	Low
Major mineral contribution:	Iron, potassium, calcium, zinc	Med, High, High, Med

Fresh figs and dried figs, are a good source of CARBOHYDRATES (sugars), fibre, iron, calcium, and potassium.

Figs have no STARCH; 92 percent of the carbohydrates in dried figs are sugars (42 percent glucose, 31 percent fructose, 0.1 percent sucrose). The rest are dietary fibres (primarily pectins and gums, plus cellulose). Figs are also a good source of the noncarbohydrate fibre lignin.

An important mineral in dried figs is iron, 100 g of uncooked dried figs provides 4.2 mg iron, 40% of the RDA for a healthy adult female. Ounce for ounce, dried figs have more calcium than milk.

The most nutritious way to serve this food
Fresh or dried

Diets that may restrict or exclude this food
Low-fibre, low-residue diets
Low-sodium (dried figs treated with sulphites)
Sucrose-restricted diet

Buying
Choose: Plump, soft fresh figs whose skin may be green, brown, or purple, depending on the variety. As figs ripen, the pectin in their cell walls dissolves and the figs grow softer to the touch.

Choose dried figs with no sign of dampness and with as little coating of white powdered sugar as possible.
Avoid: Fresh figs that smell sour. The odour indicates that the sugars in the fig have fermented; such fruit is spoiled.

Storing

Refrigerate fresh figs. Dried figs can be stored in the refrigerator or at room temperature; either way, wrap them tightly in an air- and moistureproof container to keep them from losing moisture and becoming hard. Dried figs may keep for months.

Preparation

Wash fresh figs under cool water; use dried figs straight from the packet. If you want to slice the dried figs, chill them first in the refrigerator or freezer: cold figs slice cleanly.

Cooking reactions

Fresh figs contain ficin, a proteolytic (protein-breaking) enzyme similar to papain in papayas and bromelain in fresh pineapple. Proteolytic enzymes split long-chain protein molecules into smaller units, which is why they help tenderize meat. Ficin is most effective at about 140–160°F (60–70°C), the temperature at which stews simmer, and it will continue to work after you take the stew off the heat until the food cools down. Temperatures higher than 160°F inactivate ficin; canned figs which have been exposed to very high heat in processing — will not tenderise meat.

Both fresh and dried figs contain pectin, which dissolves when you cook the figs, making them softer. Dried figs also absorb water and swell, becoming softer.

Effects of processing

Canning: Canned figs contain slightly less thiamin, riboflavin, and nicotinic acid than fresh figs, and no active ficin.

Medical uses and/or benefits

✖ POTASSIUM REPLACEMENT

Iron supplementation. Dried figs are an excellent source of iron.
As a laxative. Figs are a good source of the indigestible food fibre lignin. Cells whose walls are highly lignified retain water and, since they are impossible to digest, help bulk up the stool. In addition, ficin has some laxative effects. Together, the lignin and the ficin make figs (particularly dried figs) an efficient laxative food.

Adverse effects

✖ SULPHITE SENSITIVITY

Food/drug interactions

✖ MAO INHIBITORS

Fish

See also SHELLFISH, SQUID

Nutritional profile per 100g food (raw)				
	Cod Fillet		*Herring*	
Energy value:	Low	76 Kcal	High	234 Kcal
Protein:	High	17.4g	High	16.8g
Fat:	Low	0.7g	High	18.5g
Cholesterol:	Med	50mg	Med	70mg
Carbohydrates:	None	None	None	None
Fibre:	None	None	None	None
Sodium:	Med	77mg	Med	67mg
Major vitamin contribution:	B vitamins,	Med,		High
	vitamins A and	Med,		Med
	D (in fatty fish	Trace,		High,
	oils)			
Major mineral contribution:	Iodine,	Med,		Med,
	selenium,	Med,		Med,
	phosphorus,	Med,		Med,
	potassium, iron,	Med, Low		Med, Low
	calcium	Low		Low

Fish have no measurable CARBOHYDRATES or food fibre, but they are an excellent source of PROTEINS considered 'complete' because they contain sufficient amounts of all the essential amino acids. White fish, like cod has proportionally less fat than meat, and most fish FATS and oils are higher in UNSATURATED FATTY ACIDS and lower in saturated fatty acids than the fat in beef, pork, or lamb. The exact proportion of fat and SATURATED FATTY ACIDS varies with the kind of fish as well as when and where it is caught. Cooked tuna, for example, is 1 to 2 percent fat; the fat in canned tuna is 63 percent unsaturated fatty acids. Dark orange salmon has more fat than pale pink salmon; salmon fats and oils are about 68 percent unsaturated. Herring may be 13 to 16 percent fat; its fats and oils are 82 percent unsaturated fatty acids.

An important nutrient in fish is the omega-3 fatty acids, eicosapentaenoic acid (EPA), and docosahexanoic acid (DHA). EPA and DHA are the principal polyunsaturated fatty acids in the fat and oils of fish. They seem to lower the levels of low-density lipoproteins (LDL), the molecules that carry cholesterol into your bloodstream, and raise the level of high-density lipoproteins (HDL), the molecules that carry cholesterol away to be eliminated from the body. They also appear to inhibit the production of leuketrienes, natural inflammatory agents that transmit signals between cells. (All inflammatory diseases are the result of exaggerated eicosanoid signals.) Omega-3 fatty acids are most abundant in oils from fatty fish that live in cold water: — herring, mackerel, salmon. The oils, which stay liquid at cold temperatures, may help insulate the fish against the cold.

Fish are a good source of the B vitamins (particularly nicotinic acid), and fish oils and fatty fish are two of the few natural food sources of vitamin D. The soft edible bones of small fish or canned salmon, sardines, and mackerel are an excellent source of calcium.

The most nutritious way to serve this food
Cooked, to kill parasites and potentially pathological microorganisms living in raw fish.

Diets that may restrict or exclude this food
Low-purine (antigout) diet
Low-sodium diet (canned, salted, or smoked fish)

Buying
Choose: Fresh-smelling whole fish with shiny skin; reddish-pink, moist gills; and clear, bulging eyes. The flesh should spring back when you press it lightly.

Choose fish fillets that look moist, not dry.

Choose tightly sealed, solidly frozen packages of frozen fish.

Avoid: Fresh whole fish whose eyes have sunk into the head (a clear sign of aging); fillets that look dry; and packages of frozen fish that are stained (whatever leaked on the package may have seeped through onto the fish) or are coated with ice crystals (the package may have defrosted and been refrozen).

Storing
Refrigerate all fresh and smoked fish immediately. Fish spoils quickly because it has a high proportion of polyunsaturated fatty acids (which are oxidized much more easily than saturated or monounsaturated fatty acids).

Keep frozen fish frozen until you are ready to use it.

Store canned fish in a cool cabinet or in the refrigerator (but not the freezer). The cooler the temperature, the longer the shelf life.

Preparation
Fresh fish. Rub the fish with lemon juice, then rinse it under cold running water. The lemon juice (an acid) will convert the nitrogen compounds that make fish smell 'fishy' to compounds that break apart easily and can be

rinsed off the fish with cool running water. Rinsing your hands in lemon juice and water will get rid of the fishy smell after you have been preparing fresh fish.

Frozen fish. Defrost plain frozen fish in the refrigerator or under cold running water. Prepared frozen fish dishes should not be thawed before you cook them since defrosting will make the sauce or coating soggy.

Salted dried fish. Salted dried fish should be soaked to remove the salt. How long you have to soak the fish depends on how much salt was added in processing. A reasonable average for salt cod, mackerel, haddock (finnan haddie), or herring is 3 to 6 hours, with two or three changes of water.

Cooking reactions

The longer you cook fish, the more moisture it will lose, Cooked fish flakes because the connective tissue in fish 'melts' at a relatively low temperature.

Cooking fish thoroughly destroys parasites and microorganisms that live in raw fish, making the fish safer to eat.

Effects of processing

Marinating. Acids coagulate the proteins in fish, squeezing out moisture. Fish marinated in citrus juices and other acids such as vinegar or wine has a firm texture and looks cooked, but the acid bath may not inactivate parasites in the fish.

Canning. Fish is naturally low in sodium, but canned fish often contains enough added salt to make it a high-sodium food. Fish canned in oil is also much higher in calories than fresh fish.

Freezing. When fish is frozen, ice crystals form in the flesh and tear its cells so that moisture leaks out when the fish is defrosted. Commercial flash-freezing offers some protection by freezing the fish so fast that the ice crystals stay small and do less damage, but all defrosted fish tastes drier and less palatable than fresh fish. Freezing slows but does not stop the oxidation of fats that causes fish to deteriorate.

Curing. Fish can be cured (preserved) by smoking, drying, salting, or pickling, all of which coagulate the muscle tissue and prevent microorganisms from growing. Each method has its own particular drawbacks. Smoking adds potentially carcinogenic chemicals. Drying reduces the water content, concentrates the solids and nutrients, increases the calories and raises the amount of sodium.

Medical uses and/or benefits

Protective effects of omega-3 fatty acids. Fish oils inhibit the formation of thromboxane, a blood-platelet aggregator, and omega-3 fatty acids in fish oils are converted to a compound similar to prostacyclin, a natural body chemical that inhibits clotting. Those effects appear to reduce the risk of heart attacks and strokes.

Adverse effects

Allergies. Fish is one of the foods most often implicated as a cause of the classic food-allergy symptoms, including gastric upset, hives, and angioedema (swelling of the lips and eyes).

Environmental contaminants. Many environmental contaminants can be stored in the fatty tissues of fish from contaminated waters.

Parasitical, viral, and bacterial infections. Like raw meat, raw fish may carry various pathogens, including fish tapeworm and flukes in freshwater fish and *Salmonella* or other microorganisms left on the fish by infected food-handlers. Cooking the fish destroys these organisms.

Scombroid poisoning. Bacterial decomposition that occurs after fish is caught produces a histamine-like toxin in the flesh of mackerel and tuna. This toxin may trigger a number of symptoms, including a flushed face immediately after you eat it. The other signs of scombroid poisoning — nausea, vomiting, stomach pain, and hives — show up a few minutes later. The symptoms usually last 24 hours or less.

Food/drug interactions

—

• Flour

See also BREAD, OATS, PASTA, POTATOES, RICE

Nutritional Profile per 100g food

	Wholemeal		Plain	
Energy value:	High	318 Kcal	High	350 Kcal
Protein:	Med	13.2g	Med	9.8g
Fat:	Low	2.0g	Low	1.2g
Cholesterol:	None	None	None	None
Carbohydrates:	High	65.8g	High	80.1g
Fibre:	Med	9.6g	Low	3.4g
Sodium:	Low (except self-raising flour)	3mg	Low	2mg
Major vitamin contribution:	B vitamins	High		Med
Major mineral contribution:	Iron, potassium, phosphorus	Med, Med, Med,		Low, Low, Low

Flour is the primary source of the CARBOHYDRATES (STARCH and fibre) in bread and pasta. All wheat and rye flours provide pectins, gums, cellulose, and the noncarbohydrate food fibre lignin. Flour also contains significant amounts of PROTEIN but, like other plant foods, its proteins are 'incomplete' because they are low in the essential amino acid lysine. The fat in the wheat germ is primarily polyunsaturated; flour contains no CHOLESTEROL. Flour is a good source of iron and the B vitamins. Iodine and iodophors used to clean the equipment in grain-processing plants may add iodine to the flour.

In the UK all flour, except wholemeal, is fortified by law with iron, calcium, thiamin and nicotinic acid.

Wholemeal flours. Wholemeal flours use every part of the kernel: the fibre-rich bran with its B vitamins, the starch- and protein-rich endosperm with its iron and B vitamins, and the oily germ with its vitamin E. Because they contain bran, whole-grain flours have much more fibre than refined white flours. However, some studies suggest that the size of the fibre particles may have some bearing on their ability to absorb moisture and 'bulk up' stool. Wholemeal flour, like other grain products, also contains an antinutrient, phytic acid — which binds calcium, iron, and zinc ions into insoluble compounds your body cannot absorb. This has no practical effect so long as your diet includes foods that provide these minerals.

'White' flours. Refined ('white') flours are paler than wholemeal flours because they do not contain the brown bran and germ. They have less fibre and fat and smaller amounts of vitamins and minerals than whole wheat flours, but *enriched refined flours* are fortified with B vitamins and iron. Refined flour has less phytic acid than wholemeal flour.

Some refined flours are bleached with chlorine dioxide to destroy the xanthophylls (carotenoid pigments) that give white flours a natural cream colour. Unlike carotene, xanthophylls have no vitamin A activity; bleaching does not lower the vitamin A levels in the flour, but it does destroy vitamin E.

There are several kinds of white flours. *Plain* white flour is a finely milled soft wheat flour. *Self-raising* flour is a soft flour to which baking powder has been added and is very high in sodium. *Semolina* is a pale high-protein, low-gluten flour made from durum wheat and used to make pasta. *Strong white* flour is a high protein flour used in bread and bun baking.

Rye flours. Rye flour has less gluten than wheat flour and is therefore less elastic, which is why it makes a denser bread.

Like wholemeal flour, dark rye flour (the flour used for pumpernickel and rye bread) contains the bran and the germ of the rye grain; light rye flour (the flour used for ordinary rye bread) does not.

The most nutritious way to serve this food
As bread or as a thickener in soups and stews rather than as high sugar and fat flour confectionery — cakes, biscuits and puddings.

Diets that may restrict or exclude this food
Low-calcium diet (whole grain and self-raising flours)
Low-fibre diet (wholemeal flours)
Low-gluten diet (all wheat and rye flour)

Buying
Choose: Tightly sealed bags less than one year old.
Avoid: Old flour, especially wholemeal, as the oil can go rancid if it has not been carefully stored since harvest.

Storing
Store all flours in air- and moistureproof canisters. Wholemeal flours which contain the germ and bran of the wheat and are higher in fat than white flours, may become rancid when exposed to air.

Put a bay leaf in the flour canister to help protect against insect infestations. Bay leaves are natural insect repellents.

Preparation
—

Cooking reactions

Protein reactions. The wheat kernel contains several PROTEINS, including gliadin and glutenin. When you mix flour with water, gliadin and glutenin clump together in a sticky mass. Kneading the dough relaxes the long gliadin and glutenin molecules, allowing them to form new bonds between atoms in different molecules. The result is a network structure made of a new gliadin — glutenin compound called *gluten.*

Gluten is very elastic. The gluten network can stretch to hold the gas (carbon dioxide) formed when you add yeast to bread dough or heat a cake mixture made with baking powder or baking soda (sodium bicarbonate), trapping the gas and making the bread dough or cake mixture rise. When you bake the dough or mixture, the gluten network hardens and the bread or cake retains its finished shape.

Starch reactions. STARCH consists of molecules of the complex CARBO-HYDRATES amylose and amylopectin packed into a starch granule. When you heat flour in liquid, the starch granules absorb water molecules, swell, and soften. When the temperature of the liquid reaches approximately 140°F (60°C) the amylose and amylopectin molecules inside the granules relax and unfold, breaking some of their internal bonds (bonds between atoms on the same molecule) and forming new bonds between atoms on different molecules. The result is a network that traps and holds water molecules. The starch granules then swell, thickening the liquid. If you continue to heat the liquid (or stir it too vigorously), the network will begin to break down, the liquid will leak out of the starch granules, and the sauce will separate.

Combination reaction. Coating food with flour takes advantage of the starch reaction (absorbing liquids) and the protein reaction (baking a hard, crisp protein crust).

Effects of processing
—

Medical uses and/or benefits
—

Adverse effects

Allergic reactions. Wheat is one of the foods most commonly implicated as a cause of allergic upset stomach, hives, and angioedema (swollen lips and eyes).

Gluten intolerance (coeliac disease). Coeliac disease is an intestinal allergic disorder that makes it impossible to digest gluten. Corn flour, potato flour, rice flour, and soya flour are all gluten free.

Food/drug interactions
—

• Garlic

See also ONIONS

Nutritional profile per 100g food (raw)		
Energy value:	Low	117 Kcal
Protein:	Low	3.5g
Fat:	Low	0.3g
Cholesterol:	None	None
Carbohydrates:	Med	26.7g
Fibre:	Low	(not available)
Sodium:	Low	18mg
Major vitamin contribution:	Vitamin C, thiamin (vitamin B$_1$)	Med, High
Major mineral contribution:	Potassium, iron	High, Low

Raw garlic is high in CARBOHYDRATES, with some fibre and PROTEIN but almost no FAT. Garlic has some vitamins and minerals; the trick is to eat enough garlic to get useful amounts. For example, raw garlic provides 0.24 mg thiamin (almost the amount in 100g egg yolk), 1.4 mg iron (15 percent of the RDA for an adult woman), and 10 mg vitamin C (30 percent of the RDA for a healthy adult).

Diets that may restrict or exclude this food
Antiflatulence diet
Bland diet

Buying
Choose: Firm, solid cloves with tight clinging skin. If the skin is papery and pulling away from the cloves and the head feels light for its size, the garlic may have withered or rotted away inside.

The most nutritious way to serve this food
Fresh, raw.

Storing
Store garlic in a cool, dark, airy place to keep it from drying out or sprouting. (When garlic sprouts, diallyl disulphide — the sulphur compound that gives fresh garlic its distinctive taste and odour — goes into the new growth and the garlic itself becomes milder.) An unglazed ceramic 'garlic keeper' will protect the garlic from moisture while allowing air to circulate freely around the head and cloves. Properly stored, garlic will keep for six months.

Do not refrigerate garlic unless you live in a very hot and humid climate.

Preparation

To peel garlic easily, blanch the cloves in boiling water for about 30 seconds, then drain and cool. Slice off the root end, and the skin should come off without sticking to your fingers. Or you can put a head of fresh, raw garlic on a flat surface and press the flat end with the flat side of a knife. The head will come apart and the skin should come off easily.

To get the most 'garlicky' taste from garlic cloves, chop or mash them or extract the oil with a garlic press.

Cooking reactions

Heating garlic destroys its diallyl disulphide, the chemical which gives garlic its smell, which is why cooked garlic is so much milder than raw garlic.

Effects of processing

Drying. Drying removes moisture from garlic but leaves the oils intact. Powdered garlic and garlic salt should be stored in a cool, dry place to keep their oils from turning rancid. Garlic salt is much higher in sodium than either raw garlic, garlic powder, or dried garlic flakes.

Medical uses and/or benefits

✓ HEART DISEASE

As an antibiotic. Garlic contains alliin and allicin, two sulphur compounds with antibiotic activity. Both in nature and in laboratory experiments garlic juice has been shown to inhibit a broad variety of microorganisms (bacteria, yeast, fungi), but its effects on human beings remain to be proved.

Cholesterol. In a number of laboratory studies, animals given garlic oil showed a decrease in blood levels of low-density lipoprotein (LDL), the 'bad' CHOLESTEROL that adheres to artery walls and a corresponding increase in blood levels of high-density lipoproteins (HDL), the 'good' cholesterol that does not stick to artery walls.

Studies of patients with heart disease have shown some increases in the activity of anticlotting substances in blood when the patients were given ten cloves of garlic a day for a month.

Adverse effects

Body odour and halitosis. Diallyl disulphide is excreted in perspiration and in the air you exhale, which is why eating garlic makes you smell garlicky.

Food/drug interactions

—

• Gelatin

Nutritional profile per 100g food		
Energy value:	High	338 Kcal
Protein:	High	84.4g
Fat:	Low	Trace
Cholesterol:	Low	(not available)
Carbohydrates:	None	None
Fibre:	None	None
Sodium:	Low	(not available)
Major vitamin contribution:	None	
Major mineral contribution:	None	

Although gelatin is made from the collagen (connective tissue) of cattle hides and bones or pig skin, its PROTEINS are considered 'incomplete' because they lack the essential acid tryptophan, which is destroyed when the bones and skin are treated with acid, and is deficient in several others, including lysine. In fact, gelatin's proteins are of such poor quality that, unlike other foods of animal origin (meat, milk), gelatin cannot sustain life. Laboratory rats fed a diet in which gelatin was the primary protein did not grow as they should: half died within 48 days, even though the gelatin was supplemented with some of the essential amino acids.

Plain gelatin has no CARBOHYDRATES and fibre. It is low in FAT.

The most nutritious way to serve this food
As a thickener in low fat fish mousses and fresh fruit mousse.

Diets that may restrict or exclude this food
Low-carbohydrate diet (gelatin desserts prepared with sugar)
Low-sodium diets (commercial gelatin powders)
Sucrose-restricted diet (gelatin desserts prepared with sugar)

Buying
Choose: Tightly sealed, clean boxes.

Storing
Store gelatin boxes in a cool, dry cabinet.

Preparation
One tablespoon of gelatin will thicken about 2 cups of water. To combine the

gelatin and water, first heat $^3/_4$ cup water to boiling. While it is heating, add the gelatin to $^1/_4$ cup cold liquid and let it absorb moisture until it is translucent. Then add the boiling water. (Flavoured fruit gelatins can be dissolved directly in hot water.)

If you are going to chill the gelatin in a mould, first rinse the mould with clear, cold running water. Then rub the inside with vegetable oil to make it easy to unmould the hardened gelatin. (The oil will make the surface of the gelatin cloudy rather than shiny.)

Cooking reactions

When you mix gelatin with hot water, its protein molecules create a network that stiffens into a stable, solid gel as it squeezes out moisture. The longer the gel sits, the more intermolecular bonds it forms, the more moisture it loses and the firmer it becomes. A day-old gel is much firmer than one you've just made.

Gelatin is used as a thickener in prepared foods and can be used at home to thicken sauces.

To build a layered gelatin mould, let each layer harden before you add the next.

Effects of processing
—

Medical uses and/or benefits
—

Adverse effects
—

Food/drug interactions
—

• Grapefruit (Ugli fruit)

Nutritional profile per 100g food		
Energy value:	Low	22 Kcal
Protein:	Low	0.6g
Fat:	Low	Trace
Cholesterol:	None	None
Carbohydrates:	Low	5.3g
Fibre:	Low	0.6g
Sodium:	Low	1mg
Major vitamin contribution:	Vitamin C	High
Major mineral contribution:	Potassium	Med

Grapefruit and ugli fruit (a cross between the grapefruit and the tangerine) have some SUGARS and a little fibre but no STARCH. Like all citrus fruits, they are prized for their vitamin C. An average-size half grapefruit (3.5 inches across) provides 41 mg vitamin C, 130 percent of the RDA for a healthy adult.

Grapefruit and grapefruit juice are good sources of potassium, providing about 80 percent of the potassium in an equal amount of fresh orange or orange juice.

Because it is a low-calorie food (about 20 calories per half grapefruit), grapefruit is often included in slimming diets.

The most nutritious way to serve this fruit
Fresh fruit or juice.

Diets that may restrict or exclude this food
—

Buying
Choose: Firm fruit that is heavy for its size, which means that it will be juicy. The skin should be thin, smooth, and fine-grained. Most grapefruit have yellow skin that, depending on the variety, may be tinged with red or green. In fact, a slight greenish tint may mean that the grapefruit is high in sugar. Ugli fruit, which looks like misshapen, splotched grapefruit, is yellow with green patches and bumpy skin.
Avoid: Grapefruit or ugli fruit with puffy skin or those that feel light for their size; the flesh inside could be dry and juiceless.

Storing
Store grapefruit either at room temperature (for a few days) or in the refrigerator.

Refrigerate grapefruit juice. Properly stored and protected from oxygen, fresh grapefruit juice can hold its vitamin C for several weeks.

Preparation
Grapefruit are most flavourful at room temperatrue, which liberates the aromatic molecules that give them their characteristic scent and taste.

To section grapefruit, cut a slice from the top, then cut off the peel in strips — starting at the top and going down — or peel it in a spiral fashion. You can remove the bitter white membrane, but some of the vitamin C will go with it. Finally, slice the sections apart. Or you can simply cut the grapefruit in half and scoop out the sections with a curved, serrated grapefruit knife.

Cooking reactions
Grilling a half grapefruit or poaching grapefruit sections reduces the fruit's supply of vitamin C, which is heat-sensitive.

Effects of processing
Commercially prepared juices. How well a commercially prepared juice retains its vitamin C depends on how it is prepared, stored, and packaged. Commercial flash-freezing preserves as much as 95 percent of the vitamin C in fresh grapefruit juices. Canned juice stored in the refrigerator may lose only 2 percent of its vitamin C in three months. Prepared, pasteurized 'fresh' juices lose vitamin C because they are sold in plastic bottles or waxed-paper cartons that let oxygen in.

All commercially prepared juices taste different from fresh juice. First, frozen, canned, or pasteurized juices are almost always a blend of fruits from various crops. Second, they have all been heated to inactivate the enzymes that would otherwise rot the juice, and heating changes flavour.

Medical uses and/or benefits
✓ POTASSIUM REPLACEMENT

Antiscorbutic. All citrus fruits are good sources of vitamin C, the vitamin that prevents or cures scurvy, the vitamin C-deficiency disease.
Increased absorption of supplemental or dietary iron. If you eat foods rich in vitamin C along with iron supplements or foods rich in iron, the vitamin C will enhance your body's ability to absorb the iron.
Wound healing. Your body needs vitamin C in order to convert the amino acid proline into hydroxyproline, an essential ingredient in collagen, the protein needed to form skin, tendons, and bones. As a result people with scurvy do not heal quickly, a condition that can be remedied with vitamin C,

which cures the scurvy and speeds healing. Whether taking extra vitamin C speeds healing in healthy people remains to be proved.

Adverse effects
Contact dermatitis. The essential oils in the peel of citrus fruits may cause skin irritation in sensitive people.

Food/drug interactions
—

Grapes
See also RAISINS

Nutritional profile per 100g food (raw)		
Black Grapes		
Energy value:	Low	51 Kcal
Protein:	Low	0.5g
Fat:	Low	Trace
Cholesterol:	None	None
Carbohydrates:	Med	13g
Fibre:	Low	0.3g
Sodium:	Low	1mg
Major vitamin contribution:	B vitamins and vitamin C	Med, Low
Major mineral contribution:	Phosphorus, potassium	Low, Med

Grapes have low amounts of fibre, CARBOHYDRATES (sugars), potassium, the B vitamins, and vitamin C.

Grape skins, stems, and seeds contain tannins, astringent chemicals that coagulate PROTEINS in the mucous membrane lining your mouth and make the membrane pucker. Most of the tannins, including the pigments (anthocyanins) that make black grapes black, are found in the skin.

Grapes also contain malic acid, which makes them taste sour when they are unripe. As grapes ripen, their malic acid content declines and their sugar content rises. Ripe eating grapes are invariably sweet. However, since grapes have no stored STARCHES they can convert to sugar, they do not get sweeter after they are picked.

Diets that may restrict or exclude this food
Sucrose-restricted diet

Buying
Choose: Plump, well-coloured grapes that are firmly attached. Green grapes should have a slightly yellow tint or a pink blush; black grapes should be deep, dark red or purple.
Avoid: Mushy grapes, grapes with wrinkled skin, and grapes that feel sticky.

They are all past their prime. So are grapes whose stems are dry and brittle.

Storing
Wrap grapes in a plastic bag and store them in the refrigerator. Do not wash grapes until you are ready to use them.

Preparation
Rinse the grapes under cold, running water and drain them. To peel grapes, drop them into boiling water for a few seconds, then plunge them into cold water. The change in temperature damages a layer of cells under the skin and the skin will slip off easily.

Cooking reactions
—

Effects of processing
Juice. Black grapes are coloured with anthocyanin pigments that turn deeper red in acids and blue, purple, or yellowish in basic (alkaline) solutions. As a result, black grape juice will turn brighter red if you mix it with lemon or orange juice. Since metals (which are basic) would also change the colour of the juice, the inside of grape juice cans is coated with plastic or enamel to keep the juice from touching the metal.

Winemaking. Grapes make an ideal fruit for winemaking. They have enough sugar to produce a product that is 10 percent alcohol and are acidic enough to keep unwanted microorganisms from growing during fermentation. Some wines retain some of the nutrients originally present in the grapes from which they are made.

Drying. *See* RAISINS.

Medical uses and/or benefits
—

Adverse effects
—

Food/drug interactions
—

• Green beans (French beans [haricots verts], runner beans)

Nutritional profile per 100g food (boiled)		
French Beans		
Energy value:	Low	7 Kcal
Protein:	Low	0.8g
Fat:	Low	Trace
Cholesterol:	None	None
Carbohydrates:	Low	1.1g
Fibre:	Low	3.2g
Sodium:	Low	3mg
Major vitamin contribution:	Vitamins A, B, and C	Med, Med, Low
Major mineral contribution:	Potassium	Med

Green beans have some fibre and vitamin C. They have carotene underneath their green chlorophyll, so they are also a good source of vitamin A.

The most nutritious way to serve this food
Raw, microwaved, or steamed just to the crisp-tender stage, to preserve their vitamin C.

Diets that may restrict or exclude this food
—

Buying
Choose: Firm, crisp beans with clean, well-coloured green skin. They should snap easily when bent.
Avoid: Withered or dry beans; they have been exposed to air, heat, or sunlight and are low in vitamin A.

Storing
Wrap green beans in a plastic bag and store them in the refrigerator to protect their vitamins by keeping them from drying out.

Preparation
To prepare green beans, wash them under cool running water, pick off odd leaves or stems, snip off the ends, pull the string off if there is one, and slice or sliver the beans.

Cooking reactions

Cooking reduces the amount of vitamin C in green beans, but does not affect the vitamin A, which is insoluble in water and stable at normal cooking temperatures.

Green beans will change colour turning brownish if you cook them for a long time. To keep green beans green, the best way may be to steam or microwave them very quickly in very little water so that they hold onto their vitamin C.

Effects of processing

Canning and freezing. Commercially frozen green beans have virtually the same nutritional value as fresh beans but can be higher in vitamin C. Canned beans, however, usually have added salt that turns the naturally low-sodium beans into a high-sodium food. Canned green beans have less vitamin C than fresh beans.

Medical uses and/or benefits

—

Adverse effects

—

Food/drug interactions

—

• Greens (Chard [Swiss chard], kale, spring greens, watercress)

See also BROCCOLI, CABBAGE

Nutritional profile per 100g food (boiled)		
Spring Greens		
Energy value:	Low	10 Kcal
Protein:	Low	1.7g
Fat:	Low	Trace
Cholesterol:	None	None
Carbohydrates:	Low	0.9g
Fibre:	Low	3.8g
Sodium:	Low	10mg
Major vitamin contribution:	Vitamins A and C	High, High
Major mineral contribution:	Calcium, iron, potassium	Low, Low, Med

Greens provide some fibre. They are an excellent source of vitamin A since they contain carotene. The yellow colour of the carotene is hidden by the chlorophyll pigment that makes these vegetables green. The darker the leaf, the more vitamin A it provides.

Greens are also a good source of vitamin C, iron, and calcium. Ounce for ounce, kale has about half as much calcium as whole milk, spinach has five times as much. Chard and kale are rich in non-heme iron, the inorganic form of iron found in plants. However, non-heme iron is not as useful to the body as heme iron, the organic form of iron in foods of animal origin, and the oxalates in some greens bind the iron into insoluble compounds, further reducing its value. You can increase the yield of iron from greens by eating the greens with an iron-rich food (meat) or with a food rich in vitamin C.

The most nutritious way to serve this food

Fresh and raw, torn just before serving, or cooked in the least possible water for the shortest possible time — all to preserve vitamin C.

Diets that may restrict or exclude this food

Low-oxalate diet (to prevent the formation of kidney stones caused by calcium oxalate; Swiss chard)
Low-sodium diet

Buying
Choose: Fresh, crisp, clean, cold, dark-green leaves.
Avoid: Yellowed, blackened, wilted, or warm greens, all of which are lower in vitamins A and C.

Storing
Refrigerate all greens, wrapped in plastic to keep them from losing moisture and vitamins. Don't rinse greens before you refrigerate them or they will rot more quickly.

Preparation
Wash the greens under cool running water to flush off all sand, dirt, debris, and hidden insects.

If you plan to use the greens in a salad, pat them dry before you mix them with salad dressing; oil-based salad dressings will not cling to wet greens.

Do not tear or cut the greens until you are ready to use them; when you tear greens you damage cells, releasing ascorbic acid oxidase, an enzyme that destroys vitamin C.

Cooking reactions
Chlorophyll, the pigment that makes green vegetables green, is sensitive to acids. When you heat greens, the chlorophyll in the leaves reacts chemically with acids in the greens or in the cooking water to give a bronze hue.

To keep the cooked greens from turning bronze or olive, steam the greens in very little water, or microwave with a little water in a microwave-safe plastic bag left open at the top so that steam can escape. These methods preserve vitamin C and preserve the colour.

Effects of processing
—

Medical uses and/or benefits
✓ PROTECTION AGAINST CANCER

Adverse effects
✗ NITRATE/NITRITE POISONING

Food/drug interactions
✗ ANTICOAGULANTS

• Guavas

Nutritional profile per 100g food (raw)		
Energy value:	Med	62 Kcal
Protein:	Low	0.8g
Fat:	Low	0.6g
Cholesterol:	None	None
Carbohydrates:	Low	9.4g
Fibre:	High	(not available)
Sodium:	Low	4mg
Major vitamin contribution:	Vitamins C and A	High, Low
Major mineral contribution:	Potassium	High

The guava is a high-fibre food high in CARBOHYDRATES, that has SUGARS (but almost no STARCH) and provides indigestible food fibres (cellulose, hemicellulose, pectins, and gums). Guavas have small amounts of vitamin A, a good supply of nicotinic acid and may be extremely rich in vitamin C.

The most nutritious way to serve this food
Fresh (for the most vitamin C) or lightly stewed.

Diets that may restrict or exclude this food
Low-carbohydrate, low-fibre diet
Sucrose-restricted diet

Buying
Choose: Ripe guavas. Depending on the variety, the colour of the skin may vary from green to yellow to dark red and the size from that of a large walnut to that of an apple. A ripe guava will yield slightly when you press it with your fingertip.
Avoid: Guavas with cracked or broken skin.

Storing
Refrigerate ripe guavas.

Preparation
Wash the guava under cool running water, then slice it in half and scoop out the seeds. Never slice or peel the fruit until you are ready to use it. When you cut into the guava and damage its cells, you activate ascorbic acid oxidase,

an enzyme that oxidizes and destroys vitamin C. The longer the enzyme is working, the more vitamin C the fruit will lose.

Cooking reactions
As the guava cooks, its pectins and gums dissolve and the fruit gets softer. Cooking also destroys some water-soluble, heat-sensitive vitamin C. You can keep the loss to a minimum by cooking the guava as quickly as possible in as little water as possible. Never cook guavas (or any other vitamin C-rich foods) in a copper or iron pot; contact with metal ions hastens the loss of vitamin C.

Effects of processing
Canning. Canned guavas have less vitamin A and C and more sugar (syrup) than fresh guavas do, but their taste and texture is similar to home-cooked fruit.

Medical uses and/or benefits
✓ POTASSIUM REPLACEMENT

✓ PROTECTION AGAINST CANCER

Adverse effects
—

Food/drug interactions
—

• Honey

See also SUGAR

Nutritional profile per 100 g food		
Energy value:	High	288 Kcal
Protein:	Trace	0.4 g
Fat:	Trace	Trace
Cholesterol:	None	None
Carbohydrates:	High	76.4 g
Fibre:	None	None
Sodium:	Low	11 mg
Major vitamin contribution:	Riboflavin (vitamin B₂)	Low
Major mineral contribution:	None	

Honey is the sweet, thick fluid produced when bees metabolize the sucrose in plant nectar. Enzymes in the honeybee's sac split the sucrose, which is a disaccharide (double sugar), into its constituent molecules, fructose and glucose (see SUGARS). Honey is about 80 percent fructose and glucose and 17 percent water. The rest is dextrin (the molecules formed when starch molecules are split apart), a trace of protein and very small amounts of iron, potassium, and B vitamins. Honey has no FAT or CHOLESTEROL.

Diets that may restrict or exclude this food
Low-carboyhydrate diet
Sucrose-restricted diet

Buying
Choose: Tightly sealed jars of honey. All honeys are natural products. They may be dark or light (depending on the plant from which the bees drew their nectar); colour has no effect on the honey's nutritional value. Raw, unprocessed honey is thick and cloudy. Commercial honey is clear because it has been filtered. It pours more easily than raw honey because it has been heated to make it less viscous and to destroy potentially harmful bacteria and yeasts that might spoil the honey by turning its sugars into alcohol and other undesirable products.

Storing
Store in closed jars.

Preparation

To measure honey easily, coat your measuring spoon or cup with vegetable oil: the honey will slide out easily. To combine honey smoothly with dry ingredients, warm it with the liquids in the recipe first. And remember to reduce the liquid in a recipe when you substitute honey for sugar. For precise amounts, check the individual recipe.

Cooking reactions

When honey is heated, the bonds between its molecules relax and the honey becomes more liquid. If you heat it too long, however, its moisture will evaporate, the honey will become more viscous, and its sugars will burn.

In baking, honey is useful because it is more hydrophilic (water-loving) than granulated sugar. It retains moisture longer while a cake or bread is baking, and it may even extract moisture from the air into the finished product. As a result, breads and cakes made with honey stay moist longer then those made with sugar.

Effects of processing
—

Medical uses and/or benefits
—

Adverse effects

Infant botulism. *C. botulinum*, the organism that causes *botulinum* poisoning produces spores which can grow in an infant's digestive tract. There have been some cases reported in the USA of infants being poisoned by *botulinum* contaminated honey.

Food/drug interactions
—

• Kohlrabi

Nutritional profile per 100 g food (raw)		
Energy value:	Low	24 Kcal
Protein:	Low	1.1 g
Fat:	Low	Trace
Cholesterol:	None	None
Carbohydrates:	Low	4.9 g
Fibre	High	(not available)
Sodium:	Low	(not available)
Major vitamin contribution:	B vitamins, vitamin C	(not available)
Major mineral contribution:	Calcium, iron, phosphorus	(not available)

The kohlrabi ('cabbage-turnip') is a member of the cabbage family, a stem rather than flowers (broccoli) or buds (head cabbage or Brussels sprouts). It is a low-carbohydrate (starch), high-fibre food, an excellent source of lignin, cellulose, and hemicellulose, the woody food fibres that make up the structure of stems, leaves, roots, seed, and peel.

Kohlrabi is also an extremely good source of vitamin C. Kohlrabi also has thiamin (vitamin B_1), riboflavin (vitamin B_2), and iron.

The most nutritious way to serve this food
Steamed just until tender, to protect the vitamin C.

Diets that may restrict or exclude this food
Antiflatulence diet
Low-fibre, low-residue diet

Buying
Choose: Small vegetables the size of a tennis ball with fresh-looking green leaves on top.
Avoid: Very large kohlrabi. The older the stem, the tougher it will be. Very old kohlrabi may have so much fibre that it is inedible.

Storing
Cut off the green tops. Then, store kohlrabi in a cold, humid place (a root cellar or the refrigerator) to keep it from drying out.

Wash and refrigerate the kohlrabi's green leaves. They can be cooked and eaten like spinach.

Preparation
Peel the root and slice or quarter it for cooking.

Cooking reactions
Cooking softens kohlrabi by dissolving its soluble food fibres (pectins, gums). Like other cruciferous vegetables kohlrabi contains the natural sulphur compounds that break down into a variety of smelly chemicals (including hydrogen sulphide and ammonia) when the vegetables are heated.

Effects of processing
—

Medical uses and/or benefits
✓ PROTECTION AGAINST CANCER

Adverse effects
✗ ENLARGED THYROID GLAND

Food/drug interactions
—

• Lamb (Mutton)

Nutritional profile per 100 g food (raw)		
	Leg of Lamb	
Energy value:	High	240 Kcal
Protein:	High	17.9 g
Fat:	Med	18.7 g
Cholesterol:	Med	78 mg
Carbohydrates:	None	None
Fibre:	None	None
Sodium:	Med	52 mg
Major vitamin contribution:	B vitamins	High
Major mineral contribution:	Iron, potassium, phosphorus	Med, High, High

Like other animal foods, lamb provides 'complete' PROTEINS with all the essential amino acids. Lamb has a higher proportion of SATURATED FATTY ACIDS and more CHOLESTEROL than poultry, pork, and most cuts of beef. It has no food fibre and no CARBOHYDRATES other than the small amounts of glycogen (sugar) stored in the animal's muscles. Mutton, which is meat from a sheep more than one year old, is more muscular and thus less tender than lamb.

Lamb is an excellent source of B vitamins, particularly nicotinic acid, vitamin B_6 and vitamin B_{12} (which is plentiful in meat, fish, and poultry but is never found in fruits and vegetables). It also provides heme iron, the organic iron in foods of animal origin that is about five times more useful to the body than none-heme iron, the inorganic form of iron in plant foods.

The most nutritious way to serve this food
Grilled or roasted, to allow the fat to melt and run off the meat. Soups and stews that contain lamb should be skimmed.

Diets that may restrict or exclude this food
Controlled fat, low-cholesterol diet
Low-protein diet (for some forms of kidney disease)

Buying
Choose: Lean cuts. Meat labelled *spring lamb* comes from animals less than five months old; *lamb* comes from an animal less than a year old; mutton

comes from an animal older than a year. The older the animal, the tougher and more sinewy the meat.

Avoid: Fatty cuts especially chops and neck which can be very fatty.

Storing
Refrigerate fresh lamb immediately, carefully wrapped to prevent its drippings from contaminating other foods.

Preparation
Trim the meat carefully. By judiciously cutting away all visible fat, you can significantly reduce the amount of fat and cholesterol in each serving.

Do not salt lamb before you cook it; the salt will draw moisture out of the meat, making it stringy and less tender. Add salt when the meat is nearly done.

After handling raw meat, wash your knives, cutting board, work surface — and your hands — with warm soapy water to reduce the chance of transferring bacteria from the meat to other foods.

Cooking reactions
Cooking changes the lamb's flavour and appearance, lowers its fat and cholesterol content, and makes it safer by killing the bacteria that live naturally on the surface of raw meat.

Browning lamb before you cook it won't seal in the juices, but it will change the flavour by caramelizing proteins and sugars on the surface of the meat (see BROWNING REACTIONS). Because the only sugars in lamb are the small amounts of glycogen in its muscles, we often add sugar in the form of marinades or basting liquids that may also contain acids (lemon juice, vinegar, wine, yoghurt) to break down muscle fibres and tenderize the meat. (Note that browning has one minor nutritional drawback. It breaks amino acids on the surface of the meat into smaller compounds that are no longer useful proteins.)

When lamb is heated, it loses water and shrinks. Its pigments, which combine with oxygen, are denatured by the heat. They break into smaller fragments and turn brown, the natural colour of well-done meat. The pigments also release iron, which accelerates the oxidation of the lamb's fat.

Effects of processing
Canning. Canned lamb does not develop a 're-heated' flavour because the high temperatures used in canning food alter the structure of the proteins in the meat so that the proteins act as antioxidants. Once the can is open, however, lamb fat may begin to oxidize again.

Freezing. Defrosted frozen lamb may be less tender than fresh lamb. It may also be lower in B vitamins. Freezing may also cause freezer burn — dry spots left when moisture evaporates from the lamb's surface. Waxed freezer paper is designed specifically to protect the moisture in meat; plastic wrap and aluminium foil may be less effective.

Medical uses and/or benefits
—

Adverse effects
✖ HEART DISEASE

Food/drug interactions
✖ FALSE RESULT IN TESTS FOR CANCER

• Lemons (Limes)

Nutritional profile per 100 g food (raw)		
Energy value:	Low	15 Kcal
Protein:	Low	0.8 g
Fat:	Low	Trace
Cholesterol:	None	None
Carbohydrates:	Moderate	3.2 g
Fibre:	Low	5.2 g
Sodium:	Low	6 mg
Major vitamin contribution:	Vitamin C, B vitamins	High, Low
Major mineral contribution:	Potassium, calcium	High, Med

Lemons and limes have no STARCH, very little SUGAR (1 percent in a lemon, less in a lime), no FAT, no CHOLESTEROL, and only a trace of PROTEIN. They are valuable only for their considerable supply of vitamin C. 100 g of lemon juice provides 50 mg vitamin C, 150 percent of the RDA for a healthy adult.

The most nutritious way to serve this food
Freshly squeezed, in a fruit-juice drink. Fresh juice has the most vitamin C.

Diets that may restrict or exclude this food
—

Buying
Choose: Firm lemons and limes that are heavy for their size. The heavier the fruit the juicier it will be. The skin should be thin, smooth, and fine-grained — shiny yellow for a lemon, shiny green for a lime. Deeply coloured lemons and limes have a better flavour than pale ones. All lemons are egg-shaped, but limes are small and round.

Storing
Refrigerate fresh lemons and limes. The lemons will stay fresh for a month, the limes for up to eight weeks. Sliced lemons and limes are vulnerable to oxygen, which can destroy their flavour and their vitamin C. Wrap them tightly in plastic, store them in the refrigerator, and use them as quickly as possible.

Preparation
The skin of the lemon and lime are rich in essential oils that are liberated

when you cut into the peel and tear open its cells. To get the flavouring oil out of the peel, grate the top, coloured part of the rind (the white membrane underneath is bitter) and wrap it in cheesecloth. Then, wring out the oil onto some granulated sugar, stir thoroughly, and use the flavoured sugar in baking or for making drinks. You can freeze lemon and lime peel or zest (grated peel), but it will lose some flavour while frozen.

Lemons and limes are often treated to protect them from moisture loss enroute to the store. Before you peel or grate the fruit, scrub it with a vegetable brush to remove the coating and any fungicides.

Cooking reactions
Heating citrus fruits and juices reduces their supply of vitamin C.

Effects of processing
Canning and freezing. Canned or frozen lemon and lime juice are as rich in vitamin C as fresh juice.

Medical uses and/or benefits
Antiscorbutic. Lemons and limes, which are small and travel well, were carried on board British navy ships in the eighteenth century to prevent scurvy, the vitamin C deficiency disease.
Wound healing. Your body needs vitamin C in order to convert the amino acid proline into hydroxyproline, an essential ingredient in collagen — the protein needed to form skin, tendons, and bones. As a result, people with scurvy do not heal quickly, a condition that can be remedied with vitamin C, which cures the scurvy and speeds healing. Whether taking extra vitamin C speeds healing in healthy people remains to be proved.

Adverse effects
Contact dermatitis. The peel of lemon and lime contains limonene, an essential oil known to cause contact dermatitis in sensitive individuals. (Limonene is also found in dill, caraway seeds, and celery.)
Photosensitivity. Lime peel contains furocoumarins (psoralens), chemicals that are photosensitizers as well as potential mutagens and carcinogens. Contact with these chemicals can make skin very sensitive to light.
Apthous ulcers. Citrus fruits or juices may trigger a flare up of 'canker sores' (apthous ulcers) in sensitive people, but eliminating these foods from the diet neither cures nor prevents canker sores.

Food/drug interactions
Iron supplements. Taking iron supplements with a food rich in vitamin C increases the absorption of iron from the supplement.

• Lentils

Nutritional profile per 100 g food (raw)		
Energy value:	High	304 Kcal
Protein:	High	23.8 g
Fat:	Low	1.0 g
Cholesterol:	None	None
Carbohydrates:	High	53.2 g
Fibre:	High	11.7 g
Sodium:	Moderate	36 mg
Major vitamin contribution:	B vitamins, folic acid	High, Med
Major mineral contribution:	Magnesium, iron, zinc, potassium, phosphorus	Med, High, High, High, High

Lentils are seeds. Their covering is an excellent source of the cellulose and the noncarbohydrate food fibre lignin, and their interior is a good source of CARBOHYDRATES: STARCH, SUGARS, hemicellulose, pectins, and gums. Up to 30 percent of the calories in cooked lentils comes from their PROTEINS, which are considered 'incomplete' because they are deficient in the essential amino acids methionine and cystine. Lentils have very little FAT and no CHOLESTEROL.

Lentils are a good source of B vitamins, particularly vitamin B_6, nicotinic acid, and folic acid. They have calcium, phosphorus, and potassium and are rich in non-heme iron, the inorganic form of iron found in plant foods.

The most nutritious way to serve this food

With grains. The proteins in grains are deficient in the essential amino acid lysine but contain sufficient methionine and cystine; the proteins in beans are exactly the opposite. Together these foods provide 'complete' proteins with no cholesterol and very little fat.

With meat or with a food rich in vitamin C (tomatoes, peppers, potatoes). Both enhance your body's ability to absorb the non-heme iron in the lentils.

Diets that may restrict or exclude this food
Antiflatulence diet
Low-calcium diet
Low-carbohydrate diet

Low-fibre diet
Low-purine (antigout) diet

Buying
Look for: Smooth-skinned, uniform, evenly coloured lentils that are free of stones and debris.
Avoid: Lentils with any sign of mould or insect damage (tiny holes in the beans indicate an insect has burrowed into or through the bean).

Storing
Store lentils in air- and moistureproof containers in cool, dark cabinets where they are protected from heat, light, and insects.

Preparation
Wash the lentils and pick them over carefully, discarding damaged or withered beans and any that float. (The only beans light enough to float in water are those that have withered away inside.) Lentils do not have to be soaked before cooking.

Cooking reactions
When lentils are cooked in liquid, their cells absorb water, swell, and eventually rupture, so that the nutrients inside are more available to your body.

Effects of processing
—

Medical uses and/or benefits
✔ HEART DISEASE

✔ DIABETES THERAPY

As a slimming aid. Although beans are very high in calories, they have so much fibre that even a small serving can make you feel full. And, since beans are insulin-sparing (because they do not cause blood-sugar levels to rise quickly), they put off the surge of insulin that makes us feel hungry again and allow us to feel full longer.

Adverse effects
✘ GOUT

Intestinal gas.
All dried beans, including lentils, contain raffinose and stachyose, sugars that

the human body cannot digest. As a result these sugars sit in the gut, where they are fermented by the bacteria that live in our intestinal tract. The result is intestinal gas. Since the indigestible sugars are soluble in hot water, they will leach out into the water in which you cook the lentils. You can cut down on intestinal gas by draining the lentils thoroughly after cooking.

Food/drug interactions
—

• Lettuce (Chicory, endive)

Nutritional profile per 100 g food		
Energy value:	Low	12 Kcal
Protein:	Low	1.0 g
Fat:	Low	0.4 g
Cholesterol:	None	None
Carbohydrates:	Low	1.2 g
Fibre:	Low	1.5 g
Sodium:	Low	9 mg
Major vitamin contribution:	Vitamins A, B and C	Med, Med, Med
Major mineral contribution:	Iron, potassium	Low, Med

Lettuce has little food fibre, a little PROTEIN and FAT, but no CHOLESTEROL. Its most important nutrients are vitamin A and potassium. The vitamin A comes from carotenes, whose yellow is hidden by green chlorophyll pigments. The darkest green leaves have the most vitamin A. Lettuce is also a source of vitamin C, iron, calcium, and copper.

The most nutritious way to serve this food
Fresh.

Diets that may restrict or exclude this food
Antiflatulence diet
Low-calcium diet

Buying
Choose: Brightly coloured heads. Iceberg lettuce should be tightly closed and heavy for its size. Loose leaf lettuces should be crisp. All lettuces should be symmetrically shaped. An asymmetric shape suggests a large hidden stem that is crowding the leaves to one side or the other.
Avoid: Lettuce with faded or yellow leaves; lettuce leaves turn yellow as they age and their green chlorophyll fades, revealing the yellow carotenes underneath. Brown or wilted leaves are a sign of ageing or poor storage. Either way, the lettuce is no longer at its best.

Storing
Wrap lettuce in a plastic bag and store it in the refrigerator.
Do not discard lettuce simply because the core begins to brown or small brown specks appear on the spines of the outer leaves. This is a natural

oxidation reaction that changes the colour, but doesn't affect the nutritional value of the lettuce. Trim the end of the core (or remove the core from iceberg lettuce) to slow the reaction.

Do not store unwrapped lettuce near apples, pears, melons, or bananas. These fruits release ethylene gas, a natural ripening agent that will cause the lettuce to develop brown spots.

Preparation
Never slice, cut, or tear lettuce until you are ready to use it. When lettuce cells are torn, they release ascorbic acid oxidase, an enzyme that destroys vitamin C.

What happens when you cook this food
When you heat lettuce, it will turn brown.

To keep cooked lettuce green, the best way may be to steam it quickly in very little water.

Effects of processing
—

Medical uses and/or benefits
✓ PROTECTION AGAINST CANCER

Adverse effects
✗ NITRATE/NITRITE POISONING

Food/drug interactions
✗ ANTICOAGULANTS

• Liver
See also SAUSAGES

Nutritional profile per 100 g food (raw)		
	Lamb's Liver	
Energy value:	High	179 Kcal
Protein:	High	20.1 g
Fat:	Med	10.3 g
Cholesterol:	High	430 mg
Carbohydrates:	Low	1.6 g
Fibre:	None	None
Sodium:	Med	76 mg
Major vitamin contribution:	Vitamin A, riboflavin, nicotinic acid, vitamin B_6, vitamin B_{12}, vitamin C, vitamin D, folic acid	All high
Major mineral contribution:	Iron, copper, potassium, phosphorus, zinc	All high

Liver is a food high in CHOLESTEROL and rich in 'complete' PROTEINS (proteins that supply adequate amounts of all the essential amino acids). It has no CARBOHYDRATES other than the sugar (glycogen) normally stored in the liver and no fibre.

Liver is the single most efficient source of vitamin A (retinol), and one of the few natural sources of vitamin D. It is an excellent source of B vitamins, especially vitamin B_{12}, the vitamin that prevents or cures pernicious anaemia, and heme iron, the organic iron in foods of animal origin. 100 g of fried liver has 10 mg iron, 100 percent of the RDA for a healthy adult female.

The most nutritious way to serve this food
Fresh, lightly fried.

Diets that may restrict or exclude this food
Galactose-free diet (for control of galactosemia)
Low-calcium diet
Low-cholesterol, controlled-fat diet
Low-protein, low-purine diet

Buying
Choose: Liver that has a deep, rich colour and smells absolutely fresh.

Storing
Keep fresh liver extremely cold; it is very perishable. It should be stored in the refrigerator for no longer than a day or two and in the freezer for no longer then three to four months.

Preparation
Wipe the liver with a damp cloth. If your butcher has not already done so, pull off the outer membrane, and cut out the veins. Sheep, pork, and older beef liver are strongly flavoured; to make them more palatable, soak these livers for several hours in cold milk, cold water, or a marinade, then discard the soaking liquid when you are ready to cook the liver.

Cooking reactions
When liver is heated it loses water and shrinks. Its pigments, which combine with oxygen, are denatured by the heat, breaking into smaller fragments that turn brown, the natural colour of cooked meat. Since liver has virtually no collagen (the connective tissue that stays chewy unless you cook it for a long time), it should be cooked as quickly as possible to keep it from drying out. Pork liver, like all pork products, must be cooked until it is no longer pink in order to kill any organisms in the meat.

Effects of processing
—

Medical uses and/or benefits
As a source of iron. Liver is an excellent source of heme iron, the organic form of iron in meat that is absorbed approximately five times more easily than non-heme iron, the inorganic iron in plants.

Adverse effects
✖ HEART DISEASE

✖ GOUT

Vitamin A poisoning. Vitamin A is stored in the liver, so this organ is an extremely rich source of retinol, the true vitamin A. Retinol is poisonous if you take too much of it, although acute poisoning (drowsiness, irritability, headache, vomiting, peeling skin) is rare. Liver should not be eaten every day unless specifically directed by a physician.

Food/drug interactions
✖ MAO INHIBITORS

• Mangoes

Nutritional profile per 100 g food		
Energy value:	Med	59 Kcal
Protein:	Low	0.5 g
Fat:	Low	Trace
Cholesterol:	None	None
Carbohydrates:	Med	15.3 g
Fibre:	Low	1.5 g
Sodium:	Low	7 mg
Major vitamin contribution:	Vitamins A and C	Med, High
Major mineral contribution:	Potassium	Med

Mangoes are an excellent source of vitamins A and C. 100 g of mango provides 30 mg vitamin C (100 percent of the RDA for a healthy adult) and 200 microg of retinol equivalent (25 percent of the RDA for a healthy adult), derived from the carotene and other carotenoid pigments that make the mango yellow-orange.

Unripe mangoes contain antinutrients, protein compounds that inhibit amylases (the enzymes that make it possible for us to digest starches) and catalase (the iron-containing enzyme that protects our cells by splitting potentially damaging peroxides in our body into safe water and oxygen). As the fruit ripens the enzyme inhibitors are inactivated.

The most nutritious way to serve this food
Fresh, ripe.

Diets that may restrict or exclude this food
Sucrose-restricted diet.

Buying
Choose: Flattish, oval fruit. The skin should be yellow-green or yellow-green flecked with red; the riper the mango, the more yellow and red there will be. A ripe mango will give slightly when you press it with your finger.
Avoid: Mangoes with grey, pitted, or spotted skin; they may be rotten inside.

Storing
Store mangoes at room temperature if they aren't fully ripe when you buy them; they will continue to ripen. When the mangoes are soft (ripe), refrigerate

them and use them within two or three days. Once you have sliced a mango, wrap it in plastic and store it in the refrigerator.

Preparation
The flavour of the mango doesn't develop fully until the fruit is completely ripe. If you cut into a mango and find that it's not ripe yet, poach it in sugar syrup to improve its flavour.

Eating a mango is an adventure. The long, oval pit clings to the flesh, and to get at the fruit you have to peel away the skin and then slice off the flesh.

Cooking reactions
When you poach a mango, its cells absorb water and the fruit softens.

Effects of processing
—

Medical uses and/or benefits
✓ PROTECTION AGAINST CANCER

Adverse effects
Contact dermatitis. The skin of the mango contains urushiol, a chemical that causes contact dermatitis.

Food/drug interactions
—

• Melons (Cantaloupe, honeydew, watermelon)

Nutritional profile per 100g food (raw)				
	Canteloupe		*Watermelon*	
Energy value:	Low	24 Kcal	Low	21 Kcal
Protein:	Low	1 g	Low	0.4 g
Fat:	Low	Trace	Low	Trace
Cholesterol:	None	None	None	None
Carbohydrates:	Low	5.3 g	Low	5.3 g
Fibre:	Low	1g	Low	(not available)
Sodium:	Low	14 mg	Low	4 mg
Major vitamin contribution:	Vitamins A and C	High, High		Low, Low
Major mineral contribution:	Potassium	High		Low

All melons have small amounts of PROTEIN, FATS, CARBOHYDRATES, and fibre. Yellow melons (cantaloupe, and honeydew melons) contain carotene and carotenoid pigments that your body can convert to vitamin A. Cantaloupe and honeydew melons are good sources of vitamin C.

The most nutritious way to serve this food
Fresh and ripe.

Diets that may restrict or exclude this food
Low-carbohydrate diet
Sucrose-restricted diet

Buying
Choose: Vine-ripened melons if possible. You can identify a vine-ripened melon by checking the stem end. If the scar is clean and sunken, it means that the stem was pulled out of a ripe melon. Ripe melons also have a deep aroma: the more intense the fragrance, the sweeter the melon.
    Cantaloupes should be round and firm, with cream-coloured, coarse 'netting' that stands up all over the fruit. The rind at the stem end of the melon should give slightly when you press it and there should be a rich, melony aroma. *Honeydews* should have a smooth creamy coloured or a yellowish-white rind. If the rind is completely white or tinged with green, the melon is not ripe.

Watermelons should have a firm, smooth rind with a deep green colour. When you shake a ripe watermelon, the seeds inside will rattle; when you thump its rind, you should hear a slightly hollow sound.

Storing

Hold whole melons at room temperature for a few days. Melons have no stored starches to convert to sugar, so they can't get sweeter once they are picked, but they will begin to soften as enzymes begin to dissolve pectin in the cell walls. As the cell walls dissolve, the melons release the aromatic molecules that make them smell sweet and ripe.

Refrigerate ripe melons to slow the natural deterioration of the fruit. Sliced melons should be wrapped in plastic to keep them from losing moisture or from absorbing odours from other foods.

Preparation

Chill the melon, wash it under running water to flush dirt off the rind, slice, and serve.

Cooking reactions

—

Effects of processing

—

Medical uses and/or benefits

✓ PROTECTION AGAINST CANCER

Adverse effects

—

Food/drug interactions

—

• Milk (Goat's milk)

Nutritional profile per 100 g food				
	Silver Top		*Goat's Milk*	
Energy value:	Med	65 Kcal	Med	71 Kcal
Protein:	Med	3.3 g	Med	3.3 g
Fat:	Med	3.8 g	Med	4.5 g
Cholesterol:	Low	14 mg	(not available)	(not available)
Carbohydrates:	Med	4.7 g	Med	4.6 g
Fibre:	None	None	None	None
Sodium:	Med	50 mg	Med	40 mg
Major vitamin contribution:	Vitamin A and D, B vitamins	All med		All med
Major mineral contribution:	Calcium	High		High

Cow's milk and goat's milk are high-protein, medium carbohydrate, high-fat foods with less sugar and more protein than human milk. About 82 percent of the PROTEIN in milk is casein, a protein found only in milk. The rest are whey proteins, principally lactalbumin and lactoglobulin. Milk's proteins are considered 'complete' because they supply all the essential amino acids. Lactose, the sugar found in most mammal milks, is a disaccharide (double sugar). Each molecule of lactose is made of one molecule of glucose and one molecule of galactose (see SUGARS).

About half the calories in whole milk come from milkfat, which is composed primarily (62 percent) of SATURATED FATTY ACIDS. Milkfat, which is lighter than water, will rise to the top of the milk and can be skimmed off. *Whole milk* is 3.8 percent milkfat. Depending on how much fat is skimmed off, what remains is either *semi-skimmed or low-fat* (1 – 2 percent fat) or *skimmed* (0.5 percent fat) milk. *Homogenized milk* is milk processed through machinery that reduces its fat globules to particles small enough to remain suspended in the liquid rather than float to the top.

Jersey milk gets its creamy colour from carotenoid pigments (principally beta-carotene) that provide small amounts of vitamin A. Since vitamin A is fat-soluble, it disappears with the fat skimmed from whole milk.

Milk is a good source of thiamin (vitamin B_1), and vitamin B_6, riboflavin (vitamin B_2), a 'visible vitamin' whose green pigment, masked by the carotenes in whole milk, gives skimmed milk and whey a greenish tint.

Milk is our best source of calcium. Even though some plant foods such as beans have more calcium per ounce, the calcium in plants is less available because it is bound into insoluble compounds by phytic acids while the calcium in milk is completely available to our bodies. No calcium is lost when milk is skimmed.

The most nutritious way to serve this food
Low-fat or skimmed milk. Fresh or heat treated but not condensed which has added sugar.

Diets that may restrict or exclude this food
Lactose- and galactose-free diet
Low-calcium diet
Low-cholesterol, controlled-fat diet

Buying
Choose: Tightly sealed, dry, refrigerated cartons or bottles. Check the date on the carton and pick the latest one you can find.

Storing
Refrigerate fresh milk and cream in tightly closed containers to keep the milk from picking up odours from other foods in the refrigerator.

Protect milk from bright light. Light destroys riboflavin (vitamin B_2), and vitamin B_6. Milk stored in glass bottles exposed to direct sunlight may lose as much as 70 percent of its riboflavin in just two hours. Opaque plastic cartons reduce the flow of light into the milk but do not block it completely.

Preparation
Chill, pour, and serve

Cooking reactions
When milk is warmed, its tightly curled PROTEIN molecules relax and unfold, breaking internal bonds (bonds between atoms on the same molecule) and forming new, intermolecular bonds between atoms on neighbouring molecules. The newly linked protein molecules create a network with water molecules caught in the net. As the milk cooks, the network tightens, squeezing out the water molecules and forming the lumps we call curds.

Casein, the proteins that combine with calcium to form the 'skin' on top of hot milk, will also form curds if you lower the pH of the milk by adding an acid — lemon juice, fruit, vegetables, vinegar, or wine. Whey proteins do not coagulate when you make the milk more acid, but they precipitate (fall to the bottom of the pot) when the milk is heated to a temperature above 170°F (77°C). If the bottom of the pot gets hotter, the whey proteins will scorch and the milk will smell burnt.

Effects of processing

Drying. Dried milk tastes cooked because it has been heated to evaporate its moisture. Unopened packets of dried milk should be stored in a cool, dry cupboard where they may hold their flavour and nutrients for several months. Once a packet of dried milk is opened, its contents should be stored in a container keeping out the moisture that will encourage bacterial growth and change the taste of the milk. Once the dried milk is reconstituted, it should be refrigerated.

Condensed and evaporated milk. Evaporated or condensed milk is milk that has been cooked to evaporate its moisture; condensed milk has added sugar. Both evaporated and condensed milk have a cooked flavour. They also have less vitamin C and vitamin B_6 than fresh milk.

Once a can of milk is opened, the milk should be poured into a clean container and refrigerated.

Heat treatments that make milk safer. Raw (unpasteurized) milk may contain a variety of microorganisms, including pathogenic and harmless bacteria, plus yeasts and moulds that are destroyed when the milk is *pasteurized* (heated to 160°F (72°C) for 15 seconds). *UHT* (Ultra high temperature) *milk* has been heated to 266°F (130°C) for two seconds or more. The higher temperature destroys more microorganisms than pasteurization and prolongs the shelf life of the milk and cream (which must be refrigerated). *Sterilized milk* is heated to about 162°F (72°C) for 60 minutes. The milk or cream is then packed into presterilized containers and aseptically sealed so that bacteria that might spoil the milk cannot enter. These containers can be stored on an unrefrigerated grocery or kitchen shelf for as long as three months without spoiling or losing any of its vitamins.

Medical uses and/or benefits

Protective effects of calcium. Adequate dietary calcium early in life may offer some protection against osteoporosis ('thinning bones').

Adverse effects

✖ HEART DISEASE

Allergy to milk proteins. Milk and milk products are among the foods most often implicated as a cause of the classic symptoms of food allergy — upset stomach, hives, and angioedemia (swelling of the face, lips and tongue).

Lactose intolerance. Lactose intolerance — the inability to digest the SUGAR in milk — is not an allergy. It is an inherited metabolic deficiency that affects two-thirds of all adults, including 90 to 95 percent of all Orientals, 70 to 75 percent of all blacks, and 6 to 8 percent of Caucasians. These people do not have sufficient amounts of lactase, the enzyme that breaks lactose (a disaccharide) into its easily digested components, galactose and glucose. When they drink milk, the undigested sugar is fermented by bacteria in the gut, causing bloating, diarrhoea, flatulence, and intestinal discomfort.

Galactosemia. Galactosemia is an inherited metabolic disorder in which the body lacks the enzymes needed to metabolize galactose, a component of lactose. Galactosemia is a recessive trait; you must get the gene from both parents to develop the condition. Babies born with galactosemia will fail to thrive and may develop brain damage or cataracts if they are given milk. To prevent this, children with galactosemia are usually kept on a protective milk-free diet for several years, until their bodies have developed alternative pathways by which to metabolize galactose. Pregnant women who are known carriers of galactosemia may be advised to give up milk while pregnant lest the unmetabolized galactose in their bodies cause brain damage to the foetus (damage that is not detectible by amniocentesis). Genetic counselling is available to identify galactosemia carriers and assess their chances of producing a baby with the disorder.

Food poisoning. Raw (unpasteurized) milk may be contaminated with *Salmonella* or other organisms. Poisoning with *Salmonella* organisms may cause nausea, vomiting, and diarrhoea — which can be debilitating, and potentially serious in infants, the elderly, and people who are ill. It is also possible to be infected with organisms causing brucellosis and although rarer, tuberculosis.

Food/drug interactions
Tetracyclines. The calcium ions in milk bind to tetracyclines (antibiotic drugs), forming insoluble compounds your body cannot absorb. Taking tetracyclines with milk makes them less effective.

• Mushrooms

Nutritional profile per 100 g food (raw)		
Energy value:	Low	13 Kcal
Protein:	Low	1.8 g
Fat:	Low	0.6 g
Cholesterol:	None	None
Carbohydrates:	None	None
Fibre:	Low	2.5 g
Sodium:	Low	9 mg
Major vitamin contribution:	Vitamin B_2 (riboflavin), folic acid	Med, Low
Major mineral contribution:	Potassium, phosphorus	High, Med

Mushrooms are a good source of riboflavin (vitamin B_2). They have only small amounts of the other vitamins and minerals, a little PROTEIN and almost no FAT.

The most nutritious way to serve this food
Fresh, in salads.

Diets that may restrict or exclude this food
—

Buying
Choose: Smooth, plump, uniformly cream-coloured button mushrooms. The cap should be closed tightly, hiding the gills. Older mushrooms, or flats, are more intensely flavoured than young ones, but they also have a shorter shelf life.
Avoid: Mushrooms which are either withered or not in a closed container. Don't eat wild mushrooms unless you are sure they have been correctly identified as edible.

Storing
Refrigerate fresh mushrooms in containers that allow air to circulate among the mushrooms. The aim is to prevent moisture from collecting on the mushrooms; damp mushrooms deteriorate quickly.

Preparation

Rinse the mushrooms under cold running water and use immediately or let drain dry.

You can clean mushrooms quickly simply by peeling the cap, but that will make them less tasty. The mushroom's flavour comes from an unusually large amount of glutamic acid in the skin. Glutamic acid is the natural version of the flavour enhancer we know as MSG (monosodium glutamate).

Slicing mushrooms hastens the loss of riboflavin. Mushrooms will brown when cut (see BROWNING REACTIONS). This can be reduced by tossing in lemon juice or vinaigrette.

Button mushrooms lose moisture and shrink when you cook them. If you choose to cut off their stems before you cook them, leave a small stub to help the mushroom hold its shape.

Cooking reactions

The B vitamins in mushrooms are all water-soluble. They will leak out into the cooking water, which should be retained in your recipe along with the mushrooms.

Cooking toughens the stem of button mushrooms but does not affect their nutritional value since riboflavin is not destroyed by heat and remains stable in a neutral solution or an acid one such as a tomato sauce or a stew with tomatoes and green peppers.

Effects of processing

Canning. Canned mushrooms with their liquid may contain up to 100 times as much sodium as fresh mushrooms. Riboflavin, the most important nutrient in mushrooms, is not destroyed by heat, but it will leach out into the salty liquid. Riboflavin is sensitive to light; mushrooms in glass jars should be stored in a cool, dark cupboard.

Drying. Dried mushrooms should be sold and stored in a tightly closed package that protects the mushrooms from moisture, and they should be kept in a cool, dark place out of direct sunlight. They should be stored in the refrigerator only if the refrigerator is less humid than the kitchen cupboard. Properly stored dried mushrooms may remain usable for as long as six months. To use dried mushrooms, cover them with boiling water and let them stand for about fifteen minutes. Then rinse them thoroughly to get rid of sand and debris in the folds of the mushroom.

Medical uses and/or benefits

—

Adverse effects

Mushroom poisoning. About a hundred of the more than 1000 varieties of mushrooms are poisonous. If you pick wild mushrooms be sure you can identify the edible types. *Do not eat* any you can't be sure of.

Food/drug interactions
● FALSE RESULT IN TESTS FOR CANCER

Alcohol/disulfiram interaction. Disulfiram (Antabuse), is a drug used to treat alcoholism. It causes flushing, difficult breathing, nausea, chest pain, vomiting and rapid heart beat if taken with alcohol. Some mushrooms, including the cultivated edible varieties may contain naturally-occurring disulfiram. If taken with alcohol, these mushrooms may cause symptoms of a disulfiram-alcohol reaction in sensitive individuals. Since disulfiram lingers in your system, the symptoms may appear half an hour after you drink alcohol even if you ate the mushrooms as many as four or five days ago.

• Nuts (Almonds, Brazil nuts, cashews, chestnuts, hazelnuts, macadamias, peanuts, pistachios, walnuts)

See also COCONUTS, VEGETABLE OILS

Nutritional profile per 100 g food (raw)				
	Peanuts		*Brazil Nuts*	
Energy value:	High	570 Kcal	High	619 Kcal
Protein:	High	24.3 g	High	12.09 g
Fat:	High	49.0 g	High	61.5 g
Cholesterol:	None	None	None	None
Carbohydrates:	High	8.6 g	High	4.1 g
Fibre:	High	8.1 g	High	9.0 g
Sodium:	Low	6 mg	Low	2 mg
Major vitamin contribution:	B vitamins, vitamin E, folic acid	High, High, Med		High, High, —
Major mineral contribution:	Iron, phosphorus, potassium, zinc calcium	Med, High, High, High —		Med, High, High, High, High

Nuts are high in PROTEIN, FAT, CARBOHYDRATES, and fibre and especially rich in the indigestible food fibres cellulose and lignin.

A single 25 g serving of peanuts delivers 6 g of protein, about 10 percent of the RDA for a healthy adult. But the proteins in nuts are considered 'incomplete' because they are deficient in the essential amino acid lysine, and nuts are too high in fat to qualify as a total source of dietary protein. Raw nuts or nuts roasted without extra fat may be more than 70 percent fat, compared to beans, which are also high in proteins, carbohydrates, and fibre, but have less than 2 percent fat.

Nuts have no CHOLESTEROL. Their fats are relatively unsaturated, and a good source of vitamin E. If the nuts are exposed to air, the carbon atoms in the molecules of UNSATURATED FATTY ACIDS will pick up oxygen atoms. This natural oxidation of the SATURATED FATTY ACIDS, which turns the fats rancid, can be slowed by protecting the nuts from air, heat, and light but it can never be completely topped. Eventually, all nuts will taste rancid.

Nuts are also a good source of B vitamins, calcium, potassium, phosphorus, zinc and iron.

Plain raw or roasted nuts are low in sodium; salted nuts are a high-sodium food.

The most nutritious way to serve this food

With beans, which are legumes and provide the essential amino acid lysine needed to 'complete' the proteins in nuts. Adding raisins adds iron.

Diets that may restrict or exclude this food

Antiflatulence diet
Low-calcium diet
Low-fat diet
Low-fibre, low-residue diet
Low-oxalate diet (for people who form calcium oxalate kidney stones; almonds and cashews)
Low-protein diet
Low-sodium diet (salted nuts)

Buying

Choose: Fresh nuts with clean, undamaged shells from the last growing season. The nuts should feel heavy for their size; nuts that feel light may be withered inside.

Choose crisp, fresh shelled nuts. They should taste fresh and snap when you bite into them. Old nuts will have an off taste. Check the sell by date on packaged nuts.

Avoid: Mouldy shrivelled, or discoloured nuts. The moulds that grow on nuts may produce potentially carcinogenic aflatoxins that have been linked to liver cancer.

Storing

Store nuts in a cool, dry, dark place in a container that protects them from the air, heat, light, and moisture.

Pack nuts in a moistureproof container and store them in the freezer if you don't plan to use them immediately. The cold will slow down the oxidation of fats and the nuts will stay fresh longer.

Do not shell nuts until you are ready to use them. The shell is a natural protective shield.

Preparation

Almonds. To skin shelled almonds, boil the nuts, drain them, and plunge them into cold water. The skin should slip off easily.

Brazil nuts. Brazil nuts are easy to open if you chill them first. To slice shelled Brazil nuts, boil the nuts in water for five minutes, then cool and slice. Or you can shave them into slivers with a potato peeler.

Chestnuts. Slice an X in the flat end of the chestnut and peel off the heavy outer skin. To remove the thin inner skin, bake the chestnuts on a pastry sheet in a 400°F (204°C) oven for about twenty minutes or cover them with boiling water and simmer them for fifteen minutes. Then drain the nuts and slip off the skins.

Walnuts and hazelnuts. Crack the nut with a nutcracker.

Pistachios. Open the nuts with your fingers, not your teeth.

Cooking reactions
—

Effects of processing

Vacuum packaging. Canned nuts and nuts in glass jars stay fresh longer than nuts sold in bulk because they are protected from the oxygen that combines with oils and turns them rancid. Nuts in sealed cans and jars may stay fresh for as long as a year if stored in a cool, dark place. Once the can or jar is opened, the oils will begin to oxidize and eventually become rancid.

Medical uses and/or benefits
—

Adverse effects

Allergic reactions. Nuts are among the foods most often implicated as a cause of the classic symptoms of food allergy: upset stomach, hives, and angioedema (swelling of the lips and eyes).

Apthous ulcers. Eating nuts may trigger an episode of apthous ulcers (canker sores) in susceptible people, but avoiding nuts will not prevent or cure an attack.

Food/drug interactions

✖ FALSE RESULT IN TESTS FOR CANCER

• Oats (Oatmeal)

See also FLOUR

Nutritional profile per 100 g food (raw)		
	Oatmeal	
Energy value:	High	401 Kcal
Protein:	High	12.4 g
Fat:	Low	8.7 g
Cholesterol:	None	None
Carbohydrates:	High	72.8 g
Fibre:	High	7 g
Sodium:	Med	33 mg
Major vitamin contribution:	B vitamins	High
Major mineral contribution:	Iron, potassium, phosphorus	All high

What we call *oats* is normally oats that have been rolled (ground) into a meal, then steamed to break down some of their starches, formed into flakes, and dried.

All oatmeals are high-carbohydrate foods, rich in STARCH, with only a trace of sugar. They are an excellent source of indigestible food fibres including the complex CARBOHYDRATES, beta-glucans. They have moderate amounts of proteins. The proteins in oatmeal are considered 'incomplete' because they are deficient in the essential amino acid lysine. Oats have no CHOLESTEROL, but oatmeal may have as much as five times the FAT in rye and wheat flours. Since oats also contain an enzyme that speeds the oxidation of fats, oatmeal would become rancid very quickly if it were not for the fact that rolling and steaming the oats to make the meal also inactivates the destructive enzyme.

Oats provide B vitamins, iron, phosphorus and potassium. Uncooked oatmeal made solely of oats (no additives) has little sodium, but the milk you add in cooking may turn the cereal into a moderate- or high-sodium food.

The most nutritious way to serve this food

As porridge with milk, which will provide the essential amino acid lysine to 'complete' the proteins in the oatmeal or as low sugar oatcakes.

Diets that may restrict or exclude this food

Gluten-restriced, gliadin-free diet
Low-carbohydrate diet
Low-fibre, low-residue diet
Low-sodium diet

Buying
Choose: Tightly sealed boxes or packets.
Avoid: Bulk cereals; grains in open bins may be exposed to moisture, mould, and insect contamination.

Storing
Keep oats in air- and moistureproof containers to protect them from potentially toxic fungi that grow on damp grains. Properly stored and dry, rolled oats may keep for as long as a year. Whole-grain oats may oxidize and become rancid more quickly.

Preparation
Unlike cows and other ruminants, human beings cannot break through the cellulose and lignin covering on raw grain to reach the nutrients inside. Cooking unprocessed oats to the point where they are useful to human beings can take as long as 24 hours. The virtue of rolled oats is that they have been precooked and can be prepared in five minutes or less. Instant oatmeals, like other 'instant' cereals, are treated with phosphates to allow them to absorb water more quickly.

Cooking reactions
STARCH consists of molecules of the complex CARBOHYDRATES amylose and amylopectin packed into a starch granule. As you heat oatmeal in liquid, its starch granules absorb water molecules, swell, and soften. When the temperature of the liquid reaches approximately 140°F (60°C), the amylose and amylopectin molecules inside the granules relax and unfold, breaking some of their internal bonds (bonds between atoms on the same molecule) and forming new bonds between atoms on different molecules. The result is a network that traps and holds water molecules, making the starch granules even more bulky and thickening the liquid. Eventually the starch granules rupture, releasing the nutrients inside so that they can be absorbed more easily by the body. Oatmeal also contains hydrophilic (water-loving) gums and pectins, including beta-glucans, that attract and hold water molecules, immobilizing them so that the liquid thickens. (The beta-glucans give oatmeal its characteristic sticky texture.)

Effects of processing
—

Medical uses and/or benefits
✔ HEART DISEASE

✔ DIABETES THERAPY

To reduce the levels of serum cholesterol. The gums and pectins in oatmeal appear to lower the amount of cholesterol in the blood and offer some protection against heart disease. There are currently two theories to explain how this may happen. The first theory is that the pectins in the oats form a gel in your stomach that sops up fats and keeps them from being absorbed by your body. The second is that bacteria in the gut may feed on the beta-glucans in the oats and produce short-chain fatty acids that inhibit the production of cholesterol in your liver.

As a source of carbohydrates for people with diabetes. Cereal grains are digested very slowly, producing only a gradual rise in the level of sugar in the blood. As a result, the body needs less insulin to control blood sugar after eating plain, unadorned cereal grains than after eating some other high-carbohydrate foods (bread or potato).

Protection against some forms of cancer. In 1986 researchers at the University of Lund in Sweden suggested that the pectins and gels in oat bran may bind with quinolines, the potentially carcinogenic nitrogen compounds formed when meat is cooked at high heat and its amino acids are split apart, preventing the quinolines from inducing the gastrointestinal cancers associated with burnt meat products.

Adverse effects

Gluten intolerance. Coeliac disease is an intestinal allergic disorder whose victims are sensitive to gluten and gliadin, proteins in wheat and rye. People with coeliac disease cannot digest the nutrients in these grains; if they eat foods containing gluten, they may suffer anaemia, weight loss, bone pain, swelling, and skin disorders. Oats contain small amounts of gliadin. Corn flour, potato flour, rice flour, and soya flour are all gluten- and gliadin-free.

Food/drug interactions
—

• Offal (Brain, heart, kidney, sweetbreads, tongue, tripe)
See also BEEF, LIVER, PORK, SAUSAGES, VEAL

Nutritional profile per 100 g food (raw)				
	Lamb's Heart		*Pig's Kidney*	
Energy value:	Med	119 Kcal	Med	90 Kcal
. Protein:	High	17.1 g	High	16.3 g
Fat:	Med	5.6 g	Low	2.7 g
Cholesterol:	High	140 mg	High	700 mg
Carbohydrates:	None	None	None	None
Fibre:	None	None	None	None
Sodium:	High	140 mg	High	190 mg
Major vitamin contribution:	B vitamins	High		High
Major mineral contribution:	Iron, copper, potassium, phosphorus, zinc	All high		All high

Heart, tongue, and tripe (the muscular lining of the cow's stomach) are muscle meats. Brains, kidneys, and sweetbreads (the thymus gland) are organ meats. Like other foods of animal origin, both kinds of meats are rich sources of PROTEINS considered 'complete' because they have sufficient amounts of all the essential amino acids.

Some organ meats have more fat than muscle meats. Their fat composition varies according to the animal from which they come. Ounce for ounce, beef FAT has proportionally more SATURATED FATTY ACIDS than pork fat, slightly less CHOLESTEROL than chicken fat, and appreciably less than lamb fat. There is no food fibre in any meat and no CARBOHYDRATES other than the very small amounts of glycogen (sugar) stored in an animal's muscles and liver.

All offal is an excellent source of B vitamins, including nicotinic acid, vitamin B_6, and vitamin B_{12}, which is found only in animal foods. Sweetbreads are a good source of vitamin C. 100 g of raw sweetbreads has 18 mg vitamin C, 60 percent of the RDA for a healthy adult. Livers are a good source of vitamin A, the fat-soluble vitamin stored in fatty organs. 100 g of beef liver provides twice the RDA for a healthy adult.

Offal is rich in heme iron, the organic form of iron in meat, fish, and poultry that is up to five times more available to the body than non-heme iron, the inorganic form of iron in plant foods. Heart, kidneys, and sweetbreads as well as tongue and tripe are high in sodium. Offal is high in CHOLESTEROL.

Cholesterol content of offal

(mg/100 g food)

Lamb brains (boiled)	2200 mg
Lamb heart (raw)	140 mg
Lamb kidney (raw)	400 mg
Lamb sweetbread (raw)	260 mg
Calf tongue (boiled)	100 mg
Tripe (raw)	95 mg

Source: McCance and Widdowson's *The Composition of Foods*, HMSO, (1974).

The most nutritious way to serve this food
Lightly fried or in casseroles.

Diets that may restrict or exclude this food
Low-cholesterol, controlled-fat diet
Low-protein diet
Low-sodium diet

Buying
Choose: Refrigerated meat that looks and smells absolutely fresh. Frozen heart or tripe should be solid, with no give to the packet and no drippings staining the outside.

Choose some offal by size. The smaller the tongue, for example, the more tender it will be. The most tender kidneys come from young animals. On the other hand, all brains and sweetbreads are by nature tender, while all heart, tongue, and tripe (the most solidly muscular of the offals) require long simmering to make them tender.

Storing
Refrigerate immediately. All are highly perishable and should be used within 24 hours of purchase. Refrigeration prolongs the freshness of meat by slowing the natural multiplication of bacteria on the surface.

Wrap fresh meat carefully before storing to keep the drippings from spilling and contaminating other food or the refrigerator/freezer shelves.

Preparation
Brains. First wash the brains under cold running water and pull off the membranes. Then put the brains in a bowl of cold water and let them soak for a half hour. Change the water; let them soak for another half hour. Repeat the process. Drain and use as your recipe directs.

Kidneys. Pull off the white membrane and rinse the kidneys thoroughly under plenty of cold running water. Cut them in half, remove the inner core, and rinse once again. Slice them and use as your recipe directs. (Beef kidneys have a strong, distinctive flavour that can be toned down by soaking the kidneys for an hour in a solution of 1 teaspoon lemon juice to 1 cup of water before cooking.)

Heart. Cut out the blood vessels, rinse the heart thoroughly (inside and out) under cold running water, and prepare as your recipe directs.

Sweetbreads. Rinse the sweetbreads thoroughly under cold running water and soak in iced water for at least an hour, changing the water until it remains clear and free of blood. Then drain the sweetbreads and blanch them in water plus 2 teaspoons of acid (lemon juice or vinegar) to firm them. Drain the sweetbreads, cover them with ice water, and remove membranes and connective tissue. Then use as your recipe directs.

Tongue. Scrub the tongue with a vegetable brush under cold running water. Cover it with cold water, bring the water to a boil, and cook the tongue at a simmer for 30 minutes or soak and cook as directed on the package. Drain the tongue, peel off the skin, cut away the gristle and small bones, and prepare as your recipe directs. Some smoked tongues require long soaking, even overnight; check the directions on the package.

Tripe. Wash the tripe in several changes of cold water, boil it for several hours until tender, then use as your recipe directs.

(After handling any raw meat, always wash your knives, cutting board, work surface — and your hands — with warm soapy water to reduce the chance of transferring microorganisms from the meat to any other food.)

Cooking reactions

Heat changes the structure of proteins. It denatures protein molecules — they break apart into smaller fragments, change shape, or clump together. All these changes force moisture out of protein tissues. The longer you cook meats, the more moisture they will lose.

All offal must be cooked thoroughly.

Effects of processing

Freezing. When meat is frozen, the water inside its cells freezes into sharp ice crystals that puncture cell membranes so that water (and B vitamins) leak out of the cells when the meat is thawed. Frozen heart, kidneys, and tripe are drier when thawed than they would have been fresh. They may also be lower in B vitamins. Freezing may also cause freezer burn, dry spots left when moisture evaporates from the surface of the meat. Waxed freezer paper is designed specifically to hold the moisture in frozen meat.

Medical uses and/or benefits

As a source of heme iron. Because the body stores excess iron in the heart, kidneys, and other organs, offal is an excellent source of heme iron.

Adverse effects
✖ GOUT

✖ HEART DISEASE

Food/drug interactions
—

• Okra (ladies fingers)

Nutritional profile per 100 g food (raw)		
Energy value:	Low	17 Kcal
Protein:	Low	2 g
Fat:	Low	Trace
Cholesterol:	None	None
Carbohydrates:	Low	2.3 g
Fibre:	Med	3.2 g
Sodium:	Low	7 mg
Major vitamin contribution:	B vitamins	High
Major mineral contribution:	Potassium	Med

The okra we use as a vegetable consists of the unripe seed capsules of the okra plant. Okra is a low-carbohydrate food that contains STARCH plus considerable amounts of gums and pectins. Together, the starch and pectins make okra an excellent thickener for soups and stews. Okra also provides some potassium, B vitamins, and vitamin C.

The most nutritious way to serve this food
In a soup or stew.

Diets that may restrict or exclude this food
—

Buying
Choose: Young, green tender pods of okra no more than 4 inches long which feel firm when bent.

Storing
Keep okra in the refrigerator.

Preparation
Wash the okra under cold running water, then use it whole or sliced.

Cooking reactions
When okra is heated in water, its starch granules absorb water molecules and swell. Eventually, they rupture, releasing amylose and amylopectin molecules as well as gums and pectic substances, all of which attract and immobilize water molecules, thickening the soup or stew.

Effects of processing
Canning and freezing. Canned and frozen okra have less vitamin C per serving than fresh okra.

Medical uses and/or benefits
✓ HEART DISEASE

Adverse effects
—

Food/drug interactions
—

• Olives

See also VEGETABLE OILS

Nutritional profile per 100 g food (in brine)		
Energy value:	Med	103 Kcal
Protein:	Low	0.9 g
Fat:	High	11 g
Cholesterol:	None	None
Carbohydrates:	Low	Trace
Fibre:	Med	4.4 g
Sodium:	High	2250 mg
Major vitamin contribution:	Vitamin A	Low
Major mineral contribution:	Iron	Low

All olives are high in FAT and sodium and low in iron.

The most nutritious way to serve this food
Black olives have less sodium than either green olives or salt-cured Greek or Italian olives, but are still high sodium foods.

Diets that may restrict or exclude this food
Low-fat diet
Low-sodium diet

Buying
Choose. Tightly sealed bottles or cans. Small olives are less woody than large ones. Green olives have a more astringent taste than black olives. Greek olives have a sharp, spicy taste. Pitted olives are the best buy if you want to slice the olives into a salad, otherwise olives with pits are less-expensive.

Storing
Store unopened cans or jars of olives on a cool, dry shelf. Once you open a can of olives, take the olives out of the can and refrigerate them in a clean glass container.

Preparation
—

Cooking reactions
—

Effects of processing

Curing. Green olives were picked before they ripened. Black olives were picked ripe and dipped in an iron solution to stabilize their colour. After they are picked, green olives and black olives are soaked in a mild solution of sodium hydroxide and then washed thoroughly in water to remove oleuropein, a naturally bitter carbohydrate. Then green olives may be allowed to ferment before they are packed in a brine solution. Black olives are not allowed to ferment before packaging, which is why they taste milder than most green olives. (Green olives that do not ferment before packing taste as mild as black olives.)

Greek and Italian olives are black olives that taste sharp because they have not been soaked to remove their oleuropein. They are salt-cured and sold in bulk, covered with olive oil that protects them from oxygen and helps preserve them.

Pressing. Olives are pressed to produce olive oil, one of the few vegetable oils with a distinctive taste and aroma. Olive oils are graded according to the pressing from which they come and the amount of free oleic acid they contain. (The presence of free oleic acid means that the oil's molecules have begun to break down.) Virgin olive oil is oil from the first pressing of the olives. Pure olive oil is a mixture of oils from the first and second pressings. Virgin olive oil may contain as much as 4 percent free oleic acid. Fine virgin olive oil may contain 3 percent free oleic acid, superfine virgin olive oil 1.5 percent, and extra virgin olive oil 1 percent.

Olive oil is a more concentrated source of alpha-tocopherol (vitamin E) than olives. Because it is high in unsaturated fatty acids, whose carbon atoms have double bonds that can make room for more oxygen atoms, olive oil oxidizes and turns rancid fairly quickly if exposed to heat or light. To protect the oil, store it in a cool, dark cupboard.

Medical uses and/or benefits

✓ HEART DISEASE

Adverse effects associated with this food

—

Food/drug interactions

—

• Onions (chives, leeks, spring onions, shallots)

See also GARLIC

Nutritional profile per 100 g food (raw)		
Energy value:	Low	23 Kcal
Protein:	Low	0.9 g
Fat:	Low	Trace
Cholesterol:	None	None
Carbohydrates:	Low	5.2 g
Fibre:	Low	1.3 g
Sodium:	Low	10 mg
Major vitamin contribution:	Vitamin C, B vitamins	Low, Low
Major mineral contribution:	Potassium	Low

All members of the onion family have moderate amounts of sucrose and other SUGARS, some PROTEIN, very little FAT, and no STARCH or CHOLESTEROL. Red onions are coloured with red anthocyanins; shallots, yellow onions, white onions, and the white bulbs of the leeks, and spring onions are coloured with creamy pale-yellow anthoxanthins. Neither of these natural pigments provides any vitamin A.

The most nutritious way to serve this food
Whole fresh spring onions or spring onions chopped (green portions and all) and added to a salad or other dish.

Diets that may restrict or exclude this food
Antiflatulence diet
Low-fibre diet

Buying
Choose: Firm, clean shallots; yellow, white, or red onions with smooth, dry, crisp skin free of any black mould spots. Leeks and spring onions should have crisp green tops and clean white bulbs.
Avoid: Onions that are sprouting or soft or whose skin is wet — all signs of internal decay.

Storing
Store shallots and red, yellow, and white onions in a cool place where the

temperature is 60°F (16°C) or lower and there is plenty of circulating air to keep the onions dry and prevent them from sprouting. Properly stored, onions should stay fresh for months at 55°F (13°C) they may retain all their vitamin C for as long as six months.

Cut the roots from spring onions, and leeks; trim off any damaged tops and refrigerate the vegetables in a tightly closed plastic bag. Check daily and remove tops that have wilted.

Preparation

When you cut into an onion, you tear its cell walls and release a sulphur compound called propanethial-S-oxide that floats up into the air. The chemical, identified in 1985 by researchers at the University of St. Louis (Missouri), turns into sulphuric acid when it comes into contact with water, which is why it stings if it gets into your eyes. You can prevent this by slicing fresh onions under running water, diluting the propanethial-S-oxide before it can float up into the air.

To peel the brown papery outer skin from an onion or a shallot, heat the vegetable in boiling water briefly, then lift it out with a slotted spoon and put it in cold water. The skin should come off easily.

Cooking reactions

Heat converts an onion's sulphurous flavour and aroma compounds into sugars, which is why cooked onions taste sweet. When you 'brown' onions, the sugars and amino acids on their surface caramelize to a deep rich brown and the flavour intensifies (see BROWNING REACTIONS).

Onions may also change colour when cooked. Onions get their creamy colour from anthoxanthins, pale-yellow pigments that turn brown if they combine with metal ions. That's why onions discolour if you cook them in an aluminium or iron pot or slice them with a carbon-steel knife. Red onions contain anthocyanin pigments that turn redder in acid (lemon juice, vinegar) and bluish in a basic (alkaline) solution. And the chlorophyll molecules that make the tops of spring onions green goes brown-green when heated.

Effects of processing

Drying. Drying onions into flakes removes the moisture and concentrates the nutrients. Ounce for ounce, dried onions have approximately nine times the vitamin C, eight times the thiamin, ten times the riboflavin, nine times the nicotinic acid, five times the iron, and eleven times as much potassium as fresh onions.

Medical uses and/or benefits

✓ HEART DISEASE

Adverse effects
—

Food/drug interactions
—

• Oranges

Nutritional profile per 100 g (flesh only)		
Energy value:	Low	35 Kcal
Protein:	Low	0.8 g
Fat:	Low	Trace
Cholesterol:	None	None
Carbohydrates:	Low	8.5 g
Fibre:	Low	2.0 g
Sodium:	Low	3 mg
Major vitamin contribution:	Vitamin C	High
Major mineral contribution:	Potassium	Med

Oranges have SUGARS but no STARCH. They are a good source of pectins, and they have small amounts of the other indigestible food fibres. Their most important contribution to our diet is vitamin C, which is concentrated in the white layer just under the peel. A single glass of fresh juice has about 50 mg vitamin C, 60 percent of the RDA for a healthy adult. Oranges and orange juice are good sources of potassium.

The most nutritious way to serve this food
Fresh — quartered or squeezed.

Diets that may restrict or exclude this food
Sucrose-restricted diet

Buying
Choose: Firm fruit that is heavy for its size; the heavier the orange, the juicier it is likely to be. The skin on juice oranges should be thin, smooth, and fine-grained. The skin on navel oranges, the large seedless orange is thicker; it comes off easily when you peel the orange.

Storing
Refrigerate oranges if you plan to keep them for longer than a week or two, which is how long they will stay fresh at room temperature.
   Refrigerate fresh orange juice in a tightly closed glass bottle. The key to preserving vitamin C is to protect the juice from heat and air (which might seep in through plastic bottles). The juice should fill the bottle as high as possible, so that there is very little space at the top for oxygen to gather. Stored this way, the juice may hold its vitamin C for two weeks. Frozen juice

should be kept frozen until you are ready to use it; once reconstituted, it should be handled like fresh juice.

Preparation

Oranges may be waxed and sprayed with fungicides to prevent moisture loss and protect them in shipping. If you plan to grate orange rind and use it for flavouring, rinse the orange first. Do not grate deeper than the coloured part of the skin; if you hit the white underneath, you will be getting bitter-tasting components in with the rind.

To collect natural flavouring oils from the oranges, grate the orange, wrap the grated peel in cheesecloth, let it sit for a while at room temperature, then squeeze the oil out through the cheesecloth onto some sugar that can then be added to a cake batter or sprinkled over fruit.

Orange peel contains volatile fragrant oils whose molecules are liberated when the skin is torn and its cell walls ruptured. These molecules are also more fragrant at room temperature than when cold. Oranges have a much truer aroma and flavour if you let them come to room temperature before peeling and serving.

Cooking reactions

Heat destroys the vitamin C but not the flavouring oils in an orange. When oranges or orange peel are cooked, they add flavour but not vitamin C.

Effects of processing

Commercially prepared juices. How well a commercially prepared juice holds its vitamin C depends on how it is prepared, stored, and packaged. Sealed cans of orange juice stored in the refrigerator may lose only 2 percent of their vitamin C in three months. Prepared, pasteurized 'fresh' juices in glass bottles hold their vitamin C better than the same juice sold in plastic bottles or waxed paper cartons that let oxygen pass through.

All commercially prepared juices taste different from fresh juice. There are two reasons for this. The first is that frozen, canned, or pasteurized juices are almost always a blend of fruits from various crops. The second is that they have all been heated to inactivate the enzymes that would otherwise rot the juice; heating alters flavour.

Canned oranges and orange juice retain most of their vitamin C. As soon as the can is opened, the oranges or juice should be removed and transferred to a glass container to prevent the fruit or juice from absorbing lead used to seal the can. The absorption of lead is triggered by oxygen, which enters the can when the seal is broken. No lead is absorbed while the can is intact.

Drying. Orange peel may be dried for use as a sweet or flavouring. Dried orange peel may be treated with sulphites (sodium sulphite, sodium bisulphite, and the like) to keep it from darkening.

Medical uses and/or benefits
✓ POTASSIUM REPLACEMENT

✓ HEART DISEASE

✓ PROTECTION AGAINST CANCER

Antiscorbutics. All citrus fruits are excellent sources of vitamin C, used to cure or prevent the vitamin C-deficiency disease scurvy. Your body also needs vitamin C in order to convert the amino acid proline into hydroxyproline, an essential ingredient in collagen, the PROTEIN needed to form skin, tendons, and bones. People with scurvy find sores and wounds do not heal quickly, a condition that can be cured by feeding them foods rich in vitamin C. Whether taking extra vitamin C speeds healing in healthy people remains to be proved. Although the UK RDA for vitamin C is 30 mg per day, it is not known whether higher intakes would be beneficial or not.

Enhanced absorption of iron from plant foods. Non-heme iron, the inorganic form of iron found in plant foods, is poorly absorbed by the body because it is bound into insoluble compounds by natural chemicals in the plants. Vitamin C appears to make non-heme iron more available to your body, perhaps by converting it from ferric iron to ferrous iron, which is more easily absorbed. Eating vitamin C-rich foods along with plant foods rich in iron can increase the amount of iron you get from the plant — a nutritional benefit of a breakfast with orange juice and cereal or bread.

Adverse effects
✗ SULPHITE SENSITIVITY

Apthous ulcers. In sensitive people, eating citrus fruits may trigger an attack of apthous ulcers (canker sores), but eliminating citrus fruit from the diet neither cures nor prevents canker sores.

Contact dermatitis Although there is ample anecdotal evidence to suggest that many people are sensitive to natural chemicals in an orange's flesh or peel, the offending substances have never been conclusively identified.

Food/drug interactions
✗ FALSE RESULT IN TESTS FOR CANCER

• Papaya (Paw-paw)

Nutritional profile per 100 g food (raw)		
Energy value:	Low	45 Kcal
Protein:	Low	0.5 g
Fat:	Low	0.1 g
Cholesterol:	None	None
Carbohydrates:	Med	11.3 g
Fibre:	Low	(not available)
Sodium:	Low	4 mg
Major vitamin contribution:	Vitamins A and C	Med, High
Major mineral contribution:	Potassium	Med

Papayas (which are also known as paw-paws) are high in sugar, but they have no STARCH and very little dietary fibre. They are a good source of vitamins C and A. A single 100 g serving provides 73 mg vitamin C (twice the RDA for a healthy adult) and 15 percent of the RDA for vitamin A. Papayas are medium in potassium and have virtually no sodium.

Unripe papayas and the leaves of the papaya plant contain papain, a proteolytic (protein-dissolving) enzyme that breaks long protein molecules into smaller fragments. You can tenderize meat by cooking it wrapped in papaya leaves or by dusting it with a meat tenderizer of commercially extracted papain dried to a powder. (Soya beans, French beans, garden peas, broad beans, wheat flours, and egg white all contain proteins that inactivate papain.)

The most nutritious way to serve this food
Fresh, sliced.

Diets that may restrict or exclude this food
Sucrose-restricted diet

Buying
Choose: Medium-size, pear-shaped fruit whose skin is turning yellow. (The yellower the skin, the riper the fruit.)

Storing
Store papayas at room temperature until they are fully ripe, which means that they have turned yellow all over and are soft enough to give when you press the stem end.

Store ripe papayas in the refrigerator.

Preparation
Wash the papaya under cool running water, then cut it in half, spoon out the seeds, and sprinkle it with lemon or lime juice.

The seeds of the papaya taste like peppercorns. They can be dried and ground as a seasoning or simply sprinkled, whole, on a salad.

Cooking reactions
—

Effects of processing
Extraction of papain. Commercial meat tenderizers contain papain extracted from fresh papaya and dried to a powder. The powder is a much more efficient tenderizer than either fresh papaya or papaya leaves. At the strength usually found in these powders, papain can 'digest' (tenderize) up to 35 times its weight in meat. Like bromelain (the proteolytic enzyme in fresh pineapple) and ficin (the proteolytic enzyme in fresh figs), papain breaks down proteins only at a temperature between 140°F (60°C) and 170°F (77°C). It won't work when the temperature is higher or lower.

Medical uses and/or benefits
First aid for insect stings. Some experts recommend applying a paste of meat tenderizer and water to reduce the pain and itch of mosquito bites by destroying the proteins injected with the insect venom. *Note*: This 'home remedy' is *never* recommended for people who are sensitive to bee or insect venom.

Adverse effects
✗ MAO INHIBITORS

Irritated skin. Because it can break down proteins, papain (and/or fresh papayas) may cause dermatitis, including a hivelike reaction. This is not an allergic response: it can happen to anyone.

Food/drug interactions
—

• Parsnips

Nutritional profile per 100 g food (raw)		
Energy value:	Low	49 Kcal
Protein:	Low	1.7 g
Fat:	Low	Trace
Cholesterol:	None	None
Carbohydrates:	High	11.3 g
Fibre:	Med	4.0 g
Sodium:	Low	17 mg
Major vitamin contribution:	Vitamin C	Med
Major mineral contribution:	Potassium, calcium	High, Low

Parsnips are roots, a good source of STARCH, plus the CARBOHYDRATE food fibres gums, pectins, cellulose and hemicellulose. They are moderately high in vitamin C; a 100 g serving of drained boiled parsnips has 10 mg vitamin C, about 33 percent of the RDA for a healthy adult. They are also a source of calcium.

The most nutritious way to serve this food
Boiled and drained.

Diets that may restrict or exclude this food
Low-fibre diet

Buying
Choose: Smooth, well-shaped, cream or tan small-to-medium roots. The larger the root, the woodier and coarser it will be.
Avoid: Discoloured parsnips. Parsnips that are darker in spots may have been frozen on the way to market. Grey spots or soft spots warn of rot inside the root.

Storing
Keep parsnips cold and humid so they won't dry out. Store them in a cool place or in the refrigerator. In storage, parsnips will convert some of their starch to sugar. As a rule of thumb, the sweeter the parsnip, the longer it has been stored.

Preparation
Scrub the parsnips with a vegetable brush under cool running water or simply peel them — but not until you are ready to use them.

Cooking reactions
Heat dissolves the pectic substances in the parnsip's cell walls, making the vegetable softer. At the same time, the parsnip's starch granules absorb water, swell, and eventually rupture, releasing nutrients inside and making the vegetables easier to digest.

Effects of processing
Freezing. When parsnips are frozen, liquids inside the vegetable's cell form ice crystals that may tear the cells, allowing moisture to escape when you thaw the parsnips. As a result, when roots like carrots, potatoes, and parsnips are frozen and thawed, their texture is mushy rather than crisp.

Medical uses and/or benefits
—

Adverse effects
Photosensitivity. Like celery and parsley, parsnips contain psoralens, natural chemicals that make the skin sensitive to light. Psoralens are not inactivated by cooking; they are present in both raw and cooked parsnips.

Food/drug interactions
—

• Pasta (Lasagne, macaroni, noodles, spaghetti)
See also FLOUR

Nutritional profile per 100 g food (boiled)		
	Spaghetti	
Energy value:	Med	117 Kcal
Protein:	Med	4.2 g
Fat:	Low	0.3 g
Cholesterol:	None	None
Carbohydrates:	High	26.0 g
Fibre:	Low	(not available)
Sodium:	Low	2 mg
Major vitamin contribution:	B vitamins	Low
Major mineral contribution:	Iron, potassium	Low, Low

The basic ingredients in pasta are water plus flour or semolina (the coarsely milled inner part of the wheat kernel called the endosperm). *Whole wheat pasta*, which is darker than ordinary pasta, is made with whole wheat flour. *Egg noodles* are made with flour and water plus eggs. *Spinach pasta* adds dried spinach for taste and colour. *Rice noodles* are made with rice flour.

All pasta is high in CARBOHYDRATES (starch). The more semolina the pasta contains, the more PROTEIN it provides. The proteins in pasta are considered 'incomplete' because they are deficient in the essential amino acids, lysine and isoleucine. Pasta made without eggs has no fat and no cholesterol.

All pasta supplies some thiamin (vitamin B_1) and riboflavin (vitamin B_2). Pasta made with flour also contains small amounts of non-heme iron, the inorganic form of iron found in plants which is three to six times less available than the iron in foods of animal origin.

The most nutritious way to serve this food
With meat, eggs, or milk products (cheese), which supply lysine and isoleucine to 'complement' the proteins in the pasta.

With beans or peas. Grains are deficient in the essential amino acids lysine and isoleucine (see PROTEIN) but contain sufficient amounts of tryptophan, methionine, and cystine. Beans and peas are just the opposite. Together, their proteins are complementary.

Diets that may restrict or exclude this food
Gluten-restricted, gliadin-free diet (all pastas made with wheat flour)

Buying

Choose: Tightly sealed packets. If you can see into the box, pick the pasta that looks smooth and shiny. Dry or dusty pasta is stale; so is pasta that is crumbling. The yellower the pasta, the more durum wheat it contains. (Egg noodles get their yellow from eggs.) Whole wheat pasta is brown.

Storing

Store pasta in air- and moistureproof glass or plastic containers. Pasta will stay fresh for about a year, egg noodles for six months.

Preparation

To cook pasta most efficiently, start with salted water. At sea level, water boils at 212°F (100°C), the temperature at which its molecules have enough energy to escape from the surface as steam. If you add salt, the water molecules will need to pick up more energy to push the salt molecules aside and escape from the surface. In effect, adding salt forces the water to boil at a higher temperature, which means the pasta will cook more quickly.

The water should be boiling furiously before you add the pasta so that it can penetrate the pasta's starch granules as fast as possible. Add the pasta slowly so that the water continues to boil and the pasta cooks evenly.

Cooking reactions

STARCH consists of molecules of the complex CARBOHYDRATES amylose and amylopectin packed into a starch granule. When you boil pasta, water molecules force their way into the starch granules. When the water reaches a temperature of approximately 140°F (60°C), the amylose and amylopectin molecules inside the starch granules relax and unfold, forming new bonds between atoms on different molecules and creating a network inside the starch granule that traps water molecules. The granules bulk up and the pasta gets thicker. In fact, the starch granules can hold so much water that plain flour-and-water pastas like spaghetti, macaroni, and lasagne will actually double in size.

The longer you cook the pasta, the more likely it is that the starch granules will absorb too much water and rupture, releasing some of their starch and making the pasta sticky. One way to keep the pieces of pasta from sticking together is to cook them in a large pot, or you might add a tablespoon of olive oil. If you plan to refrigerate the cooked pasta, drain it, rinse it in warm water (to wash off the starch on the outside), and toss it with olive oil.

Effects of processing

Canning and freezing. When pasta is canned or frozen in sauce, its starch granules continue to absorb the liquid and the pasta becomes progressively more limp.

Medical uses and/or benefits
✓ DIABETES THERAPY

Adverse effects
Food allergy. Wheat is among the foods most often implicated as a cause of the classic food allergy symptoms — upset stomach, hives, skin rashes, angioedema (swelling of the face, eyes, and lips).
Gluten intolerance (coeliac disease). Coeliac disease is an intestinal allergic disorder that results in an inability to absorb the nutrients in gluten and gliadin. People with coeliac disease cannot absorb the nutrients in wheat or wheat products, such as pasta, Corn flour, potato flour, rice flour, and soya flour are gluten- and gliadin-free.

Food/drug interactions
—

• Peaches (Nectarines)

Nutritional profile per 100 g food (fresh)		
Energy value:	Low	37 Kcal
Protein:	Low	0.6 g
Fat:	Low	Trace
Cholesterol:	None	None
Carbohydrates:	Med	9.1 g
Fibre:	Low	1.2 g
Sodium:	Low	3 mg
Major vitamin contribution:	Vitamin A, vitamin C	Med, Med
Major mineral contribution:	Potassium	Med

Peaches have a little dietary fibre, primarily pectins and gums. As peaches ripen, the pectins in their cell walls dissolve and the fruit get softer.

Peaches have a trace of PROTEIN and virtually no FAT. There is some STARCH in unripe peaches, but it turns to SUGAR as the fruit ripens. Nectarines, which have been called 'peaches without fuzz,' have about twice as much fibre.

Both peaches and nectarines are coloured with yellow carotenoid pigments your body can convert to vitamin A. Nectarines and peaches are also a good source of potassium; they provide moderate amounts of vitamin C.

The most nutritious way to serve this food
Fresh and ripe.

Diets that may restrict or exclude this food
Sucrose-restricted diet

Buying
Choose: Peaches and nectarines with rich cream or yellow skin. The red 'blush' characteristic of some varieties of peaches is not a reliable guide to ripeness. A better guide is the way the fruit feels and smells. Ripe peaches and nectarines have a warm, intense aroma and feel firm, with a slight softness along the line running up the length of the fruit.
Avoid: Green or hard unripe peaches and nectarines. As peaches and nectarines ripen their concentration of bitter phenols decreases. The longer the peach is left on the tree, the lower the concentration of phenols will be, which is why late-season peaches and nectarines are the sweetest. Once you pick the peach it may shrivel, but it cannot continue to ripen.

Storing

Store firm ripe peaches and nectarines at room temperature until they soften. Once they have softened, put them in the refrigerator. The cold will stop the enzymatic action that softens the fruit.

Preparation

To peel peaches, immerse them in hot water for a few seconds, then lift them out and plunge them into cold water. The hot water destroys a layer of cells under the skin, allowing the skin to slip off easily.

Don't peel or slice peaches and nectarines until you are ready to use them as they will go brown on the cut surfaces (see BROWNING REACTIONS). You can slow the reaction (but not stop it completely) by chilling the fruit or by mixing the sliced peaches and nectarines into a fruit salad with citrus fruits.

Cooking reactions

When you cook peaches or nectarines, pectin in the cell walls dissolves and the fruit softens. Cooking peaches and nectarines also destroys polyphenoloxidase and keeps the fruit from darkening.

Effects of processing

Drying. Like other dried fruits, dried peaches may be treated with sulphites (sodium sulphite) that inhibit polyphenoloxidase and keep the peaches from darkening. People who are sensitive to sulphites may suffer serious allergic reactions, including potentially lethal anaphylactic shock, if they eat dried peaches treated with these compounds.

Medical uses and/or benefits

✓ PROTECTION AGAINST CANCER

✓ POTASSIUM REPLACEMENT

Adverse effects

✗ SULPHITE SENSITIVITY

Poisoning. Like apple seeds and apricot pits, the leaves and bark of the peach tree as well as the 'nut' inside the peach pit contain amygdalin, a naturally occurring cyanide/sugar compound that breaks down into hydrogen cyanide in your stomach. Accidentally swallowing a peach pit once in a while is not a serious hazard, but cases of human poisoning after eating peach pits have been reported (see APPLES).

Food/drug interactions

—

• Pears

Nutritional profile per 100 g food (raw)		
Energy value:	Low	29 Kcal
Protein:	Low	0.2 g
Fat:	Low	Trace
Cholesterol:	None	None
Carbohydrates:	Med	7.3 g
Fibre:	Low	2.3 g
Sodium:	Low	2 mg
Major vitamin contribution:	Vitamin C	Low
Major mineral contribution:	Potassium	Med

Pears are a source of food fibre, pectin, gums, cellulose, hemicellulose, and the noncarbohydrate food fibre lignin, which is found in the sclerenchyma cells that make up the gritty particles in the pear's flesh. The pear's starches turn to SUGAR as it ripens: only a trace of STARCH remains in ripe pears. Pears have some vitamin C, which is concentrated in the skin.

The most nutritious way to use this food
Fresh and ripe, with the skin.

Diets that may restrict or exclude this food
Sucrose-restricted diet

Buying
Choose: Large, firm, ripe pears. Most fruit and vegetables get softer after they are picked because their pectic enzymes begin to dissolve the pectin in their cell walls. With pears, this reaction occurs if the pear is left on the tree to ripen, which is why tree-ripened pears sometimes taste mushy. The best-tasting pears are ones that are picked immature and allowed to ripen in storage or on your grocer's shelf.

Choose a brightly coloured pear. The colour of a ripe pear varies with the variety. Williams pears have clear yellow skin or yellow skin with a reddish blush and smooth, juicy flesh. The skin of the Conference pear ranges from yellow to green with some russet shades in between; the flesh is juicy and spicy. Comice pears are larger than the others, with greenish-yellow skin that may have a reddish cast. The flesh is fine, sweet, and juicy.
Avoid: Cut, shrivelled, or bruised pears. They are probably discoloured inside.

Storing

Store pears at room temperature for a few days if they are not fully ripe when you buy them. A ripe pear will yield when you press it lightly with your palm.

Do not store pears in sealed plastic bags either in or out of the refrigerator. Without oxygen circulating freely around the pear, the fruit will begin to 'breathe' internally, creating compounds that turn the core brown and make brownish spots under the skin.

Preparation

Handle pears with care; never peel or slice them until you are ready to use them as they will brown (see BROWNING REACTIONS). You can slow this natural reaction (but not stop it completely) by chilling the pears, brushing the cut surface with an acid solution (lemon juice and water, vinegar and water), or mixing the peeled, sliced fruit into a fresh fruit salad with citrus fruits (they are full of vitamin C, a natural antioxidant).

Cooking reactions

Like other fruits and vegetables, pears have cell walls made of cellulose, hemicellulose, and pectic substances. As the fruit cooks and its pectins dissolve, it gets softer. But no amount of cooking will dissolve the lignin particles in the pear flesh. In fact, the softer the pear, the easier it is to feel the crunchy texture of the lignin particles.

Effects of processing

Drying. Fresh pears are sometimes treated with sulphur compounds such as sulphur dioxide to inactivate polyphenoloxidase and keep the pears from darkening when they are exposed to air while drying. People who are sensitive to sulphites may suffer serious allergic reactions, including anaphylactic shock, if they eat these treated dried pears.

Sealed packets of dried pears may be stored at room temperature for up to six months. Once the packet is opened, the pears should be refrigerated in a tightly closed container that will protect them from air and moisture.

Medical uses and/or benefits
✓ POTASSIUM REPLACEMENT

Adverse effects
✗ SULPHITE SENSITIVITY

Poisoning. Like apple seeds and peach pits, the seeds of pears contain amygdalin, a cyanide/sugar compound that breaks down into hydrogen cyanide in your stomach. Accidentally swallowing a pear seed once in a while is not necessarily hazardous, but there have been reports of serious poisoning among people who have eaten several apple seeds (see APPLES).

Food/drug interactions
—

• Peas (Mangetout, split peas)

Nutritional profile per 100 g food (raw)		
Energy value:	Med	67 Kcal
Protein:	Med	5.8 g
Fat:	Low	0.4 g
Cholesterol:	None	None
Carbohydrates:	Med	10.6 g
Fibre:	High	5.2 g
Sodium:	Low	1 mg
Major vitamin contribution:	Vitamin A, vitamin C	Med, High
Major mineral contribution:	Iron, potassium, phosphorus	Low, High Med

Peas start out high in sugar but convert it to STARCH as they age. Within a few hours after they are picked, peas may convert as much as 40 percent of their SUGARS to starch. Mangetout are eaten immature. Fresh peas are a good source of food fibre pectins, gums, hemicellulose, and cellulose and the noncarbohydrate food fibre lignin.

Peas are a high-protein food. A 100 g serving of fresh green peas has 5 grams of PROTEIN. The proteins in peas, like the proteins in other vegetables, are considered 'incomplete' because they are deficient in some of the essential amino acids, in this case tryptophan, methionine, and cystine. Peas have very little FAT and no CHOLESTEROL.

Peas are a good source of vitamin A, which comes from yellow carotenoids hidden under their green chlorophyll pigments. As peas age, the chlorophyll fades and the yellow shows through. Peas also have some non-heme iron, the inorganic form of iron found in plants.

The most nutritious way to serve this food
With grains. The PROTEINS in peas and other legumes are deficient in the essential amino acids tryptophan, methionine, and cystine but contain sufficient amounts of the essential amino acids lysine and isoleucine. The proteins in grains are exactly the opposite. Together, they complement each other and produce 'complete' proteins.

Diets that may restrict or exclude this food
Low-residue diet
Low-purine (antigout) diet

Buying
Choose: Fresh, firm bright-green pods, loose fresh peas, or mangetout peas. The pods should feel velvety; fresh pea pods should look full, with round fat peas inside.

When buying *split peas*, look for well-coloured peas in a tightly sealed box or bag. Store the peas in an air- and moistureproof container in a cool, dry cupboard. When you are ready to use them, pick the peas over, discarding any damaged, broken, or withered ones along with any pebbles or other foreign matter.

Avoid: Flat or wilted fresh pea pods (the peas inside are usually immature), fresh pea pods with grey flecks (the peas inside are usually overly mature and starchy), or yellowed fresh or mangetout pea pods.

Storing
Refrigerate fresh peas in the pod and use them quickly. As peas age their sugars turn to starch; the older the peas, the less sweet. Mangetout peas should also be stored in the refrigerator.

Do not wash pea pods before you store them. Damp pods are likely to mould.

Preparation
To prepare fresh peas, wash the pods, cut off the end, pull away the string running down the side, and shell the peas. To prepare mangetout peas, wash them under cold running water, pull away the string, snip off the ends, then stir-fry or boil quickly to keep them crisp.

Cooking reactions
When you heat green peas, the chlorophyll in the peas reacts chemically with the acids in the vegetable or in the cooking water and they lose their bright green colour.

To keep cooked peas green, steam the peas in very little water or stir-fry them so fast that they cook before the chlorophyll has time to react with the acids. No matter how you cook the peas, save the cooking liquid. It contains the peas' water-soluble B vitamins.

Effects of processing
Drying. Fresh green garden peas are immature seeds. The peas used to make dried split peas are mature seeds, may have twice as much STARCH as fresh peas, and are a good source of PROTEIN. Split peas don't have to be soaked before cooking; in fact, soaking drains the B vitamins.

Medical uses and/or benefits
✔ HEART DISEASE

✔ DIABETES THERAPY

Adverse effects

✘ GOUT

Food/drug interactions

—

• Peppers (Capsicum, chilli peppers, green peppers, red peppers)

Nutritional profile per 100 g food		
Energy value:	Low	15 Kcal
Protein:	Low	0.9 g
Fat:	Low	0.4 g
Cholesterol:	None	None
Carbohydrates:	Low	2.2 g
Fibre:	Low	0.9 g
Sodium:	Low	2 mg
Major vitamin contribution:	Vitamins A and C	Low, High
Major mineral contribution:	Iron, potassium	Low, Med

Peppers are green when immature and red, yellow, or purple when ripe. *Chillis* are distinguished from other peppers by their shape (they are longer and skinnier) and by their burning taste.

All peppers are rich in vitamin C. 100 g of fresh green pepper have 100 mg vitamin C, three times the RDA for a healthy adult. All peppers contain red or yellow carotenoid pigments your body can convert to vitamin A, but mature peppers have twice as much vitamin A as green peppers. Chilli powder, and paprika are very rich in vitamin A.

The most nutritious way to serve this food
Green and red peppers: Fresh sliced or chopped on a salad.
Chilli peppers: Sparingly in a soup or stew.

Diets that may restrict or exclude this food
Antiflatulence diet
Bland diet

Buying
Choose: Firm peppers that feel thick and fleshy. Their skin should be brightly coloured green, red, yellow, or purple.
Avoid: Dull-coloured peppers; they may be immature. If the skin is wrinkled, the peppers have lost moisture; soft spots suggest decay inside.

Storing
Refrigerate fresh peppers in the vegetable drawer to preserve their moisture and vitamin C.

Preparation
Green and red peppers. Wash the peppers under cold running water, slice, and remove the seeds.

Chillis. Never handle any variety of hot peppers without protective gloves. Hot peppers contain large amounts of the irritating chemical capsaicin which will burn unprotected skin, and does not dissolve in water; you cannot simply wash it off. Capsaicin and its chemical cousins do dissolve in milkfat or alcohol, which is why either milk or beer will soothe the burning taste of a dish spiced with curry or chilli.

Cooking reactions
To avoid green peppers losing all their bright colour in cooking, cook them as quickly as possible.

When long cooking is inevitable, as with stuffed green peppers, the only remedy is to smother the peppers in sauce so that it doesn't matter what colour the peppers are.

Because vitamin C is sensitive to heat, cooked peppers have less than fresh peppers. But peppers have so much vitamin C to begin with that even cooked peppers are a good source of this nutrient.

Effects of processing
—

Medical uses and/or benefits
Relieving the congestion of a cold. Hot spices, including hot pepper, irritate the mucous membranes lining your nose and throat and the bronchi in your lungs, making the tissues 'weep'. The watery secretions may make it easier for you to cough up mucus or blow your nose, thus helping to relieve your congestion for a while.

Adverse effects
Irritant dermatitis. See *Preparation* (Chillis), above.
Painful urination. The irritating oils in peppers are eliminated through urination. They may cause temporary irritation of the urinary tract.

Food/drug interactions
—

• Persimmons

Nutritional profile per 100 g food		
Energy value:	Low	127 Kcal
Protein:	Low	0.8 g
Fat:	Low	0.4 g
Cholesterol:	None	None
Carbohydrates:	High	33.5 g
Fibre:	Low	1.5 g
Sodium:	Low	1 mg
Major vitamin contribution:	Vitamins A and C	(not available)
Major mineral contribution:	Potassium	(not available)

There are two kinds of persimmon, the Japanese variety (sometimes called a 'kaki' or Sharon fruit) and the smaller, more seedy American persimmon. The American fruit is more valuable nutritionally, with twice the CARBOHYDRATES, sixteen times the iron, twice the potassium, and nine times as much vitamin C as the Sharon fruit. One 100 g persimmon has 66 mg vitamin C, about 100 percent the RDA for a healthy adult.

The most nutritious way to serve this food
Fresh and ripe.

Diets that may restrict or exclude this food
Sucrose-restricted diet

Buying
Choose: Firm, plump fruit with brightly coloured, smooth unbroken skin. The bright-green stem cap should be firmly anchored to the fruit.

Storing
American fruit cannot be eaten until it is so ripe it feels mushy. Eating it sooner will produce an unpleasant coating in the mouth. The Sharon or kaki types can be eaten when they are orange but still firm to touch.

Preparation
Wash the persimmon and pull off its stem cap. Then peel and slice the persimmon or put it through a food mill to mash the flesh and remove the seeds.

Cooking reactions
—

Effects of processing
—

Medical uses and/or benefits
✓ POTASSIUM REPLACEMENT

✓ PROTECTION AGAINST CANCER

Adverse effects
—

Food/drug interactions
—

• Pineapples

Nutritional profile per 100 g food (fresh)		
Energy value:	Low	46 Kcal
Protein:	Low	0.5 g
Fat:	Low	Trace
Cholesterol:	None	None
Carbohydrates:	Low	11.6 g
Fibre:	Low	1.2 g
Sodium:	Low	2 mg
Major vitamin contribution:	Thiamin, vitamin C	Low, High
Major mineral contribution:	Potassium	Med

Pineapples have little fibre (primarily pectins and gums). They are high in SUGAR but have no STARCH and only small amounts of PROTEIN and FAT. Their most important nutrient is vitamin C. A 100 g serving of fresh pineapple provides 25 mg vitamin C, 80 percent of the RDA for a healthy adult.

Diets that may restrict or exclude this food
Disaccharide-intolerance diet (for people deficient in the enzymes sucrase and invertase)
Sucrose-restricted diet

Buying
Choose: Large pineapples. The leaves in the crown on top should be fresh and green, the pineapple should feel heavy for its size (which means it's juicy), it should have a rich pineapple aroma, and you should hear a solid 'thunk' when you tap a finger against the side. While the pineapple's shell generally loses chlorophyll and turns more golden as the fruit ripens, some varieties of pineapple have more chlorophyll and stay green longer than others, so the colour of the shell is not a reliable guide to ripeness.

Storing
Store pineapples either at room temperature or in the refrigerator. Neither will have any effect on the sweetness of the fruit. Fruits and vegetables get sweeter after they are picked by converting stored STARCHES to SUGARS. Since the pineapple has no stored starch and gets its sugar from its leaves, it is as sweet as it ever will be on the day it is picked. It will get softer while stored, though, as its pectic enzymes break down pectins in its cell walls.

Preparation

The pineapple fruit and the stem of the pineapple plant contain bromelain, a proteolytic (protein-dissolving) enzyme similar to papain (in unripe papayas) and ficin (in fresh figs). Bromelain is a natural meat tenderizer that breaks down the protein molecules in meat when you add the fruit to a stew or baste a roast with the juice. Bromelain only works at a temperature between 140°F (60°C) and 170°F (77°C). It is destroyed by boiling the fruit. To get the maximum effect in stewing, keep the pot simmering, not boiling. If you add fresh pineapple to gelatin, the bromelain will break down the proteins in the gelatin and the dish will not set. To add fresh pineapple to a gelatin mould, boil the fruit first.

Cooking reaction

As you cook pineapple, the pectic substances in its cell walls dissolve and the pineapple softens. Boiling pineapple also inactivates its bromelain.

Effects of processing

Drying. Drying concentrates the calories and nutrients in pineapple. Fresh pineapple may be treated with a sulphur compound such as sulphur dioxide to protect its vitamin C and keep it from darkening as it dries. In people sensitive to sulphites, these compounds may provoke serious allergic reactions, including potentially fatal anaphylactic shock.

Medical uses and/or benefits
—

Adverse effects

✘ SULPHITE SENSITIVITY

Dermatitis. Bromelain, which breaks down proteins, may cause irritant dermatitis. Pineapples may also cause allergic dermatitis. (Irritant dermatitis may occur in anyone who touches a pineapple; allergic dermatitis occurs only in an individual who is sensitive to a particular substance.)

Food/drug interactions

✘ FALSE RESULT IN TESTS FOR CANCER

• Plums

See also PRUNES

Nutritional profile per 100 g food (fresh)		
Energy value:	Low	38 Kcal
Protein:	Low	0.6 g
Fat:	Low	Trace
Cholesterol:	None	None
Carbohydrates:	Med	9.6 g
Fibre:	Low	2.1 g
Sodium:	Low	2 mg
Major vitamin contribution:	Vitamins A, B and C	Low, Low, Low
Major mineral contribution:	Potassium	Med

Plums are high in SUGAR. They have no STARCH, and only moderate amounts of fibre, mostly soluble gums and pectins in the flesh, plus cellulose and the noncarbohydrate food fibre lignin in the peel. Plums have very little PROTEIN and only a trace of FAT. They have small amounts of vitamins A and C, the B vitamins, and potassium.

The most nutritious way to serve this food
Fresh and ripe, with the peel.

Diets that may restrict or exclude this food
Sucrose-restricted diet

Buying
Choose: Firm, brightly coloured fruit that are slightly soft to the touch, yielding a bit when you press them with your finger.

Comparing varieties of plums	
Damson	Dark skin and flesh (for preserves only)
Greengage	Green-yellow skin and yellow flesh
Mirabelles	Cherry-sized, golden colour
Pershore	Golden or purple varieties
Santa Rosa	Red-purple skin, yellow flesh (very tart)
Victoria	Golden fleshed
Zwetschen	Small purple fruit with bronze flesh

Storing

Store firm plums at room temperature. Plums have no stored STARCH to convert to SUGARS, so they won't get sweeter after they are picked, but they will soften as their pectic enzymes dissolve some of the pectin stiffening their cell walls. When the plums are soft enough, refrigerate them to stop the enzyme action.

Preparation

Wash and serve fresh plums or split them, remove the pit, and slice the plums for fruit salad. Plums can be stewed in the skin; if you prefer them skinless, put them in boiling water for a few seconds, then lift them out with a slotted spoon and plunge them into cold water. The hot water will damage a layer of cells under the skin, the plum will swell, and its skin will split and peel off easily.

Cooking reactions

When you cook a plum, its water-soluble pectins and hemicellulose will dissolve and the flesh will soften.

Cooking may also change the colour of plums with red, purple, or blue-red skin coloured with anthocyanin pigments that are sensitive to acids or bases (alkalis). The colours get more intensely red or purple in acids (lemon juice) and less so in bases (baking soda). And, cooking plums (which are acid) in an aluminium pot can create acid/metal compounds that discolour either the pot or the plum.

Effects of processing
Drying. See PRUNES

Medical uses and/or benefits
—

Adverse effects

Poisoning. Like apple seeds and peach and apricot pits, the seed inside a plum pit contains amygdalin, a natural cyanide/sugar compound that breaks down into hydrogen cyanide in your stomach (see APPLES).

Food/drug interactions

✖ FALSE RESULT IN TESTS FOR CANCER

• Pomegranates

Nutritional profile per 100 g food (raw)		
Energy value:	Low	72 Kcal
Protein:	Low	1 g
Fat:	Low	0.6 g
Cholesterol:	None	None
Carbohydrates:	Med	16.6 g
Fibre:	Low	(not available)
Sodium:	Low	1 mg
Major vitamin contribution:	Vitamin C	Low
Major mineral contribution:	Potassium	High

Pomegranates are rich in SUGAR. The juice — which we get by crushing or crunching the jellylike substance that clings to the pomegranate's seeds — contains no STARCH, no fibre, a little PROTEIN, a trace of FAT, and moderate amounts of vitamin C and the B vitamins. Pomegranate juice is also a good source of potassium.

The most nutritious way to serve this food
Fresh cut or juiced.

Diets that may restrict or exclude this food
Sucrose-restricted diet

Buying
Choose: A pomegranate that feels heavy for its size (which means it's juicy). The rind should be bright red.
Avoid: Pale pomegranates or pomegranates that look dry or wrinkled.

Storing
Store pomegranates in the refrigerator and use within a week.

Preparation
Slice through the stem end of the pomegranate and pull off the top — carefully, to avoid splashing red pomegranate juice all over yourself. Then slice the pomegranate into wedges and pull the wedges apart. Once you cut the pomegranate apart you can handle it in one of two ways, the messy way and the neat way. The messy way is to pull the seeds out of the pomegranate, crush them in your teeth to get the juice, and then spit out the crushed seeds.

The neat way is to put the seeds through a strainer, collect the juice, and discard the seeds.

Cooking reactions
—

Effects of processing
—

Medical uses and/or benefits
—

Adverse effects
—

Food/drug interactions
—

• Pork (Bacon, ham)

See also SAUSAGES

Nutritional profile per 100 g food (raw)		
	Pork leg	
Energy value:	High	269 Kcal
Protein:	High	16.6 g
Fat:	High	22.5 g
Cholesterol:	Med	72 mg
Carbohydrates:	None	None
Fibre:	None	None
Sodium:	Med	59 mg
Major vitamin contribution:	Thiamin (vitamin B_1), niacin, vitamin B_6	High, High, High
Major mineral contribution:	Iron, potassium	Low, High

Pork, like other foods of animal origin, is rich in complete PROTEINS that provide sufficient amounts of all the essential amino acids. Its FAT is higher in UNSATURATED FATTY ACIDS than the fat in beef, veal, or lamb. Pork fat is 64 percent unsaturated fatty acids, while beef and veal fat are 52 percent unsaturated fatty acids and lamb fat is 44 percent unsaturated fatty acids. Pork's CHOLESTEROL content is similar to that of beef.

Pork is a good source of B vitamins but provides less iron than beef. The iron in pork, like the iron in beef, is heme iron, the organic form of iron found in foods of animal origin. Heme iron is five times more available to the body than non-heme iron, the inorganic iron in plant foods.

The most nutritious way to serve this food
Lean pork, thoroughly cooked.

Diets that may restrict or exclude this food
Controlled-fat, low-cholesterol diet
Low-protein diet

Buying
Choose: Firm, fresh pork that is light pink or reddish and has very little visible fat. If there are any bone ends showing, they should be red, not white; the whiter the bone ends, the older the animal from which the meat was taken.

Avoid: Packets with a lot of liquid leakage. Meat that has lost moisture is likely to be dry and tough.

Storing

Refrigerate fresh pork immediately. Refrigeration prolongs the freshness of pork by slowing the natural multiplication of bacteria on the surface of meat.

Fresh roasts and chops usually stay fresh for three to five days. For longer storage, store the pork in the freezer where the very low temperatures will slow the bacteria even more.

Store unopened smoked or cured pork products like bacon in the refrigerator in the original wrapper and use according to the date and directions on the packet.

Preparation

Trim the pork carefully. You can significantly reduce the amount of fat and cholesterol in each serving by judiciously cutting away all visible fat.

Do not add salt to the pork before you cook it; the salt will draw moisture out of the meat, making it stringy and tough. Add salt near the end of the cooking process.

After handling raw meat, wash your knives, cutting board, work surface — and your hands — with hot soapy water to reduce the chance of transferring microorganisms from the pork to other foods.

Cooking reactions

Cooking changes the way pork looks and tastes, alters its nutritional value, makes it safer, and extends its shelf life.

Browning meat before you cook it does not seal in the juices, but it does change the flavour by caramelizing proteins and sugars on the surface (see BROWNING REACTIONS). Because the only sugars that occur naturally in pork are the small amounts of glycogen in its muscles, we add sugars in the form of marinades or basting liquids that may also contain acids (vinegar, lemon juice, wine) to break down muscle fibres and tenderize the meat. Browning has one minor nutritional drawback. It breaks amino acids on the surface of the meat into smaller compounds that are no longer useful proteins.

When pork is heated, it loses water and shrinks. Its pigments, which combine with oxygen, are denatured (broken into smaller fragments) by the heat and turn brown, the natural colour of cooked meat. This colour change is more dramatic in beef (which starts out red) than in pork (which starts out grey-pink). In fact, you can pretty much judge how well beef is cooked from its colour, but you must use a meat thermometer to measure the internal temperature of the meat before you can say it is thoroughly cooked.

Pork is considered done (and safe to eat) when it reaches an average uniform internal temperature of 170°F (77°C), hot enough to kill *Trichinella spiralis*, the organism that causes trichinosis.

Effects of processing

Freezing. Freezing changes the flavour and texture of fresh pork. When fresh pork is frozen, the water in its cells turn into ice crystals that can tear the cell walls so that liquids leak out when the pork is thawed. That's why defrosted pork, like defrosted beef, veal, or lamb, may be drier and less tender than fresh meat.

Curing, smoking, and aging. *Curing* preserves meat by osmotic action. The dry salt or a salt solution draws liquid out of the cells of the meat and the cells of any microorganisms living on the meat. *Smoking* — hanging meat over an open fire — gives meat a rich, 'smoky' flavour that varies with the wood used in the fire. Meats smoked over an open fire are exposed to carcinogenic chemicals in the smoke, including a-benzopyrene. Meats treated with artificial smoke flavouring are not, since the flavouring is commercially treated to remove tar and a-benzopyrene. Cured and smoked meats sometimes have less moisture and proportionally more fat than fresh meat. They are also saltier. *Aging* — letting the meat hang exposed to air — further reduces the moisture content and shrinks the meat.

Medical uses and/or benefits
—

Adverse effects
✖ HEART DISEASE

Trichinosis. You get trichinosis by eating meat that contains cysts of *Trichinella spiralis*, a parasitic roundworm that lives in animals that eat meat. Pigs are not the only animals that carry trichinosis. It can show up in any animal that eats uncooked flesh infested with the worms. In the arctic, for example, explorers got trichinosis from polar bear meat.

When we swallow encysted *Trichinella* larvae, the wall of the cyst breaks down in our stomach, freeing the larvae, which burrow into the membranes of the stomach and gut, where they mature within two days The mature *Trichinellae* burrow into the intestinal wall, where the females begin to discharge larvae that are carried into the bloodstream and throughout the body, infesting and eventually destroying muscle fibres. The worms can damage the retina and other tissues in the eye. Untreated, trichinosis can cause death from paralysis of the respiratory muscles.

Food/drug interactions
—

• Potatoes

See also FLOUR, SWEET POTATOES

Nutritional Profile per 100 g food (raw)		
	Old Potatoes	
Energy value:	Med	87 Kcal
Protein:	Low	21.0 g
Fat:	Low	0.1 g
Cholesterol:	None	None
Carbohydrates:	High	20.8 g
Fibre:	Low	2.1 g
Sodium:	Low	7 mg
Major vitamin contribution:	Vitamins C and B vitamins	Med, Low
Major mineral contribution:	Potassium, iron	High, Low

Potatoes are high-carbohydrate food with much STARCH and a little SUGAR. In storage, the potato's starch turns to sugar, so the longer a potato is stored, the sweeter it will taste. Potatoes have cellulose, hemicellulose, pectins, and gums plus lignin, the noncarbohydrate food fibre found in plant stems, leaves, and peel.

The proteins in potatoes are considered incomplete because they are deficient in the essential amino acids (see PROTEIN) methionine and cystine. Potatoes have very little FAT and no CHOLESTEROL at all.

Potatoes are a good source of vitamin C. A 100 g baked potato provides 10 mg vitamin C, 30 percent of the RDA for a healthy adult. Potatoes are a source of B vitamins, particularly thiamin (vitamin B_1) and nicotinic acid, and they are a good source of potassium.

Diets that may exclude or restrict this food
Low-carbohydrate diet
Low-salt diet (canned potatoes, potato crisps, potato sticks, and the like)
Sucrose-restricted diet

The most nutritious way to serve this food
Boiled or baked in their jackets.

Buying
Choose: Firm potatoes with unscarred, unblemished skin. Different varieties

of potatoes have skins of different thickness. This has no effect at all on the nutritional value of the potato.

Avoid: Potatoes with peeling skin (an immature vegetable that won't store well) except for new potatoes; potatoes with wrinkled or blemished skin (there may be decay inside); potatoes with green spots or sprouts growing out of the eyes (higher than normal levels of solanine); or mouldy potatoes (potentially hazardous toxins).

Storing

Store potatoes in a dark, dry cupboard to prevent sprouting and protect them from mould. The temperature should be cool, but not cold, since temperatures below 50°F (10°C) encourage the conversion of the potato's starches to sugar. If the potatoes are accidentally frozen, they will develop black rings inside.

Vitamin C is sensitive to oxygen, so the longer potatoes are stored, the less vitamin C they will have.

Do not wash potatoes before you store them or store them in the refrigerator; dampness encourages the growth of moulds.

Preparation

Discard potatoes with green spots, sprouting eyes, or patches of mould on the skin, and scrub the rest with a stiff vegetable brush under cool running water. When you peel and slice potatoes, throw out any that have rot or mould inside.

Don't peel or slice potatoes until you are ready to use them as they brown on cut surfaces (see BROWNING REACTIONS). You can slow this reaction (but not stop it completely) by soaking the peeled sliced fresh potatoes in iced water, but many of the vitamins in the potatoes will leach out into the soaking water.

Cooking reactions

Starch consists of granules packed with the molecules of amylose and amylopectin. When you cook a potato, its starch granules absorb water molecules that cling to the amylose and amylopectin molecules, making the granules swell. If the granules absorb enough water, they will rupture, releasing the nutrients inside. If you are cooking potatoes in a stew or soup, the amylose and amylopectin molecules that escape from the ruptured starch granule will attract and hold water molecules in the liquid, thickening the dish. Cooked potatoes have more nutrients available than raw potatoes.

Effects of processing

Freezing. A potato's cells are like a balloon whose stiff wall is held rigidly in place by the air inside. When you freeze a cooked potato, the water in its cells forms ice crystals that can tear the cell walls, allowing liquid to leak out when the potatoes are defrosted, which is why defrosted potatoes taste mushy. Commercial processors get around this by partially dehydrating potatoes before they are frozen or by freezing potatoes in a sauce that gives an interesting flavour to take your mind off the texture.

Dehydrating. Potato 'flakes' and 'granules' have fewer vitamins and minerals than fresh potatoes; potato crisps are usually much higher in salt.

Medical uses and/or benefits
—

Adverse effects
✖ SULPHITE SENSITIVITY

Solanine poisoning. Potatoes contain solanine, a natural toxin. Solanine, which is produced in the green parts of the potato (the leaves, the stem, and any green spots on the skin), is a nerve poison. It interferes with your body's ability to use acetylcholinesterase, a chemical that facilitates the transmission of impulses between body cells.

Potatoes that are exposed to light will produce solanine more quickly than potatoes stored in the dark, but all potatoes produce some solanine all the time. Solanine does not dissolve in water, nor is it destroyed by heat; any solanine present in a raw potato will still be there after you cook it.

Food/drug interactions
—

• Poultry (Chicken, duck, goose, turkey)

Nutritional profile per 100 g of food (raw)		
	Meat only	
Energy value:	Med	121 Kcal
Protein:	High	20.5 g
Fat:	Low	4.3 g
Cholesterol:	Med	90 mg
Carbohydrates:	None	None
Fibre:	None	None
Sodium:	Med	81 mg
Major vitamin contribution:	B vitamins	High
Major mineral contribution:	Zinc, potassium, iron	Med, High, Low

All poultry provides high-quality, 'complete' PROTEINS (proteins with adequate amounts of all the essential amino acids). Most poultry has less FAT than beef, veal, pork, or lamb. Its fat is proportionally higher in UNSATURATED FATTY ACIDS, but cooked chicken and turkey have about the same amount of CHOLESTEROL as cooked lean beef (74-79 mg/100 g).

Poultry is a good source of the B vitamins and heme iron, the organic form of iron found in foods of animal origin that is five times more available to the body than non-heme iron, the inorganic form of iron in plant foods.

The most nutritious way to serve this food
Grilled or roasted, with the skin removed to reduce the fat. Soups and stews should be skimmed.

Diets that may restrict or exclude this food
Controlled-fat, low-cholesterol diet (duck, goose)
Low-protein diet

Buying
Choose: Poultry with fresh, unblemished skin and clear unblemished meat. If you buy whole fresh chickens that have not been prepacked, try to bend the breastbone — the more flexible it is, the younger the bird and the more lean and tender the flesh.

Choose the bird that fits your needs. Young birds are good for grilling, frying, and roasting. Older birds have tougher muscle fibre, which requires long stewing or steaming to tenderize the meat.

Avoid: Poultry whose skin is dry or discoloured.

Storing

Refrigerate fresh poultry immediately. Refrigeration prolongs freshness by slowing the natural multiplication of bacteria on the surface of the chicken, turkey, duck, or goose. The bacteria multiply most on poultry wrapped in plastic, which is why it often smells bad when you unwrap it at home. Never use, store or freeze any poultry that does not smell absolutely fresh. Throw it out or return it to the shop.

Cover fresh poultry and refrigerate it in a dish that keeps it from dripping and contaminating other foods or the refrigerator. Properly wrapped fresh poultry will keep for one or two days at 40°F (5°C). For longer storage, freeze the poultry.

Preparation

Wash the poultry under cool running water.

Discard any poultry that feels slimy to the touch. If you are preparing duck or goose, pull as much fat out of the abdominal cavity as possible. To cut down on the fat in chicken, remove the skin before cooking.

After preparing fresh poultry, always wash your implements, the work surface, and your hands with hot soapy water to avoid contaminating other foods with bacteria from the poultry.

Cooking reactions

Cooking changes the way poultry looks and tastes, alters its nutritional content, and makes it safer to eat.

Heat changes the structure of the poultry's proteins. It denatures the protein molecules so that they break apart into smaller fragments or change shape or clump together. These changes force moisture out of the tissues so that the poultry turns opaque as it cooks. As it loses water, the poultry also loses water-soluble B vitamins, which drip out into the pan. Since they are not destroyed by heat, they can be saved by using the skimmed pan drippings for gravy. Cooking also caramelizes proteins and the small amounts of sugar on the bird's surface, a BROWNING REACTION that gives the skin of the bird its characteristic sweet taste. As moisture escapes from the skin; it turns crisp. At the same time, the heat liquifies the fat in the bird, which runs off into the pan, lowering the FAT and CHOLESTEROL content.

Finally, cooking kills the *Salmonella* and other microorganisms on the skin and flesh of poultry. For maximum safety, poultry should be cooked to a uniform internal temperature of 180°F (82°C). If you are cooking your poultry in a microwave oven, check to be sure that the surface of the bird — which is cooled by evaporating moisture — is as hot as the inside, otherwise bacteria on the skin may remain alive.

Effects of processing

Freezing. When poultry is frozen, the water in its cells turns into ice crystals which rupture the cell walls. When you thaw the poultry, liquid escapes from the cells and the chicken, turkey, duck, or goose may taste dry and stringy.

The UNSATURATED FATTY ACIDS in poultry will continue to oxidize (and eventually turn rancid) while the bird is frozen. Poultry cut into pieces will spoil more quickly than a whole bird because it has more surfaces exposed to the air. Fresh whole chicken and turkey will keep for up to twelve months at 0°F; chicken pieces will keep for nine months; turkey pieces and whole duck and goose for six months.

'Self-basting' poultry. To make these birds 'self-basting,' fat or oil is inserted under the skin of the breast before the bird is packed or frozen. As the bird cooks, the fat warms, melts, and oozes out, basting the bird. 'Self-basting' poultry are higher in fat; depending on what kind of fat is inserted into the breast, they may also be higher in cholesterol.

Medical uses and/or benefits

To relieve the congestion of a cold. Hot chicken soup, the quintessential folk remedy, does appear to relieve the congestion that comes with a head cold. Exactly why remains a mystery but some researchers have suggested that the hot steam from the soup helps liquify mucus and clear the nasal passages.

Adverse effects

✘ HEART DISEASE

Food/drug interactions

—

• Prunes

See also PLUMS

Nutritional profile per 100 g food (raw)		
Energy value:	Med	161 Kcal
Protein:	Low	2.4 g
Fat:	Low	Trace
Cholesterol:	None	None
Carbohydrates:	High	40.3 g
Fibre:	High	16.1 g
Sodium:	Low	12 mg
Major vitamin contribution:	Vitamin A	Med
Major mineral contribution:	Potassium, iron	High, High

Prunes are high-fibre food. Ounce for ounce, they have more food fibre than dry beans. Prunes are also high-sugar fruit. Thirty percent of the weight of a prune is glucose, 15 percent is fructose, and 2 percent is sucrose (see SUGARS). Prunes have very little FAT and no CHOLESTEROL.

Prunes are a source of vitamin A. A 100 g serving of uncooked dried prunes has nearly 22 percent of the RDA for a healthy adult. They are also a good source of B vitamins and an excellent source of iron, the form of iron found in plants. Ounce for ounce, they provide one third as much iron as liver. Prunes are also a rich source of potassium.

The most nutritious way to serve this food
With meat or a food rich in vitamin C to increase the absorption of iron from the prunes. Meat makes the stomach more acid (iron is absorbed better in an acid medium), while vitamin C changes the iron from ferric iron to ferrous iron, a more easily absorbed form.

Diets that may restrict or exclude this food
Antiflatulence diet
Low-fibre diet
Low-residue diet
Low-potassium diet
Low-sodium diet (prunes treated with sodium bisulphite, sodium metabisulphite, sodium sulphite)
Sucrose-restricted diet

Buying
Choose: Tightly sealed boxes or bags of fruit that are protected from air, moisture, and insects. Prunes come in different sizes, but size has no bearing on taste or quality. Seeded prunes are more convenient but also more expensive than prunes with their seeds still in place.

Storing
Store prunes in a tightly closed container at room temperature, where they may stay fresh for up to six months. Check periodically to be sure that there is no insect infestation and no mould.

Preparation
Do not soak prunes before you cook them. The sugars that make prunes so distinctively sweet are soluble and will leach out into the soaking water.

Cooking reactions
When you stew dried prunes, their water-soluble pectins and hemicellulose dissolve, and their cells absorb water. Since the water displaces nutrients, ounce for ounce stewed prunes may have only one-third as much vitamin C and B vitamins, vitamin A, iron and fibre as uncooked prunes.

Effects of processing
—

Medical uses and/or benefits
✓ PROTECTION AGAINST CANCER

✓ POTASSIUM REPLACEMENT

To relieve or prevent constipation. Prunes are a high-fibre food that helps relieve constipation. However, since prune juice, which has only a trace of fibre, is also a laxative, some food chemists suggest that what makes the prune such an effective laxative is not its fibre but another constitutent, an unidentified derivative of the organic chemical isatin, which is related to another natural substance, biscodyl. Biscodyl, which is the active ingredient in some over-the-counter laxative tablets and suppositories, is a contact laxative that induces the secretion of fluid in the bowel and stimulates contractions of the intestines that push waste through the colon more quickly and efficiently.

Adverse effects
✗ SULPHITE SENSITIVITY

Food/drug interactions
—

• Pumpkin

Nutritional profile per 100 g food (raw)		
Energy value:	Low	15 Kcal
Protein:	Low	0.6 g
Fat:	Low	Trace
Cholesterol:	None	None
Carbohydrates:	Low	3.4 g
Fibre:	Low	0.5 g
Sodium:	Low	1 mg
Major vitamin contribution:	Vitamin A, B vitamins	Med, Med
Major mineral contribution:	Potassium	Med

Pumpkins are really two foods: the orange-yellow flesh (whose nutritional profile appears above) and the brown edible seeds.

Like the flesh of other winter squashes, the pumpkin's has moderate amounts of SUGAR, some STARCH, some fibre but little PROTEIN and FAT. Pumpkins are packed with yellow-orange carotenoids tht your body can convert to vitamin A. One 100 g serving of canned pumpkin may provide as much as 30 percent of the RDA for a healthy adult.

The pumpkin's seeds are edible and highly nutritious, rich in protein, high in unsaturated vegetable oil (the source of vitamin E), and an excellent source of B vitamins and iron.

The most nutritious way to serve this food.
Pumpkin. Baked. Boiled pumpkin absorbs water, which displaces nutrients; ounce for ounce, baked pumpkin has more nutrients than boiled pumpkin.
Pumpkin seeds. Oven-toasted without salt.

Diets that may restrict or exclude this food
Low-fat (the seeds)
Low-fibre (particularly the seeds)

Buying
Choose: A pumpkin with a bright-orange, blemish-free rind. The pumpkin should feel heavy for its size.

Storing
Store pumpkins in a cool, dry place and use within a month. Vitamin A is

vulnerable to oxygen; the longer the pumpkin is stored, the less vitamin A it will have especially if not kept cool.

Preparation

Wash the pumpkin under cold running water, then cut it in half or in quarters or in smaller portions, as you wish. Pull off the stringy parts and collect and set aside the seeds. Leave the rind on if you plan to bake large pieces of the pumpkin; peel it off for boiling. If the pumpkin is small enough and/or your oven is large enough, you can simply scoop out the strings and seeds and bake the pumpkin whole.

Cooking reactions

Pumpkin. When you bake a pumpkin, the soluble food fibres in its cell walls dissolve and the pumpkin gets softer. If you bake it too long, the moisture inside the cells will begin to evaporate and the pumpkin will shrink. When you boil pumpkin, it's just the opposite. The cell walls still soften, but its cells absorb water and the vegetable swells. Boil it too long, though, and the cells will rupture, moisture will escape, and the pumpkin will collapse.

Pumpkin seeds. When you toast pumpkin seeds, their moisture evaporates and they turn crisp and brown. (Commercially toasted pumpkin seeds are usually salted and must be considered high-sodium food.)

Effects of processing

Canned. According to the United States Department of Agriculture, canned 'pumpkin' may be a mixture of pumpkin and other yellow-orange winter squash, all of which are similar in nutritional value.

Medical uses and/or benefits

PROTECTION AGAINST CANCER

Adverse effects

—

Food/drug interactions

—

• Quinces

Nutritional profile per 100g food (raw)		
Energy value:	Low	25 Kcal
Protein:	Low	0.3 g
Fat:	Low	Trace
Cholesterol:	None	None
Carbohydrates:	Low	6.3 g
Fibre:	Low	6.4 g
Sodium:	Low	3 mg
Major vitamin contribution:	Vitamin C	Med
Major mineral contribution:	Potassium	Med

Quinces, which look like pears and are (like pears) members of the same family as apples, are high in SUGAR, with moderate amounts of food fibre. Like apples, they are a good source of pectins. Fresh quinces are rich in vitamin C, but, since quince is always cooked before it is served and vitamin C is heat-sensitive, it has only moderate amounts of vitamin C when it reaches your plate. Quinces are a moderately good source of potassium.

The most nutritious way to serve this food
Baked or stewed without sugar to save calories

Diets that may restrict or exclude this food
Sucrose-restricted diet

Buying
Choose: Firm, round, or pear-shape fruit with a pale-yellow, furry skin.
Avoid. Small, knobby fruit or fruit with bruised skin.

Storing
Store quinces in the refrigerator and use them within two weeks.

Preparation
Wash the quince under cold running water, wipe off the fur, cut off the stem and the blossom ends, core the fruit, and bake or stew it.

Cooking reactions
When you cook a quince, heat and the acids in the fruit convert the quince's colourless leucoanthocyanin pigments to red anthocyanins, turning the flesh

from pale yellow to pink or red. Cooking also transforms the raw quince's strong, unpleasant, astringent taste to a more mellow flavour, halfway between that of an apple and a pear.

Effects of processing
—

Medical use and/or benefits
✓ HEART DISEASE

Adverse effects
Poisoning. The seed of the quince, like apple seeds, pear seeds, and apricot, cherry, peach, and plum pits, contain amygdalin, a natural cyanide/sugar compound that breaks down into hydrogen cyanide in your stomach (see APPLES).

Food/drug interactions
—

• Radishes (Horseradish)

See also CABBAGE

Nutritional profile per 100g food (raw)		
Energy value:	Low	15 Kcal
Protein:	Low	1.0 g
Fat:	Low	Trace
Cholesterol:	None	None
Carbohydrates:	Low	2.8 g
Fibre:	Low	0.5 g
Sodium:	Med	59 mg
Major vitamin contribution:	Vitamin C, B vitamins	High, Med
Major mineral contribution:	Iron, potassium	High, Med

Radishes are roots, members of the cabbage family. They have moderate amounts of food fibre, plus some STARCH and SUGAR. All varieties of radish — the common red 'eating' radish, and the horseradish — are excellent sources of vitamin C. Ounce for ounce, they have half as much vitamin C as fresh oranges.

The most nutritious way to serve this food
Fresh, crisp red radishes; freshly grated fresh horseradish or recently opened prepared horseradish.

Diets that may restrict or exclude this food
Antiflatulence diet

Buying
Choose: Firm, well-shaped radishes. The skin should be clear, clean, and free of blemishes. If there are green tops on the radish, they should be crisp and fresh. If you are buying radishes in plastic bags, check them carefully through the plastic to see that they are free of mould.
Avoid. Misshapen radishes, spongy radishes, or radishes with soft spots (which suggest decay or discolouration underneath), and withered or dry radishes (they have lost vitamin C, which is sensitive to oxygen).

Storing
Cut off any green tops and refrigerate fresh radishes in plastic bags to keep them from drying out.

Preparation

Scrub the radishes under cold running water. Cut off the tops and the roots. Don't slice or grate radishes until you are ready to use them. When you cut into a radish, you tear its cells, releasing moisture — which converts an otherwise mild chemical called sinigrin into an irritant mustard oil that gives radishes their hot taste.

Cooking reactions
—

Effects of processing

Prepared horseradish. Prepared horseradish should be used within a few weeks after you open the bottle. The longer it is exposed to air, the more bitter (rather than spicy) its mustard oils will be.

Medical uses and/or benefits
✔ PROTECTION AGAINST CANCER

Adverse effects
✘ ENLARGED THYROID GLAND

Food/drug interactions
✘ FALSE RESULT IN TESTS FOR CANCER

• Raisins (Currants, muscatels, sultanas)

See also GRAPES

Nutritional profile per 100g food		
Energy value:	High	246 Kcal
Protein:	Low	1.1 g
Fat:	Low	Trace
Cholesterol:	None	None
Carbohydrates:	High	64.4 g
Fibre:	Med	6.8 g
Sodium:	Med	64.4 mg
Major vitamin contribution:	B vitamins	High
Major mineral contribution;	Iron, potassium	High, High

All raisins are high-carbohydrate food, rich in SUGARS with no STARCH at all. They are also rich in food fibre, primarily gums, pectins, and hemicellulose. Raisins have little PROTEIN and FAT.

Raisins are a good source of B vitamins and potassium, but they have no vitamin C, which disappears when the raisins are dried. Raisins are also rich in non-heme iron, the inorganic form of iron found in plant foods. Ounce for ounce, seedless raisins have as much iron as cooked mince and nearly one-third the iron in cooked liver.

The most nutritious way to serve this food
Straight from the packet.

Diets that may restrict or exclude this food
Low-fibre diet
Sucrose-restricted diet

Buying
Choose: Tightly sealed packets that protect the raisins from air (which will make them dry and hard) and insects.

Storing
Store sealed packages of raisins in a cool, dark cupboard, where they may stay fresh for as long as a year. Once the package is opened, the raisins should be stored in an air- and moistureproof container at room temperature and used within a few months. Check periodically for mould or insect infestation.

Preparation
To use raisins in a bread or cake, 'plump' them first by soaking them in water (or wine, rum or brandy for a fruit cake) for about fifteen minutes. Otherwise the raisins will be hard and dry when the cake or bread is baked.

Cooking reactions
If you cook raisins in water, their pectins and gum will dissolve and the raisins will soften. They will also absorb liquids and swell up. Cook them long enough and the water will leak out again, allow the raisins to collapse.

Effects of processing
—

Medical uses and/or benefits
—

Adverse reactions
✘ SULPHITE SENSITIVITY

Food/drug interactions
✘ MAO INHIBITORS

• Rhubarb

Nutritional profile per 100g food (raw)		
Energy value:	Low	6 Kcal
Protein:	Low	0.6 g
Fat:	Low	Trace
Cholesterol:	None	None
Carbohydrates:	Low	1 g
Fibre:	Low	2.6 g
Sodium:	Low	2 mg
Major vitamin contribution:	Vitamins C and A	Med, Low
Major mineral contribution:	Potassium, calcium	High, Med

Despite its crunchy stringiness, rhubarb provides only small amounts of fibre, including the insoluble cellulose and lignin in the stiff cells of its stalk and 'strings' and the soluble pectins in the flesh. Rhubarb has some SUGAR, no STARCH, and only a trace of PROTEIN and FAT.

Rhubarb is a moderately good source of vitamin C; a 100g serving of cooked rhubarb with sugar added has 7mg vitamin C, 25 percent of the RDA for a healthy adult. It has calcium, but oxalic acid (one of the natural chemicals that gives rhubarb its astringent flavour) binds the calcium into calcium oxalate, an insoluble compound your body cannot absorb.

The most nutritious way to serve this food
Cooked. Only the stalks of the rhubarb are used as food; *the leaves are poisonous, whether raw or cooked.*

Diets that may restrict or exclude this food
Low-oxalate diet (for people who form calcium oxalate kidney stones)

Buying
Choose: Crisp, bright, fresh stalks of rhubarb. Although colour is not necessarily a guide to quality, the deeper the red, the more flavourful the stalks are likely to be. The medium-size stalks are generally more tender than large ones, which, like large stalks of celery, may be stringy.

Storing
Wrap rhubarb in plastic and store it in the refrigerator to keep cool and humid. Rhubarb is fairly perishable; use it within a few days after you buy it.

Preparation

Remove and discard all leaves on the rhubarb stalk. *Rhubarb leaves are not edible, they are poisonous, raw or cooked.*

Wash the rhubarb under cool running water. Trim the end and cut off any discoloured parts. If the stalks are tough, peel them to get rid of hard 'strings.' (Most of the rhubarb we buy is grown in hothouses and bred to have a thin skin that doesn't have to be peeled.)

Cooking reactions

Rhubarb is coloured with red anthocyanin pigments that turn redder in acid and turn bluish in bases (alkalis) and brownish if you cook them with sugar at very high heat. If you cook rhubarb in an aluminium or iron pot, metal ions flaking off the pot will interact with acids in the fruit to form brown compounds that darken both the pot and the rhubarb.

Effects of processing

—

Medical uses and/or benefits

—

Adverse effects

Kidney stones. More than 50 per cent of all kidney stones are composed of calcium oxalate, or calcium oxalate plus phosphate. People with a metabolic disorder that leads them to excrete large amounts of oxalates in their urine or who have had ileal disease or who eat large amounts of foods high in oxalic acids are the ones most likely to form these stones. Rhubarb, like beets, cocoa, nuts, parsley, spinach, and tea, is high in oxalic acid.

Tannins. Rhubarb also contains astringent tannins and phenols that coagulate proteins on the surface of the mucous membrane lining of your mouth, which is why your mouth puckers when you eat rhubarb. Tannins, which are also found in tea, red wines, and many unripe fruits, may be constipating.

Food/drug interactions

—

• Rice

See also FLOUR

Nutritional profile per 100g food (raw)		
	White Rice	
Energy value:	High	361 Kcal
Protein:	Med	6.5 g
Fat:	Low	1.0 g
Cholesterol:	None	None
Carbohydrates:	High	86.8 g
Fibre:	Med	2.4 g
Sodium:	Low	6 mg
Major vitamin contribution:	B vitamins	Med
Major mineral contribution:	Iron, potassium	Low, Med

Brown rice is rice that retains its outer bran and its germ. *White rice* has been milled to remove the bran and germ.

All rice is high-carbohydrate food, rich in STARCH, with moderate amounts of all the CARBOHYDRATE food fibres (cellulose, hemicellulose, pectins, and gums). Brown rice, which still has its bran, also has the noncarbohydrate food fibre lignin, found in stems, leaves, and seed coverings.

Rice is high in PROTEIN, but its proteins are considered 'incomplete' because they are limited in the essential amino acids lysine and isoleucine. White rice has only a trace of fat. Brown rice, with its fatty germ, has more fat. There is no CHOLESTEROL in rice.

Brown rice has more vitamins and minerals than plain milled white rice, but enriched white rice may have even more nutrients than the natural brown product. All rice is a good source of B vitamins, has non-heme iron, the inorganic form of iron found in plant foods. However, since rice (like other grains) contains phytic acids that bind its iron and calcium into insoluble compounds, it is not necessarily a good source of these minerals.

The most nutritious way to serve this food

With legumes (beans, peas). The PROTEINS in rice are deficient in the essential amino acids lysine and isoleucine and rich in the essential amino acids tryptophan, methionine, and cystine. The proteins in legumes are exactly the opposite. Combining the two foods in one dish 'complements' or 'completes' their proteins.

With meat or a food rich in vitamin C (tomatoes, peppers). Both will increase the availability of the iron in the rice. Meat increases the secretion of stomach acids (iron is absorbed better in an acid environment); vitamin C changes the iron in the rice from ferric iron (which is hard to absorb) to ferrous iron (which is easier to absorb).

Diets that may restrict or exclude this food
Low-calcium diet (brown rice)
Low-fibre diet

Buying
Choose. Tightly sealed packages that protect the rice from air and moisture, which can oxidize the fats in the rice and turn them rancid.

Choose the rice that meets your needs. *Long-grain rice*, which has less starch than *short-grain* ('Oriental') rice, will be fluffier and less sticky when cooked. *Brown rice* has a distinctive nutty taste.

Avoid. Stained boxes of rice, even if they are still sealed. Whatever spilled on the box may have seeped through the cardboard onto the rice inside.

Storing
Store rice in air- and moistureproof containers in a cool, dark cupboard to keep it dry and protect its fats from oxygen. White rice may stay fresh for as long as a year. Brown rice, which retains its bran and germ and thus has more fats than white rice, may stay fresh for only a few months before its fats (inevitably) oxidize. All rice spoils more quickly in hot, humid weather. Aging or rancid rice usually has a distinctive stale and musty odour.

Preparation
Check for stones or other debris.

Cooking reactions
STARCH consists of molecules of complex CARBOHYDRATES amylose and amylopectin packed into a starch granule. When you cook rice, the starch granules absorb water molecules. When the temperature of the water reaches approximately 140°F (60°C), the amylose and amylopectin molecules inside the starch granules relax and unfold, breaking some of their internal bonds (bonds between atoms on the same molecule) and forming new bonds between atoms on different molecules. The result is a starch network of starch molecules that traps and holds water molecules, making the starch granules even more bulky. In fact, rice holds so much water that it will double or even triple in bulk when cooked.

If you continue to cook the rice, the starch granules will eventually break open, the liquid inside will leak out, the walls of the granules will collapse, and the rice will turn sticky — the reason why overcooked rice clumps together.

To keep rice from clumping when you cook it, cook the rice in just as much water as it can absorb without rupturing its starch granules and remove the rice from the heat as soon as the water is almost absorbed. Fluff the cooked rice with a fork as it is cooling, to separate the grains.

Effects of processing
'Quick-cooking' rice. This is rice that has been cooked and dehydrated. Its hard, starchy outer covering and its starch granules have already been broken so it will reabsorb water almost instantly when you cook it.

Medical uses and/or benefits
As a substitute for wheat flour in a gluten-free diet. People with coeliac disease have an inherited metabolic disorder which makes it impossible for them to digest gluten and gliadin, proteins found in wheat and some other grains. Rice and rice flour, which are free of gluten and gliadin, may be a useful substitute in some recipes.

Adverse effects
Mould toxins. Rice, like other grains, may support the growth of toxic moulds, including *Aspergillus flavus*, which produces carcinogenic aflatoxins. Other toxins found on mouldy, rice include citrinin, a penicillium mould too toxic to be used as an antibiotic; rubratoxins, mould products known to cause haemorrhages in animals who eat the mouldy rice; and nivalenol, a mould toxin that suppresses DNA and protein synthesis in cells. Because mould may turn the rice yellow, mouldy rice is also known as yellow rice.

Food/drug interactions
—

• Sausages (Frankfurter, liver sausage, salami)

See also BEEF, LIVER, PORK, POULTRY

Nutritional profile per 100g food (raw)				
	Beef Sausage		*Salami*	
Energy value:	High	299 Kcal	High	491 Kcal
Protein:	High	9.6 g	High	19.3 g
Fat:	High	24.1 g	High	45.2 g
Cholesterol:	Med	40 mg	Med	79 mg
Carbohydrates:	Med	11.7 g	Low	1.9 g
Fibre:	None	None	None	None
Sodium:	High	810 mg	High	1850 mg
Major vitamin contribution:	B vitamins	Med		Med
Major mineral contribution:	Iron, phosphorus, potassium	High, High, Med		High, High, Med

Like other meat, sausage contains PROTEINS considered 'complete' because they contain adequate amounts of all the essential amino acids. But sausage is higher in FAT and thus proportionally lower in protein than beef, veal, lamb, pork, or poultry. The composition of the fat (its ratio of SATURATED to UNSATURATED FATTY ACIDS) varies according to the meat used to make the sausage.

All sausage, like all meat, contains B vitamins and heme iron, the organic form of iron found in meat, fish, poultry, milk, and eggs. Liver sausage, like liver, is high in vitamin A and iron.

The most nutritious way to serve this food

In moderation. For example, adding a moderate amount of sausages to a casserole with beans combines a high-fat, low-fibre meat with high-fibre, low-fat beans and allows you to enjoy the sausages' taste while using its 'complete' proteins to complement the tryptophan, methionine, and cystine-limited proteins in the beans.

Diets that may restrict or exclude this food

Controlled-fat, low-cholesterol diet
Lactose-free diet
Low-protein diet
Low-sodium diet

Low-purine diet (liverwurst, liver sausages)
Sucrose-restricted diet

Buying
Choose. Fresh sausage that meets the test for any fresh meat: it should look fresh — not grey or dry. Pick packaged sausage by the date on the packet and the ingredient label. Check for 'hidden ingredients.'

Storing
Refrigerate all sausages. *Fresh* (raw) *sausages* and *uncooked smoked sausages*, which are highly perishable, should be wrapped carefully to keep them from dripping and contaminating the refrigerator shelves or other foods and used within two or three days (or according to the directions on the packet). Whole *cooked sausages* and *cooked smoked sausages* such as frankfurters, liver sausage, and salami may stay fresh for five or six days in the refrigerator. (Unopened packets may have a shelf life of weeks or months; check the label.) Whole *dry sausages* such as pepperoni and mortadella may keep months in the refrigerator, but when sliced these sausages spoil more quickly. All should be wrapped in plastic to keep other foods from absorbing their strong odours.

Preparation
—

Cooking reactions
Cooking sausage changes its flavour, reduces its fat content, and makes raw sausage safer by killing any pathogenic microorganisms, including those that cause trichinosis.

Browning the sausage caramelizes PROTEINS and SUGARS on the surface of the meat, giving the sausage a richer flavour (see BROWNING REACTIONS). At the same time, browning breaks up protein molecules, making them less valuable nutritionally. As the sausage cooks, it loses moisture and shrinks. Its pigments, which combine with oxygen, are denatured (broken into smaller fragments) by the heat and turn brown, the natural colour of cooked meat.

Effects of processing
—

Medical uses and/or benefits
—

Adverse reactions
✘ HEART DISEASE

✘ GOUT

Allergy to milk proteins and/or lactose intolerance. Milk proteins or lactose (milk sugar) are present in sausages that contain nonfat milk solids as binders, extenders, or sweeteners. Milk proteins or sugars may cause upset stomach or other reactions in people sensitive to the proteins or unable to digest lactose (see MILK).

Artificial colourings. Sausages are allowed to contain colourings in the filling and casing. The presence of colour or other permitted additives will be listed on the label of prepacked food or on the wall of the butcher making his or her own. Ask if in doubt.

Food/drug interactions

✘ MAO INHIBITORS

• Shellfish (Cockles, crabs, crayfish, lobster, mussels, oysters, prawns, scallops, scampi, shrimp, whelks)

Nutritional profile per 100g food (boiled)				
	Prawns		*Whelks*	
Energy value:	Med	107 Kcal	Med	91 Kcal
Protein:	High	22.6 g	High	18.5 g
Fat:	Low	1.8 g	Low	1.9 g
Cholesterol:	High	200 mg	High	100 mg
Carbohydrates:	Trace	None	Low	Trace
Fibre:	None	None	None	None
Sodium:	High	1590 mg	High	270 mg
Major vitamin contribution:	B vitamins	Med		Med
Major mineral contribution:	Iron,	Med,		High,
	iodine,	High,		High,
	potassium,	High,		High,
	phosphorus,	High,		High,
	calcium	High		Med

Shellfish are an excellent source of high-quality PROTEINS that are considered 'complete' because they contain sufficient amounts of all the essential amino acids. Shellfish are relatively low in FAT. Like other saltwater seafood, they contain omega-3 fatty acids, which appear to offer some protection against a variety of inflammatory conditions. Unlike other seafood, shellfish are relatively high in CHOLESTEROL.

Cholesterol content of shellfish (mg/100 grams)	
Crab (fresh or canned)	60-120 mg
Lobster	150 mg
Mussels (raw)	100 mg
Oysters (raw)	50 mg
Prawns	200 mg
Scallops	40 mg
Shrimp	200 mg

Source: McCance and Williamson's *The Composition of Foods, 4th ed, HMSO (1978)*

All shellfish are a good source of B vitamins, and heme iron, the organic form of iron found in meat, fish, poultry, milk, and eggs.

Shellfish are also a source of the trace minerals copper, iodine, and zinc.

The most nutritious way to serve this food
Thoroughly cooked, to take advantage of the nutrients while destroying any potentially hazardous microorganisms.

Diets that may restrict or exclude this food
Controlled-fat, low-cholesterol diet
Low-protein diet
Low-sodium diet

Buying
Choose. Mussels and oysters live in the shell. Live mussels and oysters should be tightly shut or close when you touch them and should be plump and smell absolutely fresh.

Choose live lobsters that look fresh, smell good, and are moving about actively. Cooked lobsters should have a bright-red shell and a fresh aroma. If the tail curls back when you pull it down, the lobster was alive when cooked. Female lobsters, which have fluffy fins ('swimmerettes') at the juncture of tail and body, may contain roe or coral that turns red when you cook the lobster.

Choose dry, creamy, sweet-smelling scallops. Unlike oysters and mussels, they can't be kept alive out of the water. Sea scallops may be sold fresh or frozen.

Choose fresh shrimp and prawns that look dry and firm in the shell.

Storing
Refrigerate all shellfish and use as quickly as possible. Like other seafood, shellfish are extremely perishable once they are no longer alive and should be used the day you buy them.

Preparation
When you are ready to prepare shellfish, sniff them first. If they don't smell absolutely fresh, throw them out.
Crabs. Snap off the claws, and pull off the shell. Cut away the gills and the digestive organs in the middle of the body and pull the meat away from the skeleton.
Lobsters and crayfish. If you plan to boil the lobsters, you can cook them just as they come. If you plan to grill a lobster, kill it first by inserting a knife into the space between the head and the body and slicing through the spinal cord. Then split the lobster and remove the internal organs. Live crayfish that have been stored in fresh running water do not have to be eviscerated before you boil them. If you wish to eviscerate the crayfish grasp

the middle fin on the tail, twist, and pull hard to pull out the stomach and intestine.

Mussels. In the shells mussels are apt to be sandy. To get rid of the grit, scrub the mussels under cold running water, then put them in a pot of cold water and let them stand for an hour or two. Discard any that float to the top. Rinse the rest once more under cold running water, trim the 'beard' with scissors, and prepare as your recipe directs.

Oysters. Unlike mussels, oysters in the shell are free of sand when you buy them. To prepare them, just wash the oysters thoroughly under cold running water. Discard any that don't close tight when you touch them or that float in water. Cook them in the shell or pry open the shell, strain the liquid for any stray grit, and use the oysters with or without the shell, as your recipe directs.

Scallops. Shelled scallops should be relatively free of liquid. Rinse them in cold running water and use as your recipe directs.

Shrimp and prawns. Wash the shrimp or prawns in cold running water. Then cook them in the shell to enhance the flavour of a soup or stew, or peel off the shell and remove the black 'vein' (actually the digestive tract) running down the back, and prepare the shellfish as your recipe directs.

Cooking reactions

When you cook shellfish, heat changes the structure of its proteins. The protein molecules are 'denatured,' which means they may break apart into smaller fragments, change shape, or clump together. All these changes force moisture out of protein tissues, making the shellfish opaque. The loss of moisture also changes the texture of the shellfish; the longer they are cooked, the more rubbery they will become. Shellfish should be cooked long enough to turn the flesh opaque and destroy any microorganisms living on the food.

Effects of processing

Freezing. When you freeze shellfish, the water in their cells forms ice crystals that can tear the cell membranes so the liquids inside leak out when the shellfish is defrosted — which is the reason defrosted shellfish tastes tougher and has less B vitamins than fresh shellfish. Defrosting the shellfish slowly, in the refrigerator, lessens the loss of moisture and B vitamins. Frozen shrimp and prawns can be boiled whole, in the shells, without defrosting.

Canning. Canning prolongs the shelf life of shell fish. Virtually all canned shellfish is higher in sodium than fresh shellfish. To reduce the sodium content, rinse the shellfish in cold water before you use it.

Medical uses and/or benefits

Protective effects of omega-3 fatty acids. Like other saltwater seafood, shellfish contain omega-3 fatty acids. Research has suggested that fish oils inhibit the formation of thromboxane, a chemical that causes red blood cells to clump together, and that omega-3 fatty acids are converted to a compound similar to prostacyclin, a natural body chemical that inhibits clotting.

Fish oils also appear to lower the levels of triglycerides in the blood. A high level of triglycerides, like a high level of CHOLESTEROL, increases the risk of heart disease and may reduce the anti-inflammatory response in the body tissues, perhaps by inhibiting the production of leuketrienes, the natural inflammatory agents that trigger a wide range of inflammatory diseases ranging from arthritis to hay fever.

As a source of calcium. Ground oyster shells, which are rich in calcium carbonate, are the calcium source in many over-the-counter supplements. Calcium carbonate is a less efficient source of the mineral than calcium lactate, the form of calcium in milk; it is also likely to cause constipation.

Adverse effects

✖ GOUT

Allergic reactions. Shellfish are among the foods most often implicated as the cause of the classic symptoms of food allergy — upset stomach, hives, and angioedema, (swelling of the face, lips, and eyes). In addition, shrimp, which are often treated with sulphites to keep them from darkening, may provoke serious allergic reactions, including anaphylactic shock, in people who are sensitive to sulphites.

Worms or parasites. Raw shellfish, like raw meat, may be host to worms, parasites, or their eggs and cysts. These organisms are killed by cooking the shellfish until the flesh is completely opaque.

Shellfish-transmitted infectious diseases. In the past ten years food scientists have identified an increasing number of bacteria and viruses, including the cholera organism, the hepatitis virus, and *Vibrio vulnificus* in live shellfish.

Food/drug interactions
—

• Soya beans

See also BEAN CURD, BEAN SPROUTS, BEANS

Nutritional profile per 100g food (raw)		
Energy value:	High	403 Kcal
Protein:	High	34.1 g
Fat:	High	17.7 g
Cholesterol:	None	None
Carbohydrates:	High	28.6 g
Fibre:	High	(not available)
Sodium:	Low	5 mg
Major vitamin contribution:	B vitamins, folic acid	High, High
Major mineral contribution:	Iron, potassium, calcium	High, High, High

Soya beans are an excellent source of food fibre, cellulose, pectins, gums, and the noncarbohydrate food fibre lignin, STARCH, and SUGARS, including the indigestible complex sugars raffinose and stachyose which make beans 'gassy' when they are fermented by bacteria in the human gut.

100g of soya beans provides 34 grams of protein, the amount found in 200g of meat, fish, and poultry.

Unlike other legumes (beans and peas), soya beans store FAT as well as starch. The oils in soya beans are primarily UNSATURATED FATTY ACIDS (62 percent polyunsaturated, 23 percent monounsaturated).

Soya beans are a good source of B vitamins, particularly vitamin B_6. They are rich in non-heme iron (the inorganic iron found in plant foods) but, like grains, beans contain phytic acid — which binds their iron into insoluble compounds your body cannot absorb. As a result, non-heme iron is five to six times less available to the body than heme iron, the organic form of iron in meat, fish, and poultry.

The most nutritious way to serve this food
With meat or a food rich in vitamin C to increase the amount of iron you can absorb from the soya beans. Vitamin C may convert the iron in soya beans from ferric iron (which is hard to absorb) to ferrous iron (which is easier to absorb).

Diets that may restrict or exclude this food
Low-calcium diet
Low-fibre diet
Low-protein diet

Low-purine (antigout) diet

Buying
Choose. Tightly sealed packets that protect the beans from air and moisture. The beans should be smooth-skinned, uniformly sized, evenly coloured, and free of stones and debris. It is easy to check beans sold in plastic bags, but the transparent material lets in light that may destroy pyridoxine.

Storing
Store beans in air- and moistureproof containers in a cool, dark cupboard where they are protected from heat, light, and insects.

Preparation
Wash the beans and pick them over carefully, discarding damaged beans, withered beans, or beans that float. (The only beans light enough to float in water are those that have withered away inside.)

Soak 'fresh' dried soya beans as directed on the package and then discard the water. If you used canned beans, discard the liquid in the can and rinse the beans in cool running water. In discarding this liquid, you are getting rid of some of the soluble indigestible sugars that may cause intestinal gas when you eat beans.

Cooking reactions
When soya beans are cooked in liquid, their cells absorb water, swell, and eventually rupture, releasing pectins, gums, and the nutrients inside the cell. In addition, cooking destroys antinutrients in beans, making them safe to eat.

Effects of processing
Soy sauce. Soy sauce is made by adding salt to cooked soya beans and setting the mixture aside to ferment. Soy sauce is particularly useful in Japanese cuisines because it inactivates antinutrient enzymes in raw fish.

Like soya beans, soy sauce is high in protein (1mg/4 tsp.). Unlike plain soya beans cooked without salt, it is high in sodium.

Milling. Soya flour is very high in protein (37-47 percent) and fat (0.9 percent-20 percent). It can be used as a substitute for up to 20 percent of the wheat flour in any recipe. Unlike wheat flour, it has no gluten or gliadin, which makes it useful for people who have coeliac disease, a metabolic disorder that makes it impossible for them to digest these wheat proteins (*see* FLOUR).

Canning. The heat of canning destroys some of the B vitamins in soya beans. Since the B vitamins are water-soluble, you could save them by using the liquid in the can. But the liquid also contains the indigestible sugars that cause intestinal gas when you eat beans.

Preprocessing. Preprocessed dried soya beans have already been soaked. They take less time to cook, but they are lower in B vitamins.

Medical uses and/or benefits
✓ HEART DISEASE

✓ DIABETES THERAPY

As a slimming aid. Although beans are high in calories, they are also high in fibre; even a small serving can make you feel full. And, because they are insulin-sparing, they put off the rise in insulin levels that makes us feel hungry again soon after eating. Research at the University of Toronto suggests the insulin-sparing effect may last for several hours after you eat the beans, perhaps until after your next meal.

Adverse effects
✗ MAO INHIBITORS
✗ GOUT

Intestinal gas. All legumes contain raffinose and stachyose, complex SUGARS that human beings cannot digest. The sugars sit in the gut, where they are fermented by intestinal bacteria, which then produce gas that distends the intestines and makes us uncomfortable. You can lessen this effect by covering the beans with boiling water and soaking them for four to six hours before you cook them so that the indigestible sugars leach out into the soaking water, which can be discarded. Or you may soak the beans for four hours in water, discard the soaking water, and add new water as your recipe directs. Then cook the beans and drain them before serving.

Food/drug interactions
—

• Spinach

Nutritional profile per 100g food (boiled)		
Energy value:	Low	30 Kcal
Protein:	Low	5.1 g
Fat:	Low	0.5 g
Cholesterol:	None	None
Carbohydrates:	Low	1.4 g
Fibre:	Med	6.3 g
Sodium:	High	120 mg
Major vitamin contribution:	Vitamins A, B and C	High, Med, High
Major mineral contribution:	Potassium, calcium, iron	High, High, High

Spinach has little STARCH; a moderate amount of PROTEINS; very little FAT; and no CHOLESTEROL. It has moderate amounts of cellulose, and the noncarbohydrate food fibre lignin, which is found in roots, seed coverings, stems, and the ribs of leaves.

Spinach is a good source of vitamin C. 100g serving of fresh raw spinach provides 25 mg vitamin C, 80 percent of the RDA for a healthy adult. Spinach is rich in yellow carotenes, which are converted to vitamin A in your body. 100g boiled, drained spinach has 130 percent of the RDA for vitamin A. Spinach is also rich in riboflavin (vitamin B_2), which is more plentiful in the leaves than in the stems.

Spinach is rich in calcium but it also has a lot of oxalic acid, which binds the calcium into an insoluble salt (calcium oxalate) that your body cannot absorb. The oxalic acid also binds iron; only 2 to 5 percent of spinach's seemingly plentiful supply of iron is actually available to your body.

The most nutritious way to serve this food
Fresh, lightly steamed, to protect its vitamin C.

Diets that may restrict or exclude this food
Low-calcium, low-oxalate diet (for people who form calcium-oxalate kidney stones)
Low-sodium diet

Buying
Choose. Fresh, crisp dark-green leaves that are free of dirt and debris.
Avoid. Yellowed leaves. These are aging leaves whose chlorophyll pigments

have faded, allowing the carotenoids underneath to show through. Wilted leaves or leaves that are limp and brownish have lost vitamin C.

Storing
Refrigerate loose leaves in a roomy plastic bag.

Preparation
Wash the spinach thoroughly under cool running water to remove all sand and debris. Discard damaged or yellowed leaves. Trim the ribs and stems but don't remove them entirely; they are rich in food fibre. If you plan to use the spinach in a salad, refrigerate the damp leaves to make them crisp.

Cooking reactions
When you heat spinach, the chlorophyll in its leaves will react with acids in the vegetable or in the cooking water, forming pheophytin, which is brown.

To keep cooked spinach green steam quickly in very little water so that it retains its vitamin C and cooks before there is time for the chlorophyll/acid reaction to occur.

Spinach also contains astringent tannins that react with metals to create dark pigments. If you cook the leaves in an aluminium or iron pot, these pigments will discolour the pots and the spinach. To keep the spinach from darkening, cook in an enamelled or glass pot.

Effects of processing
Canning and freezing. Canned spinach, which is processed at high heat, is olive or bronze rather than green. Like cooked spinach, canned spinach has only 50 percent of the vitamin C in fresh spinach.

Medical uses and/or benefits
✓ PROTECTION AGAINST CANCER

Adverse effects
✗ NITRATE/NITRITE POISONING

Food/drug interactions
✗ ANTICOAGULANTS

✗ MAO INHIBITORS

• Squid (Calamari, octopus)

Nutritional profile per 100g food (raw)		
Energy value:	Low	75 Kcal
Protein:	High	15.3 g
Fat:	Low	0.8 g
Cholesterol:	High	(not available)
Carbohydrates:	Low	0.7 g
Fibre:	None	None
Sodium:	High	176 mg
Major vitamin contribution:	B vitamins	Med
Major mineral contribution:	Iron, potassium	Med, Med

Squid (also known by its Italian name, *calamari*) and octopus are cephalopods (*cephalo* = head; *pod* = foot), a class of molluscs. They are lean, muscular animals, high in PROTEIN and very low in FAT.

The proteins in squid and octopus are considered 'complete' because they provide all the essential amino acids. The fats are proportionally higher in CHOLESTEROL than the fat in many other forms of seafood, but they are also high (30 percent) in the omega-3 fatty acids, eicosapentaenoic acid (EPA), and docosahexanoic acid (DHA). EPA and DHA are the primary polyunsaturated fatty acids in the fat and oils of fish.   Both squid and octopus are good sources of B vitamins and provide heme iron, the organic form of iron found in meat, fish, and poultry. They are high in sodium and have traces of calcium and phosphorus.

The most nutritious way to serve this food
Prepared with little or no added fat, to preserve the seafood's status as a low-fat food.

Diets that may restrict or exclude this food
Low-cholesterol diet
Low-protein diet
Low-sodium diet (frozen squid or octopus)

Buying
Choose. Fresh whole squid with clear, smooth skin. The squid should smell absolutely fresh. Squid larger than 8 inches may be tough.

Choose, fresh, whole baby octopus or octopus meat that looks and smells absolutely fresh. Octopus larger than 1 kg may be tough.

Storing
Refrigerate fresh, cleaned octopus or squid immediately and use it within a day or two. Frozen squid or octopus will keep for one month in a freezer.

Preparation
Squid. Whole squid are usually sold cleaned, like any other seafood. If you are cleaning the squid yourself, your goal is to throw out everything but the empty saclike body and the tentacles. Start by removing the beak. Then reach into the body cavity and pull out all the innards, including the cartilage. (If you tear or puncture the ink sac and spill the ink, just wash it off your hands.) Cut the innards away from the body and throw them out. Peel off the skin. Squeeze the thick end of the tentacles and discard the small yellowish piece of meat that pops out. Rinse the squid meat thoroughly, inside and out, under cool running water. Stuff the sac whole for baking or cut it into rings and stew it along with the tentacles.

Octopus. Cleaned, dressed octopus needs only be rinsed thoroughly under cold running water. To prepare a small whole octopus, remove the beak, eyes, anal area, and ink sac. Cut off the tough ends of the tentacles, slice the tentacles into rounds or chunks, rinse them thoroughly under cold running water to remove all the gelatinous cartilage, and pound the meat to tenderize it.

Cooking reactions
Squid cooks fairly quickly. Its thin-walled body can be fried or sautéed in less than a minute and stewed in half an hour. Octopus, on the other hand, may need to be simmered for as long as three hours. But take care: the longer you cook the octopus, the more moisture you squeeze out of its protein tissues and the more rubbery it becomes.

Effects of processing
Freezing. Commercially processed squid are soaked in brine before freezing, which makes them much higher in sodium than fresh squid.

Medical uses and/or benefits
Protective effects of omega-3 fatty acids. Research shows that fish oils inhibit the formation of thromboxane, a chemical that makes red blood cells clump together, and that omega-3 fatty acids are converted to a compound similar to prostacyclin, a natural body chemical that inhibits clotting.

Fish oils also appear to lower the levels of triglycerides in the blood to reduce the anti-inflammatory response in body tissues, perhaps by inhibiting the production of leuketrienes, the natural inflammatory agents that trigger a wide range of inflammatory diseases ranging from arthritis to hay fever. Unlike fatty fish which can be over 16 percent fat, squid and octopus have much less fat so supply less omega-3 fatty acids.

Adverse effects

✘ HEART DISEASE

Allergic reactions. Shellfish are among the foods most likely to cause the classic symptoms of food allergy, including upset stomach, hives, and angioedema (swelling of the lips and eyes).

Parasitical, viral, and bacterial infections and/or food poisoning. Like raw meat, raw shellfish may carry various pathogens, including *Salmonella* bacteria. These organisms are destroyed by thorough cooking.

Food/drug interactions

—

• Strawberries

Nutritional profile per 100g food		
Energy value:	Low	26 Kcal
Protein:	Low	0.6 g
Fat:	Low	Trace
Cholesterol:	None	None
Carbohydrates:	Med	6.2 g
Fibre:	Low	2.2 g
Sodium:	Low	2 mg
Major vitamin contribution:	Vitamin C	High
Major mineral contribution:	Iron, potassium	Low, Med

Strawberries have moderate amounts of SUGAR, no STARCH, and are a good source of food fibre, particularly pectin and the noncarbohydrate food fibre lignin, which is found in the tiny seeds that dot the surface of the berry.

Strawberries are an excellent source of vitamin C. Ounce for ounce, they have as much vitamin C as fresh oranges. Strawberries also have some non-heme iron, the inorganic form of iron found in plants.

The most nutritious way to serve this food
Fresh and ripe, to preserve the vitamin C.

Diets that may restrict or exclude this food
Low-fibre diet
Sucrose-restricted diet

Buying
Choose. Bright red berries with fresh green caps. Pale berries are immature; berries with dark red wet spots are overmature; berries whose caps have browned are aging. Small berries are generally more flavourful than large ones.

Storing
Refrigerate strawberries with their caps on.

Preparation
When you are ready to use the berries, rinse them thoroughly under cool running water. Then remove the caps. (If you hull the berries before you rinse them, water may run into the berry and dilute the flavour.)

Don't slice the berries until you are ready to use them.

Cooking reactions

The red anthocyanin pigments in strawberries are heat-sensitive; they break apart and turn brown when you heat them. Adding sugar speeds up the process even further because some of the chemicals produced when sugars are heated also break down anthocyanins. That's why strawberries cooked in boiling, sugared water turn brown faster than strawberries steamed quickly without sugar.

Red anthocyanins also change colour in acids and bases (alkalis). They are bright-red in acids such as lemon juice and bluish or purple in bases such as baking soda. If you cook strawberries in an aluminium or iron pot, their acids will react with metal ions from the surface of the pot to create dark brown compounds that darken either the pot or the fruit.

Strawberries also lose heat-sensitive vitamin C when you cook them.

Effects of processing

Heat processing (canning; making jams, jellies, and preserves). As noted above, strawberries turn brown when you heat them with sugar. Lemon juice added to jams, jellies, and preserves makes the taste tart and helps preserve the colour.

Medical uses and/or benefits

PROTECTION AGAINST CANCER

An as antiscorbutic. Strawberries, which (ounce for ounce) have more vitamin C than citrus fruits, help protect against scurvy, the vitamin C-deficiency disease.

Adverse effects

Allergic reactions. Strawberries are among the foods most often implicated as a cause of the classic food-allergy symptoms: upset stomachs, hives, angioedema (swelling of the face, lips, and eyes), and a hay-feverlike reaction.

Food/drug interactions

—

• Sugar (Corn syrup, fructose, golden syrup, maple syrup, molasses, treacle)

See also HONEY

Nutritional profile per 100g food		
	White Granulated	
Energy value:	High	394 Kcal
Protein:	None	None
Fat:	None	None
Cholesterol:	None	None
Carbohydrates:	High	99.9 g
Fibre:	None	None
Sodium:	None	Trace
Major vitamin contribution:	None	
Major mineral contribution:	None	

SUGARS are CARBOHYDRATES, members of the class of nutrients that includes STARCHES and some food fibres.

Table sugar, (also known as *granulated sugar, white sugar, refined surar*, or simply *sugar*) is sucrose crystallized from sugar cane or sugar beets. Sucrose is a disaccharide ('double sugar') that contains one molecule of fructose and one molecule of glucose. Sucrose cannot be absorbed into your body until it is split into fructose and glucose.

Table sugar has no nutrients. They are left behind when sucrose is crystallized out of cane or beet juice. Treacle and golden syrup have some potassium, calcium and iron.

The most nutritious way to serve this food
In moderation.

Diets that may restrict or exclude this food
Low-calorie diet
Low-carbohydrate diet
Sucrose-restricted diet

Buying
Choose: Tightly sealed boxes or sacks of dry sugars. Avoid stained packages; whatever stained the outside may have seeped through into the sugar.

Choose tightly sealed bottles of liquid sugars. The liquid inside should be clear; tiny bubbles and a grey scum on the surface of the sugar suggest that it has fermented.

Molasses and *golden syrup*, which are by-products of the production of table sugar, retain minute amounts of nutrients. *Raw sugar* (also known as *muscavado sugar*) is cane sugar with some of the molasses left in.

Fructose, which is twice as sweet as sucrose, is a monosaccharide (a 'single sugar'). Unlike sucrose, which must be broken down by enzymes before you can use it, fructose can be absorbed directly into your body. Eating fructose does not trigger the insulin rush that occurs when you eat sucrose.

Glucose syrup, a liquid syrup processed from corn, is made of glucose, a monosaccharide extracted from corn starch, plus some sucrose or fructose to make it sweeter. (Glucose is only half as sweet as sucrose.)

Storing
Store solid sugars in air- and moistureproof containers in a cool, dry cabinet. Sugars are hydrophilic, which means that they will absorb moisture. If sugars get wet (or pick up excess moisture from hot, humid air), they will harden or cake.

Store tightly sealed, unopened containers of liquid sugars such as glucose syrup, golden syrup, and molasses at room temperature. Once the container is opened, you can store the sugar in the refrigerator to protect it from moulds and keep the sugars from fermenting.

Preparation
Because they contain different amounts of water and have different levels of sweetness, sugars cannot simply be substituted equally for each other. As a general rule, one cup of white table sugar = one cup of firmly packed brown sugar = 1.75 cups of icing sugar (which cannot be substituted in baking).

To measure granulated white sugar, pour into a cup and use a knife to level. To measure brown sugar, pack tightly into a cup. Icing sugar can be sifted or not, as the recipe dictates.

Cooking reactions
When you heat sugar its molecules separate. The sugar liquifies, then turns brown. The browning is called carmelization. When you heat sugar in water it attracts molecules of water and forms a syrup that can be thickened by heating the solution long enough to evaporate some of the water.

Effects of processing
—

Medical use and/or benefits
—

Adverse effects

✖ HEART DISEASE

Tooth decay. Fermentable carbohydrates, including sugars, may cling to the teeth and nourish the bacteria that produce acid that causes cavities. Regular flossing and brushing remove the sugars mechanically; fluoridated water hardens the surface of the teeth so that they are more resistant to bacterial action.

Sugar in the urine. People with diabetes cannot use sucrose efficiently either because they do not produce enough insulin (which promotes the metabolism of carbohydrates) or because they do not have enough of the receptors to which insulin binds when it is released by the pancreas. Eating sugar will not cause diabetes, but it may exacerbate existing cases so that unmetabolized glucose will be present in the urine and blood.

Behavioural problems. The National Institutes of Health in the USA has conducted double-blind studies in which childen were given drinks sweetened with glucose, sucrose, or saccharin without their knowing which drink had which sweetener. These studies show no correlation between eating the sugars and developing behavioural problems, even in children whose parents had claimed that the children were hyperactive after eating sugared foods. In fact, the children were quieter after the sugared beverages, an observation consistent with research at the Massachusetts Institute of Technology which shows that eating carbohydrates facilitates the brain's ability to absorb tryptophan and produce serotonin, a naturally calming chemical.

Hypoglycaemia. Reactive hypoglycaemia, an oversecretion of insulin in response to eating sugar, is a rare condition that causes trembling, anxiety, headache, fast heartbeat, and difficulty in thinking clearly. Hypoglycaemia may also be caused by the presence of a pancreatic tumour or an overdose of insulin. This is a more serious condition that, uncorrected, may lead to coma or death.

Food/drug interactions

—

• Sweet corn (Maize)

See also VEGETABLE OILS

Nutritional profile per 100g food (raw)		
Energy value:	Med	127 Kcal
Protein:	Med	4.1 g
Fat:	Low	2.4 g
Cholesterol:	None	None
Carbohydrates:	High	23.7
Fibre:	Med	3.7 g
Sodium:	Low	1 mg
Major vitamin contribution:	B vitamins, vitamin C, vitamin A (in yellow corn)	High, Med, Low
Major mineral contribution:	Potassium, iron, zinc	High, Med, Med

Sweet corn is high in CARBOHYDRATES and STARCH.

Corn is a moderately good source of plant proteins, but zein (its major protein) is deficient in the essential amino acids lysine, cystine, and tryptophan. Corn is low in fat but its oils are composed primarily of UNSATURATED FATTY ACIDS.

Yellow corn, which gets its colour from the xanthophyll pigments lutein and zeaxanthine plus the vitamin A-active pigments carotene and crypto-xanthin, contains a little vitamin A; white corn has very little.

All varieties of sweet corn are sources of vitamin C. Corn is rich in nicotinic acid, but as much as 80 percent of it is unavailable to the human body because it is bound into insoluble carbohydrate-protein-nitrogen compounds. Sweet corn also has some non-heme iron (the organic form of iron found in plants) that the body does not absorb as well as heme iron (the organic form of iron in foods of animal origin). You can get more non-heme iron from corn by eating the sweet corn with meat or with a food rich in vitamin C.

The most nutritious way to serve this food
Boiled, on the cob. With meat or a food rich in vitamin C, to make the iron in the sweet corn more useful.

Diets that may restrict or exclude this food
Low-fibre diet
Sucrose-free diet

Buying
Choose: Cobs that feel cool or are stored in a refrigerated cabinet. Keeping sweet corn cool helps retain its vitamin C and slows the natural conversion of the corn's sugars to starch.

Choose fresh sweet corn with medium-sized kernels that yield slightly when you press them with your fingertip. Very small kernels are immature; very large ones are older and will taste starchy rather than sweet. Both yellow and white kernels may be equally tasty, but the husk of the sweet corn should always be moist and green. A dry yellowish husk means that the sweet corn is old enough for the chlorophyll pigments in the husk to have faded, letting the carotenes underneath show through.

Storing
Refrigerate fresh sweet corn. At room temperature, fresh-picked sweet corn will convert nearly half its sugar to starch within 23 hours and lose half its vitamin C in four days. In the refrigerator, it may keep all its vitamin C for up to a week and may retain its sweet taste for as long as ten days.

Preparation
Strip off the husks and silk, and plunge into boiling water for four to six minutes, depending on the size of the sweet corn.

Cooking reactions
Heat denatures (breaks apart) the long-chain protein molecules in the liquid inside the sweet corn kernel, allowing them to form a network of protein molecules that will squeeze out moisture and turn rubbery if you cook the corn too long. Heat also allows the starch granules inside the kernel to absorb water so that they swell and eventually rupture, releasing the nutrients inside. When you cook sweet corn, the trick is to cook it just long enough to rupture its starch granules while keeping its protein molecules from turning tough and chewy.

Cooking fresh sweet corn for several minutes in boiling water may destroy at least half of its vitamin C. Cooking fresh sweet corn in the microwave oven (2 ears/without water if very fresh/4 minutes/600-700 watts) preserves most of the vitamin C.

Effects of processing
Canning and freezing. Canned sweet corn and frozen sweet corn both have less vitamin C than fresh-cooked sweet corn. The vitamin is lost when the sweet corn is heated during canning or blanched before freezing to destroy the natural enzymes that would otherwise continue to ripen it. Blanching in a microwave oven rather than in boiling water can preserve the vitamin C in frozen sweet corn (see above).
Processed corn cereals. All processed, ready-to-eat corn cereals are much higher in sodium and sugar than fresh sweet corn.

Medical uses and/or benefits

As a wheat substitute in baking. People who are allergic to wheat or cannot tolerate the gluten in wheat flour or wheat cereals can often use corn flour instead.

Bath powder. Corn starch, a fine powder refined from the endosperm (inner part) of the sweet corn kernel, can be used as an inexpensive, unperfumed body or face powder. Because it absorbs oils, it is also used as an ingredient in dry shampoos.

Adverse effects

Allergy. Corn is one of the most commonly implicated as a cause of the classic food allergy symptons: hives, angioedema (swelling of the lips and eyes), and upset stomachs. The pollen of the sweet corn plant is also an airborne allergen that can trigger hay feverlike symptoms in sensitive people.

Pellegra. Pellegra is a niacin-deficiency disease that occurs most commonly among people for whom corn is the staple food in a diet lacking PROTEIN foods with the essential amino acid tryptophan, which can be converted to niacin in the human body. Pellegra is not an inevitable result of a diet high in corn, however, since the niacin in corn can be made more useful by soaking the corn in a solution of calcium carbonate (lime) and water. In Mexico, for example, the corn used to make tortillas is boiled in a dilute solution of calcium carbonate (from shells or limestone) and water, then washed, drained, and ground. The alkaline bath appears to release the bound niacin in corn so that it can be absorbed by the body.

Food/drug interactions

—

• Sweet potatoes (Yams)

See also POTATOES

Nutritional profile per 100g food (raw)		
Energy value:	Med	91 Kcal
Protein:	Low	1.2 g
Fat:	Low	0.6 g
Cholesterol:	None	None
Carbohydrates:	High	21.5 g
Fibre:	Med	2.5 g
Sodium:	Low	19 mg
Major vitamin contribution:	Vitamin A, vitamin C	High, High
Major mineral contribution:	Potassium	High

Sweet potatoes are high in STARCH, with moderate amounts of food fibre, a little PROTEIN, a trace of FAT, and no CHOLESTEROL. Sweet potatoes contain alpha amylase, an enzyme that converts starches to SUGARS as the potato matures, when it is stored, or as it begins to heat up when you cook it.

Sweet potatoes are an excellent source of vitamin A, derived from the carotene pigments that make the potato orange-yellow. The deeper the colour the higher the vitamin A content. On average, a 100g boiled sweet potato provides 80 percent of the RDA for a healthy adult. Sweet potatoes also have vitamin C, some B vitamins, potassium and iron.

True yams, which are native to Africa, are available in this country. The 'yams' sold here are actually a variety of sweet potato with copper-coloured skin, orange flesh, a moist texture, less vitamin A, and more vitamin C than sweet potato.

The most nutritious way to serve this food
Baked or boiled.

Diets that may restrict or exclude this food
Low-fibre diet
Sucrose-restricted diet

Buying
Choose: Solid, well-shaped sweet potatoes, thick in the centre and tapering towards the ends. The potatoes should feel heavy for their size and the skin should be evenly coloured and free of blemishes, bruises, and mould. Mouldy sweet potatoes may be contaminated with a number of toxins including the

liver toxin ipomeamarone and a toxin derivative, ipomeamaronol. These toxins cannot be destroyed by normal boiling or baking.

Storing
Handle sweet potatoes gently to avoid bruising. When you bruise a sweet potato you tear some of its cells, releasing polyphenoloxidase, an enzyme that hastens the oxidation of phenols in the potato, creating brown compounds that darken the potato.

Store sweet potatoes in a cool, dark cupboard, not in the refrigerator. Like bruising, very cold temperatures damage the potato's cells, darkening the potato.

Store home-grown sweet potatoes at 85°F (29°C) for four to six days right after harvesting to sweeten them by increasing the natural conversion of starches to sugars.

Preparation
Scrub sweet potatoes under cool running water. Boiling the potatoes in their skin will save more vitamins since you will be able to peel them more closely after they are cooked. If you plan to bake the sweet potatoes, pierce the skin with a cake tester to let the steam escape as the potato cooks.

Cooking reactions
Cooking sweetens the potato by converting some of its STARCHES to SUGARS.

Cooking also changes the potato's texture. When you bake a sweet potato, the water inside its cells dissolves some of the pectins in its cell walls, so the potato gets softer. As it continues to bake, moisture begins to evaporate from the cells and the potato shrinks. When you boil sweet potatoes, the initial reaction is just the opposite: at first, the starch granules in the potato absorb moisture and swell so that the potato looks bigger. If you continue to boil the potato, however, its starch granules will absorb so much water that they rupture. The water inside will leak out and the potato, once again, will shrink.

Effects of processing
Canning. Sweet potatoes canned in water have the same nutrients as cooked fresh sweet potatoes. Sweet potatoes canned in sugar syrups have more carbohydrates and more calories.

Medical uses and/or benefits
✓ PROTECTION AGAINST CANCER

Adverse effects
—

Food/drug interactions
—

• Tangerines (Clementine, satsuma, tangelo)

Nutritional profile per 100g food		
Energy value:	Low	34 Kcal
Protein:	Low	0.9 g
Fat:	Low	Trace
Cholesterol:	None	None
Carbohydrates:	Med	8 g
Fibre:	Low	1.9 g
Sodium:	Low	2 mg
Major vitamin contribution:	Vitamin C	High
Major mineral contribution:	Potassium	Med

The tangerine (also known as Mandarin orange), the tangelo (a cross between the grapefruit and the tangerine), and the clementine (a small-to-medium-size Algerian tangerine) are all medium in SUGAR, with no STARCH and moderate amounts of food fibre, particularly soluble gums and pectins. A tangerine provides about as much pectin as an apple.

Ounce for ounce, tangerines have about 60 percent as much vitamin C as oranges.

Tangerines, tangelos, and clementines are a good source of potassium, and tangerines have more vitamin A than other citrus fruit.

The most nutritious way to serve this food
Freshly peeled.

Diets that may restrict or exclude this food
Low-fibre diet
Sucrose-restricted diet

Buying
Choose: Tangerines that are heavy for their size (which means they will be juicy). The skin should be deep orange, almost red, and naturally puffy and easy to peel.

Choose firm, heavy tangelos, with a thin, light-orange skin that is less puffy than the tangerine's.

Choose small-to-medium clementines with bright-orange skin. They should be heavy for their size.

Storing

Store tangelos at room temperature for a few days. Refrigerate them for longer storage.

Refrigerate tangerines and clementines. Tangerines are very perishable; use them within a day or two.

Preparation

Wash the fruit under cold running water. Don't peel it until you are ready to use it; peeling tears cells and activates ascorbic acid oxidase, an enzyme that destroys vitamin C.

Cooking reactions
—

Effects of processing

Canning. Before they are canned, tangerines are blanched briefly in steam to inactivate ascorbic acid oxidase, an enzyme that would otherwise destroy the fruit's vitamin C. Canned tangerines contain approximately as much vitamin C as fresh ones.

Medical uses and/or benefits

✔ PROTECTION AGAINST CANCER
✔ POTASSIUM REPLACEMENT

As an antiscorbutic. Although tangerines, tangelos, and clementines provide less vitamin C per ounce than other citrus fruits, they are still useful in preventing scurvy, the vitamin C-deficiency disease.

Adverse effects

Contact dermatitis. The oils in the peel of the tangerine, tangelo, or clementine may be irritating to sensitive individuals.
Apthous ulcers. Eating citrus fruit, including tangerines, tangelos, and clementines, may trigger an attack of apthous ulcers (canker sores) in sensitive people, but eliminating these foods from your diet will neither cure nor prevent an attack.

Food/drug interactions
—

• Tea

Nutritional profile per 100g food		
	Infusion of Indian tea	
Energy value:	None	None
Protein:	Low	0.1 g
Fat:	Low	Trace
Cholesterol:	None	None
Carbohydrates:	Low	Trace
Fibre:	None	None
Sodium:	None	Trace
Major vitamin contribution:	Folic acid	Low
Major mineral contribution:	Fluoride	Low

All teas are a good source of folic acid. Teas are rich in fluorides. They ordinarily provide about 0.3-0.5 mg fluoride per cup, and tea plants with a fluoride concentration of 100 ppm (parts per million) are not uncommon. (Fluoridated water is generally 1 ppm fluoride). Tea also provides small amounts of magnesium and potassium.

Like coffee and chocolate, tea contains the methylxanthine stimulants caffeine, theophylline, and theobromine. Depending on how you brew it, a cup of tea may have anywhere from 30-110 percent as much caffeine as a cup of coffee. Brewed tea is higher in caffeine than tea made from bags or instant teas.

Caffeine content of brewed teas (mg/5 oz. cup)	
Tea bags (black tea)	
5-min. brew.	47 mg
1-min. brew.	29 mg
Loose tea	
Black, 5-min. brew	41 mg
Green, 5-min. brew	36 mg
Green (Japanese), 5-min. brew	21 mg
Filter coffee	139 mg

Source: The American Dietetic Association, *Handbook of Clinical Dietetics* (New Haven: Yale University Press, 1981).

Tea leaves also contain antinutrient enzymes that can split the thiamin (vitamin B_1) molecule so that it is no longer nutritionally useful. This is not generally considered a problem for healthy people who eat a balanced diet and consume normal amounts of tea, but it might trigger a thiamin deficiency if you drink a lot of tea and your diet is marginal in thiamin. The tannins in tea are also potential antinutrients that bind calcium and iron into insoluble compounds your body cannot absorb. High consumption of tea might substantially reduce the absorption of iron from foods. Tannins also interfere with the absorption of thiamin (vitamin B_1) and vitamin B_{12}. Finally, tea contains oxalates that can bind calcium and might contribute to the formation of calcium-oxalate kidney stones in people predisposed to form stones.

The most nutritious way to serve this food
With milk. Milk protein (casein) binds and inactivates tannins.

Diets that may restrict or exclude this food
Bland diet
Low-oxalate diet (for people who form calcium oxalate kidney stones)

Buying
Choose: Tightly sealed packages. Tea loses flavour and freshness when it is exposed to air, moisture, or light.

Green tea, black tea, and oolong all come from the same plant. The difference lies in the way they are processed. *Green tea* is made from leaves that are dried right after harvesting; the leaves are still green, with a delicate flavour. *Black tea* is made of leaves allowed to ferment after harvesting. During fermentation polyphenolaxidase, an enzyme in the leaves, hastens the oxidation of phenols in the leaves, creating brown pigments that darken the leaves and intensify their flavour. *Oolong tea* is made from leaves allowed to ferment for only a short time. The leaves are brownish-green and the flavour is somewhere between the delicate green tea and the strong black tea. (*Souchong, pekoe*, and *orange pekoe* are terms used to describe grades of black-tea leaves. Souchong leaves are round; orange pekoe leaves are thin and wiry; pekoe leaves are shorter and rounder than orange pekoe.)

Storing
Store tea in a cool, dark cupboard in an air- and moistureproof container, preferably a glass jar.

Preparation
When brewing tea, always start with an absolutely clean glass, china, or enamel pot and, if possible, soft, mineral-free water. The tannins in tea leaves react with metals and minerals to create the compounds that make up the film sometimes seen floating on top of a cup of tea.

Cooking reactions

When tea leaves are immersed in water they begin to release flavouring agents plus bitter tannins, the astringent chemicals that coagulate proteins on the surface of the mucous membrane lining the mouth, making the tissues pucker. The best tea is brewed at the boiling point of water, a temperature that allows the tea leaves to release flavouring agents quickly without overloading the tea with bitter tannins. If the brewing water is below boiling point, the leaves will release their flavouring agents so slowly that by the time enough flavour molecules have been released into the brew, the ratio of bitter tannins will be so high that the tea tastes bitter. Brewing tea in water that is too hot also makes a bitter brink. At temperatures above boiling, the tannins are released so fast that they turn tea bitter in a minute or two.

You cannot judge the flavour of brewed tea by its colour. Brewed black teas turn reddish-brown and brewed green teas are almost colourless, but they are both distinctively flavoured. Brewing time is a much better guide, three to five minutes for the most flavourful brew. Once the tea is brewed, swirl a spoon through it before serving, to make sure the flavouring oils are evenly distributed.

Effects of processing

Iced tea. Hot water can dissolve more pigments from tea leaves than cold water. When tea brewed in hot water is chilled, as for iced tea, the 'extra' pigments will precipitate out and the tea will look cloudy.

Medical uses and/or benefits

Methylxanthine effects. All methylxanthines are stimulants. Theophylline and caffeine are central-nervous system stimulants, vasoactive compounds that dilate the skeletal blood vessels and constrict blood vessels in the brain. Theophylline, which effectively relaxes the smooth muscles in the bronchi — the small passages that carry air into the lungs — is used as an asthma medication, but the relatively low concentrations of theophylline in brewed tea are too small to produce therapeutic effects.

Protection against tooth decay. Tea contains natural fluorides that may protect against tooth decay, but if you are a steady tea drinker, the fluorides also stain your teeth.

Adverse effects

Stimulation of the central nervous system. Taken in excessive amounts, caffeine and theophylline may cause rapid heartbeat, restlessness, sleeplessness, and/or depression in sensitive individuals. Since different people can tolerate different amounts of caffeine and theophylline without suffering ill effects, exactly which dose produces problems varies from person to person.

Constipation. The tannins in tea may be constipating.

Food/drug interactions

✖ ANTICOAGULANTS

Allopurinol. Tea and other beverages containing the methylxanthine stimulants (caffeine, theophylline, and theobromine) reduce the effectiveness of the xanthine inhibitor, antigout drug allopurinol.

Antibiotics. Drinking tea increases stomach acidity, which reduces the absorption of some antibiotics.

Antiulcer medication. Drinking tea makes the stomach more acid and may reduce the effectiveness of normal doses of cimetidine and other antiulcer medication.

Iron supplements. Caffeine and tannic acid bind with iron to form insoluble compounds your body cannot absorb. Ideally, iron supplements and tea should be taken at least two hours apart.

Nonprescription drugs containing caffeine. The caffeine in brewed tea may add to the stimulant effects of the caffeine in some cold remedies, diuretics, pain relievers, stimulants, and weight-control products. Some over-the-counter cold pills contain 30 mg caffeine, some pain relievers 130 mg, and some weight-control products as much as 280 mg caffeine. There are 21 to 47 mg caffeine in a cup of brewed tea.

Sedatives. The caffeine in tea may counteract the drowsiness caused by sedative drugs.

Theophylline. The theophylline and caffeine in brewed tea may intensify the effects and/or increase the risk of side effects from this antiasthmatic drug.

• Tomatoes

Nutritional profile per 100g food		
Energy value:	Low	14 Kcal
Protein:	Low	0.9 g
Fat:	Low	Trace
Cholesterol:	None	None
Carbohydrates:	Med	2.8 g
Fibre:	Low	1.5 g
Sodium:	Low	3 mg
Major vitamin contribution:	Vitamins A, B, C	Low, High, High
Major mineral contribution:	Potassium	High

Tomatoes are medium in SUGAR (fructose, glucose, and sucrose), but they have no STARCH and only moderate amounts of food fibre, including cellulose and the noncarbohydrate food fibre lignin in the seeds and peel. Tomatoes have a little PROTEIN, a trace of FAT, and no CHOLESTEROL at all.

Tomatoes are an excellent source of vitamin C, most of which is found in the 'jelly' around each seed. 100g of fresh tomato has 25 mg vitamin C, 80 percent of the RDA for a healthy adult. Tomatoes grown outdoors have almost twice as much vitamin C as hothouse tomatoes; a garden-grown tomato picked just as it is beginning to turn yellow already has more vitamin C than fully ripened red hothouse tomatoes. Tomatoes are not a rich source of vitamin A since most of their colour comes from lycopene, a red carotenoid that the body cannot convert into vitamin A. Tomatoes are a good source of potassium.

The most nutritious way to serve this food
Fresh and ripe.

Diets that may restrict or exclude this food
Low-fibre diet
Sucrose-restricted diet

Buying
Choose: Smooth round or oval tomatoes. The tomatoes should feel heavy for their size; their flesh should be firm, not watery. If you plan to use them immediately, pick ripe ones whose skin is a deep orange-red. If you plan to store the tomatoes for a few days, pick tomatoes whose skin is still slightly yellow or pink.
Avoid: Bruised tomatoes or tomatoes with mould around the stem end. The

damaged tomatoes may be rotten inside; the mouldy ones may be contaminated with mycotoxins, poisons produced by moulds.

Storing

Store unripe tomatoes at room temperature until they turn fully orange-red. Tomatoes picked before they have ripened on the bush will be at their most nutritious if you let them continue to ripen at a temperature between 60° and 75°F (16-24°C). Keep them out of direct sunlight, which can soften the tomato without ripening it and destroy vitamins A and C. At room temperature, yellow to light-pink tomatoes should ripen in three to five days.

Refrigerate ripe tomatoes to inactivate enzymes that continue to soften the fruit by dissolving pectins in its cell walls. Fully ripe tomatoes should be used within two or three days.

Preparation

Remove and discard all leaves and stalks; they are poisonous. Wash the tomatoes under cool running water, then slice and serve. Or peel the tomatoes by plunging them into boiling water, then transferring them on a slotted spoon into a bowl of cold water. The change in temperature damages a layer of cells just under the skin so that the skin slips off easily.

To get rid of the seeds, cut the tomato in half across the middle and squeeze the halves gently, cut side down, over a bowl. The seeds should pop out easily.

Cooking reactions

When a tomato is heated the soluble pectins in its cell walls dissolve and the flesh of the tomato turns mushy. But the seeds and peel, which are stiffened with insoluble cellulose and lignin, stay hard. This is useful if you are baking or grilling a tomato (the peel will act as a natural 'cup') but not if you are making a soup or stew. If you add an unpeeled tomato to the dish the peel will split and separate from the tomato flesh.

Vitamin C is sensitive to heat. A cooked tomato has less vitamin C than a fresh one, but it has the same amount of vitamin A. Carotenoid pigments are impervious to the heat of normal cooking.

Effects of processing

Artifical ripening. Tomatoes are available all year round. In the summer, when they can be picked close to the market and have less distance to travel, they are picked bush-ripened. In the winter, when they have to travel farther, they are picked while the skin is still a bit green so they will not spoil on the way to market. On the bush, in shipping, or in your kitchen, tomatoes produce ethylene, a natural ripening agent that triggers the change from green to red skin. In winter, if the tomatoes are still green when they reach the market, they are sprayed with ethylene — which turns them red. These tomatoes are called hard-ripened (as opposed to bush-ripened). You cannot soften hard-ripened tomatoes by storing them at room temperature. They should be refrigerated to keep them from rotting.

Canning. Most canned tomatoes are salted. Unless otherwise labelled, they should be considered high-sodium foods.

The *botulinum* organism whose toxin causes botulism thrives in an airless, nonacid environment like the inside of a vegetable can. Because tomatoes are an acid food, many people assume that canned tomatoes will not support the growth of the *botulinum* organism, but there have been reports of canned tomatoes contaminated with *botulinum* toxins. Tomatoes should therefore be treated like any other canned food. Cook them thoroughly before you use them. Throw out any unopened can that is bulging. And discard — *without tasting* — any canned tomatoes that look or smell suspicious.

Medical uses and/or benefits

As an antiscorbutic. Fresh tomatoes, which are rich in vitamin C, help protect against scurvy, the vitamin C-deficiency disease.

Adverse effects

Orange skin. Lycopene, the red carotenoid pigment in tomatoes, can be stored in the fatty layer under your skin. If you eat excessive amounts of tomatoes (or tomatoes and carrots), the carotenoids may turn your palms, the soles of your feet, and even some of your other skin yellow-orange. The colour (which is harmless) will disappear as soon as you cut back your consumption of these vegetables. This reaction is extremely unusual.

Poisoning. The roots and leaves of the tomato plant are poisonous. They contain the nerve toxin solanine, which interferes with your body's ability to use acetylcholinesterase, a chemical that facilitates the transmission of impulses between body cells. Solanine does not dissolve in water, nor is it destroyed by heat. (Tomatoes also contain solanidine, a less-toxic derivative of solanine.)

Food/drug interaction

✘ FALSE RESULT IN TESTS FOR CANCER

• Turnips (Swedes)

See also CABBAGE, GREENS

Nutritional profile per 100g food (raw)		
Energy value:	Low	20 Kcal
Protein:	Low	0.8 g
Fat:	Low	0.3 g
Cholesterol:	None	None
Carbohydrates:	Med	3.8 g
Fibre:	Low	2.8 g
Sodium:	Med	58 mg
Major vitamin contribution:	Vitamins B and C	Med, High
Major mineral contribution:	Calcium, iron	Low, High

White turnips and swedes (which are members of the same plant family) are taproots of plants belonging to the cabbage family (cruciferous vegetables). The white turnip is a creamy globe, tinged with rose at the top and capped with greens that may be used on their own as a rich source of calcium. The swede is a large globe with bumpy tan skin and a yellow interior.

Both turnips and swedes are moderately good sources of food fibre, particularly pectins, and SUGARS. They have no STARCH, very little PROTEIN, a trace of FAT, and no CHOLESTEROL.

The most nutritious way to serve this food

White turnips. Raw or steamed to preserve the vitamin C. The peeled raw turnip may be grated into a salad or eaten like an apple.

Swede. Steamed as quickly as possible, to protect the vitamin C.

Diets that may restrict or exclude this food

Low-fibre diet
Low-sodium diet (white turnips)
Sucrose-restricted diet

Buying

Choose: Firm, smooth, medium-sized white turnips with fresh green leaves on top.

Choose medium-sized swede with smooth, unscarred skin.

Avoid: White turnips with wilted greens or swedes with mould on the surface.

Storing
Refrigerate the turnips in the vegetable drawer.

Preparation
White turnips. Wash the turnips under cool running water and peel to just under the line that separates the peel from the flesh.
Swedes. Cut the vegetables into quarters (or smaller pieces if necessary) and then cut away the skin.

Cooking reactions
When turnips and swedes are cooked, the pectins in their cells walls dissolve and the vegetable softens.

Like other cruciferous vegetables, turnips and swedes contain mustard oils bound to sugar molecules. These compounds are activated when you cook a turnip or swede or cut into it, damaging its cell walls and releasing enzymes that separate the sugar and oil compounds into their smelly components (which include hydrogen sulphide, the chemical that makes rotten eggs smell rotten). Compared to the mustard oil in cabbage, Brussels sprouts, and broccoli, the ones in turnips and swedes are very mild. They produce only a faint odour when these vegetables are cut or cooked, but the longer you cook them, the more smelly chemicals you will produce and the stronger the taste and odour will be.

Cooking white turnips in an aluminium or iron pot will darken the turnips or discolour the pot. The turnips contain pale anthoxanthin pigments that interact with metal ions escaping from the surface of the pot to form brown or yellow compounds. Swedes which get their colour from carotenes that are impervious to the heat of normal cooking, stay bright-yellow in any pot.

Effects of processing
Freezing. Crisp fruit and vegetables like apples, carrots, potatoes, turnips, and swedes snap when you break or bite into them because their cells are so full of moisture that they pop when the cell walls are broken. When these vegetables are cooked and frozen, the water inside their cells leaks out when the vegetable is defrosted and the cells collapse inward (which is the reason defrosted turnips and swedes, like defrosted carrots and potatoes, have a softer texture).

Medical uses and/or benefits
✓ PROTECTION AGAINST CANCER

Adverse effects
✗ ENLARGED THYROID GLAND

Food/drug interactions
✗ FALSE RESULT IN TESTS FOR CANCER

• Veal

Nutritional profile per 100g food (raw)		
	Fillet	
Energy value:	Med	109 Kcal
Protein:	High	21.1 g
Fat:	Low	2.7 g
Cholesterol:	Med	97 mg
Carbohydrates:	None	None
Fibre:	None	None
Sodium:	Med	110 mg
Major vitamin contribution:	B vitamins	High
Major mineral contribution:	Iron, zinc, potassium	High, High, High

Veal is meat from cattle usually under three months of age, weighing less than 400 pounds.

Veal is more subtly flavoured than beef from older animals. It has proportionally more PROTEIN and less FAT. Like other animal foods, veal provides proteins considered 'complete' because they have adequate amounts of all the essential amino acids. Veal has no food fibre and no CARBOHYDRATES other than small amounts of glycogen (sugar) stored in the animal's muscles.

Veal is an excellent source of B vitamins, including nicotinic acid, vitamin B₆, and vitamin B₁₂, which is found only in animal foods. and heme iron, the organic form of iron found in foods of animal original. Heme iron is approximately five times more available to the body than non-heme iron, the inorganic form of iron found in plant foods.

The most nutritious way to serve this food
Lightly fried.

Diets that may restrict or exclude this food
Controlled-fat, low-cholesterol diet
Low-protein diet (for some forms of kidney disease)

Buying
Choose: The cut of veal that fits your recipe. Thick cuts, such as roasts, have much connective tissue. They need long, slow cooking to gelatinize the connective tissue and keep the veal from drying out. A breast with bones, however, has more fat than a solid roast. Veal fillet and cutlets are the only

kinds of veal that can be sautéed or grilled quickly.

Storing
Refrigerate raw veal immediately, carefully wrapped to prevent its drippings from contaminating the refrigerator shelves or other foods.

Fresh veal will keep for three to five days in the refrigerator. As a general rule, large cuts of veal will keep a little longer than small ones. Minced veal, which has many surfaces where bacteria can live, should be used within 48 hours.

Preparation
To lighten the colour of veal cover the meat with milk and soak it overnight in the refrigerator. Or marinate it in lemon juice. Trim the meat carefully. By judiciously cutting away all visible fat you can significantly reduce the amount of fat and cholesterol in each serving.

Do not salt the veal before you cook it. The salt dissolves in water on the surface of the meat to form a liquid denser than the moisture inside the veal's cells. As a result the water inside the cells will flow out across the cell toward the denser solution, a phenomenon known as osmosis. The loss of moisture will make the veal less tender and stringy.

After handling raw meat, *always* wash your knives, cutting board, work surface — and your hands — with warm soapy water to reduce the chance of transferring microorganisms from the meat to other foods.

Cooking reactions
Cooking changes the way veal looks and tastes, alters its nutritional value, makes it safer, and extends its shelf life.

Browning meat before you cook it does not seal in the juices, but does change the flavour by caramelizing proteins and sugars on the surface (see BROWNING REACTIONS). Since meat has no sugars other than the small amounts of glycogen in its muscles, we usually add sugars in the form of marinades or basting liquids that may also contain acids (vinegar, lemon juice, wine) to breakdown muscle fibres and tenderize the meat. Browning has one minor nutritional drawback. It breaks amino acids on the surface of the meat into smaller compounds that are no longer useful proteins.

Heat changes the structure of PROTEINS. It denatures the protein molecules, which means they break up into smaller fragments or change shape or clump together. All these changes force water out of protein tissues, which is why meat gets dryer the longer it is cooked. In addition, heat denatures the pigments in meat, which combine with oxygen and turn brown.

An obvious nutritional benefit of cooking is that it liquifies the fat in the meat so that it can run off. And, of course, cooking makes veal safer by killing *Salmonella* and other organisms.

Effects of processing

Freezing. When you thaw frozen veal it may be less tender than fresh veal. It may also be lower in B vitamins. While the veal is frozen, the water inside its cells turns into sharp ice crystals that can puncture cell membranes. When the veal thaws, moisture (and some of the B vitamins) will leak out through these torn cell walls. The loss of moisture is irreversible.

Freezing can also cause freezer burn, the dry spots where moisture has evaporated from the surface of the meat. Waxed freezer paper is designed specifically to hold the moisture in meat.

Freezing slows the oxidation of fats and the multiplication of bacteria so that the veal stays usable longer than it would in a refrigerator. At 0°F fresh veal will keep for four to eight months. (Beef, which has fewer oxygen-sensitive unsaturated fatty acids than veal, will keep for up to a year.)

Medical uses and/or benefits
—

Adverse effects
 HEART DISEASE

Antibiotic-resistant Salmonella and toxoplasmosis. Veal treated with antibiotics may produce meat contaminated with antibiotic-resistant strains of *Salmonella*, and all raw beef may harbour *T. gondii*, the parasite that causes toxoplasmosis. Toxoplasmosis is particularly hazardous for pregnant women. It can be passed on to the foetus and may trigger a series of birth defects, including blindness and mental retardation. Both the drug-resistant *Salmonella* and *T. gondii* can be eliminated by cooking meat thoroughly and washing all utensils, cutting boards, and work surfaces as well as your hands with hot soapy water before touching any other food.

Food/drug interactions
✖ MAO INHIBITORS

• Vegetable oils (Coconut oil, corn oil, cottonseed oil, olive oil, peanut oil, safflower oil, sesame oil, soya bean oil)

See also COCONUT, NUTS, OLIVES, SOYA BEANS

Nutritional profile per 100g oil		
	Typical culinary oil	
Energy value:	High	899 Kcal
Protein:	Low	Trace
Fat:	High	99.9 g
Cholesterol:	None	None
Carbohydrates	None	None
Fibre:	None	None
Sodium:	Low	Trace
Major vitamin contribution:	Vitamin E	High
Major mineral contribution:	None	None

Vegetable oils are derived from nuts, seeds, and vegetables. They are concentrated sources of energy. Ounce for ounce, fats contain twice as many calories as PROTEINS and CARBOHYDRATES; because they are digested more slowly, they produce a feeling of satiety and keep us from being hungry again quickly.

FATS provide the ESSENTIAL FATTY ACIDS linoleic acid and arachidonic acid. Our bodies cannot manufacture linoleic acid, but we can make arachidonic acid from the linoleic acid we get from foods. The best sources of linoleic acid are vegetable oils other than olive oil and coconut oil. The best sources of arachidonic acid are the fats in dairy foods, meat, fish, and poultry.

Vegetable oils are also our best source of vitamin E, a natural antioxidant. (*Vitamin E* is the collective name for a group of chemicals known as tocopherols.)

Vegetable oils are composed primarily of UNSATURATED FATTY ACIDS, fatty acids whose molecule can accommodate extra hydrogen atoms. Monounsaturated fatty acids can accommodate two extra hydrogen atoms; polyunsaturated fatty acids can accommodate four or more hydrogen atoms. Most of the fatty acids in olive oil and peanut oil are monounsaturated; most of the fatty acids in maize oil, safflower oil, and soya bean oil are polyunsaturated.

The most nutritious way to serve this food
Used only once and certainly not after repeated use in the chip fryer.

Fatty acid composition of various dietary fats				
	% saturated	% mono-unsaturated	% poly-unsaturated	% other
Maize oil	13	24	59	4
Olive oil	13	73	8	5
Peanut oil	15	46	32	5
Safflower oil	19	12	75	5
Soya bean oil (partially hydrogenated)	15	43	38	4
Butter	62	29	4	5

Source: 'Provisional table on the fatty acid and cholesterol count of selected foods' (USDA, 1984)

Diets that may restrict or exclude this food
Low-fat diet

Buying
Choose: Tightly sealed bottles of vegetable oil, protected from light and heat.

Storing
Store vegetable oils in a cool, dark cupboard. The oils should be protected from light, heat, and air. When exposed to air, fatty acids become rancid, which means that they combine with oxygen to form hydroperoxides, natural substances that taste bad, smell bad, and may destroy the vitamin E in the oil. The higher the proportion of polyunsaturated fatty acids in the oil, the more quickly it will turn rancid. Many salad and cooking oils contain antioxidant preservatives (BHT, BHA) to slow this reaction.

Preparation
—

Cooking reactions
Heat promotes the oxidation of fats, a chemical reaction accelerated by cooking fats in iron pots. Cooked fats are safe at normal temperatures, but when they are used over and over, they may break down into components known as free radicals — which are suspected carcinogens.

Most fats begin to decompose well below 500°F (260°C), and they may catch fire spontaneously with no warning without boiling first. The point at which they decompose and burn is called the smoking point. Vegetable shortening will burn at 375°F (191°C), vegetable oils at close to 450°F (232°C). Safflower, soya bean, cottonseed, and maize oils have higher smoking points than peanut and sesame oils.

Effects of processing
Margarine and shortening. Margarine is made of hydrogenated vegetable oils (oils to which hydrogen atoms have been added). Adding hydrogen atoms hardens the oils into a semi-solid material than can be moulded into bars or packed in tubs as a margarine or shortening. Hydrogenation also changes the structure of some of the polyunsaturated fatty acids in the oils from a form known as 'cis fatty acids' to a form known as 'trans fatty acids'. Questions have been raised as to the safety of trans fatty acids, but there is no proof so far that they are more likely to clause atherosclerosis. Margarines may also contain colouring agents (to make the margarine look like butter), emulsifiers, and milk or animal fats (including butter).

Margarine should be refrigerated, closely wrapped to keep it from picking up odours from other foods. It will keep for several weeks in the refrigerator before its fatty acids oxidize to produce off odours and taste. Shortening can be stored, tightly covered, at room temperature.

Medical uses and/or benefits
✓ HEART DISEASE

Adverse effects
—

Food/drug interactions
—

• Water

Nutritional profile		
Energy value:	None	None
Protein:	None	None
Fat:	None	None
Cholesterol:	None	None
carbohydrates:	None	None
Fibre:	None	None
Sodium:	Low to high	Varied
Major vitamin contribution:	None	None
Major mineral contribution:	Calcium, magnesium, fluoride	Varied

About the nutrients in this food

Water has no nutrients other than the minerals it picks up from the earth or the pipes through which it flows or that are added by a bottler to give the water a specific taste. *Hard* water contains dissolved calcium and magnesium salts, usually in the form of bicarbonates, sulphates, and chlorides. *Soft* water has very little calcium and magnesium, but it may still contain sodium. Some bottled 'mineral waters' may contain as much as 200 to 400 mg sodium per glass.

The only absolutely 'pure' water is *distilled water*, which has been vaporized, condensed, and collected free of any impurities. *Spring water* is water that flows up to the earth's surface on its own from an underground spring. *Well water* is water that must be reached through a hole drilled into the ground. *Naturally sparkling water* is spring water with naturally occurring carbon dioxide. *Sparkling water*, is artificially carbonated with added carbon dioxide. *Soda water* is sparkling water flavoured with salts, including sodium bicarbonate.

The most nutritious way to serve this food

Filtered, if required, to remove impurities. Change the filter frequently.

Diets that may restrict or exclude this food

Low-sodium diets ('softened' water, some bottled waters)

Buying

Choose: Tightly sealed bottles, preferably with a protective foil seal under the cap. If you are on a low-sodium diet, read the label on bottled waters carefully. Many bottled mineral waters contain sodium chloride or sodium bicarbonate.

Storing

Water bottled in glass will keep longer than water bottled in plastic which may begin to pick up the taste of the container after about two weeks.

Improve the taste of heavily chlorinated tap water by refrigerating it overnight in a glass bottle. The chlorine will evaporate and the water will taste fresh.

Preparation

—

Cooking reactions

When you heat a liquid, you excite its molecules (increase their thermal energy) and disrupt the forces holding them together. As the molecules continue to absorb energy, they separate from each other and begin to escape from the liquid. When the concentration of the molecules escaping from the liquids equals the pressure of air above the surface, the liquid will *boil* and its molecules will *vaporize*, converting the liquid to a gas that floats off the surface as the liquid *evaporates*.

At sea level, plain water boils at 212°F (100°C), the temperature at which its molecules have absorbed enough energy to begin to escape from the surface as steam. If you add salt to the water before it starts to boil, the water molecules will need to pick up extra energy in order to overcome the greater attractive forces between the salt and water molecules. Since the energy comes from heat, adding salt raises the boiling point of water. Salted water boils at a higher temperature than plain water does.

Effects of processing

Freezing. Water is the only compound that expands when it freezes. A water molecule is shaped roughly like an open triangle, with an oxygen atom at the centre and a hydrogen atom at the end of either arm. When water is frozen, its molecules move more slowly, and each hydrogen atom forms a temporary bond to the oxygen atom on a nearby water molecule. The phenomenon, known as hydrogen bonding, creates a rigid structure in which the molecules stretch out rather than pack closely together, as normally happens when a substance is cooled. An ounce of frozen water (ice) takes up more room than an ounce of liquid water.

'Softening'. Home water softeners that filter out 'hard' calcium carbonate and replace it with sodium may increase the sodium content of tap water by as much as 100 mg per quart.

Medical uses and/or benefits

Antacid, diuretic, and laxative effects. Mineral waters are natural mild diuretics and, because they contain sodium bicarbonate, naturally antacid. Any kind of water, taken warm about a half hour before breakfast, appears to be mildly laxative, perhaps because it stimulates contraction of the muscles in the digestive tract.

Protection against cavities. Fluorine is a natural element, present in soil and rocks. Fluoridated drinking water provides fluoride ions that are incorporated into the crystalline structure of dental enamel and bones, making our teeth more resistant to decay and possibly offering some protection against osteoporosis. A concentration of one part fluoride ions to one million parts water (1 ppm) is considered both safe and protective.

Protection against hypertension and heart disease. People whose drinking water is 'hard' (more than 15-50 ppm calcium and magnesium salts) appear to have lower rates of coronary heart disease than people whose drinking water is 'soft' (less than 15-50 ppm calcium and magnesium salts). Exactly how hard water might protect against heart disease remains to be explained.

Adverse effects

Contaminants. Drinking water may pick up a variety of chemical contaminants as it travels through the ground or through pipes. Even chlorine, which is added to the water supply to eliminate potentially hazardous microorganisms, can be a problem. The free chlorine generated during the purification process may react with organic compounds in the water to produce trihalomethanes, such as chloroform, which are suspected carcinogens or mutagens (substances that alter the structure of DNA).

Food/drug interactions
—

• Yoghurt (Buttermilk, kefir, sour cream)

Nutrutional profile per 100g food		
	Natural, Low Fat Yoghurt	
Energy value:	Med	52 Kcal
Protein:	Med	5 g
Fat:	Low	1 g
Cholesterol:	Low	7 mg
Carbohydrates:	Low	6.2 g
Fibre:	None	None
Sodium:	Med	76 mg
Major vitamin contribution:	B vitamins	Med
Major mineral contribution:	Calcium, potassium	High, High

Cultured milks are fermented products. Their lactose has been digested by any one or two of a number of strains of bacteria that produce lactic acid as a waste product. The lactic acid coagulates proteins in the milk to form curds that thicken the milk. *Cultured buttermilk* is pasteurized low-fat or skimmed milk cultured with *Streptococcus lactis*. *Sour cream* is made either by culturing pasteurized sweet cream with bacteria that produce lactic acid or by curdling the cream with vinegar. *Yoghurt* is pasteurized whole, low-fat, or skimmed sweet milk cultured with *Lactobacilli bulgaricus* and *Streptococcus thermophilus*. Some yoghurt also contains *Lactobacillus acidophilus*.

Cultured milk products are an excellent source of PROTEINS considered complete because they contain sufficient amounts of all the essential amino acids. They contain moderate amounts of SUGARS, (unless they are artificially sweetened when they can be high in sugar), but they have no STARCH or fibre. They contain butterfat, which is high in SATURATED FATTY ACIDS. Their CHOLESTEROL content varies with their fat; skimmed-milk products have less cholesterol than whole-milk products.

Like other milks, cultured milks contain moderate amounts of carotenoids that your body can convert into vitamin A. Vitamin A is fat-soluble; low-fat and skimmed-milk products have less vitamin A than whole-milk products. All milk products are relatively good sources of thiamin (vitamin B₁) and riboflavin (vitamin B₂).

Milk products are an important source of calcium. They are also a good source of iodine, which we ordinarily associate with seafood or plants grown near the sea. In fact, dairy products may now be our most important source of iodine. The iodine in milks comes from supplements fed to dairy cattle and, perhaps, from the iodates and iodophors in the agents used to clean the machinery in plants where milk is processed.

The most nutritious way to serve this food
For adults skimmed-milk products, without added fruit and sugars.

Diets that may restrict or exclude this food
Controlled-fat, low-cholesterol diet
Lactose- and galactose-free diets
Sucrose-restricted diet (flavoured yoghurt or yoghurt made with fruit)

Buying
Choose: Tightly sealed, refrigerated containers. Check the date on the container to buy the freshest product.

Storing
Refrigerate all cultured milk products immediately. At 40°F (4°C), buttermilk will stay fresh for two to three weeks, sour cream for three to four weeks, and yoghurt for three to six weeks. Keep the containers tightly closed so the milks do not pick up odours from other foods.

Preparation
Do not 'whip' yoghurt before adding to any dish. You will break the curd and make the yoghurt watery.

Cooking reactions
Cultured milk products, which are more unstable than plain milks, separate quickly when heated. Stir them gently but do not boil.

Effects of processing
Freezing. Cultured milk products separate easily when frozen. Commercially frozen yoghurt contains gelatin and other emulsifiers to make the product creamy and keep it from separating. Freezing inactivates but does not destroy the bacteria in yoghurt; if there were live bacteria in the yoghurt when it was frozen, they will still be there when it's thawed.

Medical uses and/or benefits
HEART DISEASE

Cholesterol. Research has shown that cholesterol levels are low in people consuming natural, fermented milks. The explanation appears to lie with the bacteria in the yoghurt.

Adverse effects
Allergy to milk proteins. Milk and milk products are among the foods

most often implicated as a cause of the classic symptoms of food allergy: upset stomach, hives, and angioedema (swelling of the face, lips, and tongue).

Lactose intolerance. Lactose intolerance is not a food allergy. It is an inherited metabolic deficiency. People who are lactose-intolerant lack sufficient amounts of lactase, the intestinal enzyme that breaks the disaccharide ('double sugar') lactose into glucose and galactose, its easily digested constituents. Two-thirds of all adults, including 90 to 95 percent of all Orientals, 70 to 75 percent of all blacks, and 6 to 8 percent of Caucasians are lactose-intolerant to some extent. When they drink milk or eat milk products, the lactose remains undigested in their gut, to be fermented by bacteria that produce gas and cause bloating, diarrhoea, and intestinal discomfort. According to researchers at Oklahoma State University in Stillwater, the *Lactobacillus acidophilus* bacteria added to acidophilus milk and some yoghurts may supply lactase, the enzyme needed to digest lactose. Lactase-deficient adults may be able to drink acidophilus-treated milks or yoghurts without ill effects.

Galactosemia. Galactosemia is an inherited metabolic disorder in which the body lacks the enzymes needed to metabolize galactose, a component of lactose. Galactosemia is a recessive trait: you must get the gene from both parents in order to develop the condition. Babies born with galactosemia will fail to thrive and may develop brain damage or cataracts if they are given milk. To prevent this, children with galactosemia are usually kept on a protective milk-free diet for several years, until their bodies have developed alternative pathways by which to metabolize galactose. Pregnant women who are known carriers of galactosemia may be advised to give up milk while pregnant lest the unmetabolized galactose in their bodies cause brain damage to the foetus (damage not detectible by amniocentesis). Genetic counselling is available to identify galactosemia carriers and assess their chances of producing a baby with the disorder.

Food/drug interactions

Tetracyclines. The calcium ions in milk products bind with tetracyclines to form insoluble compounds your body cannot absorb. Taking tetracyclines with buttermilk, sour cream, or yoghurt makes the drug less effective.

• Further reading

Chemical children.   Mansfield P; Monro. J; Century.
Eating for health,   Robbins. C; Grafton.
E for additives,   Hanssen. M; Thorsons.
Food additives,   Millstone. E; Penguin.
Gluttons for punishment,   Erlichman. J; Penguin.
Manual of nutrition,   Ministry of Agriculture, Fisheries and Food; HMSO
Nutritional medicine,   Davies. S; Stewart. A; Pan.
Open University guide to healthy eating,   Rambletree Pelham.
Shopping for health,   Marshall. J; Penguin.
The fat counter,   Thomas. J; Pan.
The health and fitness handbook,   Polunin. M (Ed); Windward and
  Here's Health.
The salt counter,   Wright. M; Pan.

262 . FOOD FACTS

• Useful addresses

British Diabetic Association
10 Queen Anne Street
LONDON W1M 0BD

British Dietetic Association
Daimler House
Paradise Circus, Queensway
BIRMINGHAM B1 2BJ

Coeliac Society
PO Box 181
LONDON NW2 2QY

Coronary Prevention Group
60 Great Ormond Street
LONDON WC1N 3HR

Health Education Authority
78 New Oxford Street
LONDON WC1A 1AH

Hyperactive Children's
Support Group
59 Meadowside
ANGMERING
West Sussex BN16 4BW

Scottish Health Education
Unit
Woodburn House
Canan Lane
EDINBURGH EH10 4SG

Vegetarian Society
53 Marloes Road
LONDON W8 6LA

• Index